BRAIN LOCK

BRAIN LOCK

Free Yourself from
Obsessive-Compulsive Behavior

**A Four-Step Self-Treatment Method to
Change Your Brain Chemistry**

Jeffrey M. Schwartz, M.D.
with Beverly Beyette

ReganBooks
An Imprint of HarperPerennial
A Division of HarperCollins*Publishers*

A hardcover edition of this book was published in 1996 by ReganBooks.

BRAIN LOCK. Copyright © 1996 by Jeffrey M. Schwartz, M.D. All rights reserved. Printed in the United States of America. No part of this book may be used or reproduced in any manner whatsoever without written permission except in the case of brief quotations embodied in critical articles and reviews. For information address HarperCollins Publishers, Inc., 10 East 53rd Street, New York, NY 10022.

HarperCollins books may be purchased for educational, business, or sales promotional use. For information please write: Special Markets Department, HarperCollins Publishers, Inc., 10 East 53rd Street, New York, NY 10022.

First ReganBooks/HarperPerennial edition published 1997.

Designed by Jessica Shatan

ISBN 0-06-039166-9
ISBN 0-06-098711-1 (pbk.)

97 98 99 00 01 ❖/RRD 10 9 8 7 6 5 4

This book is dedicated to the memory of my grandfather
HARRY WEINSTEIN

and to the memory of
VEN. MAHĀSI SAYADAW
for his monumental contribution to the practice of
mindful awareness in this century

The names and some of the external circumstances of the patients in this book have been changed to protect their confidentiality. All of the symptoms and therapeutic efforts are as they actually occurred.

Note: Part III of this book is a Self-Treatment Manual which contains a practical summary of the Four-Step Method. It can be read independently from the rest of the book, and can be referred to at any time for concrete guidance.

Contents

Acknowledgments

This book could not have been created without the efforts of the many patients who helped me learn the Four-Step Method. Without the generous support of the Charles and Lelah Hilton family, the scientific work on which this book is based could not have been done. Jessica Klein and Steve Wasserman encouraged me to write this book and introduced me to my publisher, Judith Regan, who has recognized from the first the potential implications of the work described here. Christine Juska helped prepare early drafts. Julie Sherman earned special thanks for her contributions. Will Weston was very helpful with artwork, A. Lorre with photography.

The OCD Research Group at UCLA Medical Center created an excellent environment for doing these studies. Beverly Beyette made a tremendous effort to help the book be as good and useful to as many people as we could make it. Iver Hand was generous with his time and input. Jan Jablonsky, Marty Wax, and Dave Richmond, among others, made helpful comments. Pam and Roy Norman provided much-needed moral support during the hectic final stage of preparation. James Q. Wilson and Don Jefferys encouraged me to pursue some of the broader potential applications of this method.

All in all, you need a lot of help to write a book about self-treatment. Thanks to all the people who provided it.

Foreword

Howard Hughes was dining with actress Jane Greer at Ciro's on the Sunset Strip in Los Angeles one evening in 1947. At one point in the meal, he excused himself to go to the rest room. To Greer's amazement, he did not return for an hour and a half. When he finally reappeared, she was astonished to see that he was soaking wet from head to toe.

"What on earth happened to you?" she asked. "Well," Hughes said, "I spilled some catsup on my shirt and pants and had to wash them out in the sink." He then let them dry for a while, hanging them over one of the toilet stalls. Once he put his clothes back on, he explained, "I couldn't leave the bathroom because I couldn't touch the door handle. I had to wait for someone to come in."

According to Peter H. Brown, coauthor with Pat Broeske of *Howard Hughes: The Untold Story,* Jane Greer never went out with Hughes again.

Howard Hughes was eccentric, certainly, but he was not a freak. He was suffering from obsessive-compulsive disorder (OCD), a classic and severe case. By the end of his life, in 1976, he was overwhelmed by the disease. He spent his last days in isolation in his top-floor suite at the Princess Hotel in Acapulco, where he had sealed himself in a hospital-like atmosphere, terrified of germs.

Blackout curtains at every window kept all sunlight out; the sun, he thought, might transmit the germs he so dreaded. Aides with facial tissues covering their hands brought him food, which had to be precisely cut and measured.

Rumors abounded that he was this reclusive because of drug abuse, a syphilitic condition, or terminal dementia. Actually, all his strange behaviors are readily understandable as symptoms of a severe case of OCD.

Sadly, there was no treatment for OCD in Howard Hughes's lifetime. It would be another decade before the disease would be identified as a brain-related disorder.

I frequently cite the case of Howard Hughes to help my patients understand that this disease, OCD, is an insatiable monster. The more you give in, the hungrier it gets. Even Hughes, with all his millions—and a retinue of servants to perform the bizarre rituals his OCD told him to perform—could not buy his way out. Eventually, the false messages coming from his brain overwhelmed him.

If you are one of many who suffer from OCD, whether it is a mild case or one as severe as Howard Hughes's, this book will show you how to fight and beat it. OCD is a tenacious enemy, but a strong-willed, motivated person can overcome it.

Along the way, you will also learn a good deal about your brain and how you can control it better. You will read the stories of courageous people who, by applying the Four-Step Method, learned how to overcome the dreaded feelings of "Brain Lock" that are caused by OCD. This method, which has been scientifically demonstrated to enable people to change their own brain function, will be described in such a way that you can readily apply it yourself.

Introduction

Obsessions, Compulsions, and
the Four-Step Self-Treatment Method

We all have our little quirks—habits and behaviors—that we know we'd be better off without. We all wish we had more self-control. But when thoughts spin out of control, becoming so intense and intrusive that they take over against our will, when habits turn into all-consuming rituals that are performed to rid us of overwhelming feelings of fear and dread, something more serious is happening.

THIS IS OBSESSIVE-COMPULSIVE DISORDER (OCD)

The victims of OCD engage in bizarre and self-destructive behaviors to avert some imagined catastrophe. But there is no realistic connection between the behaviors and the catastrophes they so fear. For example, they may shower forty times a day to "ensure" that there will not be a death in the family. Or they may go to great lengths to avoid certain numbers so as to "prevent" a fatal airplane crash. Unlike compulsive shoppers or compulsive gamblers, people with OCD derive no pleasure from performing their rituals. They find them extremely painful.

Almost certainly, OCD is related to a biochemical imbalance in the brain that we now know can be treated very effectively without drugs. We know, too, that the Four-Step Self-Treatment Method you will learn in this book enables people with OCD to change their own brain chemistry. Furthermore, this method can be applied effectively to take control over a wide variety of less serious, but troublesome and annoying, compulsive habits and behaviors. (If you think you may have OCD, the University of Hamburg Obsession-Compulsion Inventory Screening Form on page 198 may help you find out. If you don't, the techniques you learn in this book may help you overcome other troubling and annoying habits and behaviors.)

Simply defined, OCD is a lifelong disorder identified by two general groups of symptoms: obsessions and compulsions. Once thought of as a curious and rare disease, it, in fact, affects one person in forty in the general population, or more than five million Americans. A disorder that typically has its onset in adolescence or early adulthood, OCD is more common than asthma or diabetes. It is a devastating disease that often creates chaos in the lives of its victims—and those who love them. The preoccupation with repetitive behaviors, such as washing, cleaning, counting, or checking, causes trouble on the job and leads to marital strife and difficulty with social interaction. Family members may become impatient and angry, demanding, "Why don't you just stop!" Or they may aid and abet the performance of the silly rituals to buy an hour's peace (a very bad idea).

WHAT ARE OBSESSIONS?

Obsessions are intrusive, unwelcome, distressing thoughts and mental images. The word *obsession* comes from the Latin word meaning "to besiege." And an obsessive thought is just that—a thought that besieges you and annoys the hell out of you. You pray for it to go away, but it won't, at least not for long or in any controllable way. These thoughts always create distress and anxiety. Unlike other unpleasant thoughts, they do not fade away, but keep intruding into your mind over and over, against your will. These thoughts are, in fact, repugnant to you.

Say that you've seen a beautiful woman and can't get her out of your mind. That is not an obsession. That is a *rumination*, something not inappropriate, something quite normal and even pleasant. If Calvin Klein's marketing department had really understood the word *obsession* properly, the perfume would have been called "Rumination."

GETTING THE (WRONG) MESSAGE

Because these obsessions don't go away, they are extremely difficult to ignore—difficult, but not impossible. We now know that OCD is related to a biochemical problem in the brain. We call this problem "Brain Lock" because four key structures of the brain become locked together, and the brain starts sending false messages that the person cannot readily recognize as false. One of the main signal-processing centers of the brain, made up of two structures called the *caudate nucleus* and the *putamen,* can be thought of as similar to a gearshift in a car. The caudate nucleus works like an automatic transmission for the front, or thinking part, of the brain. Working with the putamen, which is the automatic transmission for the part of the brain that controls body movements, the caudate nucleus allows for the extremely efficient coordination of thought and movement during everyday activities. In a person with OCD, however, the caudate nucleus is not shifting the gears properly, and messages from the front part of the brain get stuck there. In other words, the brain's automatic transmission has a glitch. The brain gets "stuck in gear" and can't shift to the next thought.

When the brain gets stuck, it may tell you, "You must wash your hands again"—and you'll wash, even though there is no real reason to do so. Or the brain may say, "You'd better check that lock again"—and you'll check again and again, unable to shake off the gnawing feeling that the door *may* be unlocked. Or an intense urge to count things or to reread words may arise for no apparent reason.

By applying behavior therapy techniques, you can change how you respond to these thoughts and urges, and **you can physically change the way your brain works.** The use of these techniques actually makes the automatic transmission in the brain shift more smoothly, so that over time the intrusive urges decrease. One patient at UCLA, Dottie, on being told that her problem was caused by a biochemical imbalance in her brain, immediately brightened and coined the catchphrase "**It's not me—it's my OCD.**" To most people with OCD, this realization alone comes as a great relief.

Washing, checking, and other OCD rituals consume hours of time each day and make the lives of people with OCD miserable. People with OCD may even fear they are going crazy—they know that their behavior is not normal. Indeed, the behavior is apt to be foreign to their personalities or self-image. Yet until they learn the Four-Step Self-Treatment Method, they are unable to stop themselves from responding to the brain's false alarms.

WHAT ARE COMPULSIONS?

Compulsions are the behaviors that people with OCD perform in a vain attempt to exorcise the fears and anxieties caused by their obsessions. Although a person with OCD usually recognizes that the urge to wash, check, or touch things or to repeat numbers is ridiculous and senseless, the feeling is so strong that *the untrained mind* becomes overwhelmed and the person with OCD gives in and performs the compulsive behavior. Unfortunately, performing the absurd behavior tends to set off a vicious cycle: It may bring momentary relief, but as more compulsive behaviors are performed, the obsessive thoughts and feelings become stronger, more demanding, and more tenacious. The afflicted person ends up with both an obsession and an often embarrassing compulsive ritual to go with it. It is not surprising that many people with OCD come to see themselves as doomed and may even have suicidal thoughts by the time they seek professional help. In addition, years of traditional psychotherapy may have served only to confuse them further.

A Checklist of Common OCD Symptoms

Obsessions

Obsessions about Dirt and Contamination
Unfounded fears of contracting a dreadful illness
Excessive concerns about dirt; germs (including the fear of spreading germs to others); and environmental contaminants, such as household cleaners
Feelings of revulsion about bodily waste and secretions
Obsessions about one's body
Abnormal concerns about sticky substances or residues

Obsessive Need for Order or Symmetry
An overwhelming need to align objects "just so"
Abnormal concerns about the neatness of one's personal appearance or one's environment

Obsessions about Hoarding or Saving
Stashing away useless trash, such as old newspapers or items rescued from trash cans
The inability to discard anything because it "may be needed sometime," a fear of losing something or discarding something by mistake

Obsessions with Sexual Content
Sexual thoughts that one views as inappropriate and unacceptable

Repetitive Rituals
Repeating routine activities for no logical reason
Repeating questions over and over
Rereading or rewriting words or phrases

Nonsensical Doubts
Unfounded fears that one has failed to do some routine task, such as paying the mortgage or signing a check

Religious Obsessions (Scrupulosity)
Troublesome blasphemous or sacrilegious thoughts
Excessive concerns about morality and right or wrong

Obsessions with Aggressive Content
The fear of having caused some terrible tragedy, such as a fatal fire
Repeated intruding images of violence
The fear of acting out a violent thought, such as stabbing or shooting someone
The irrational fear of having hurt someone, for example, the fear of having hit someone while driving

Superstitious Fears
The belief that certain numbers or colors are "lucky" or "unlucky"

COMPULSIONS

Cleaning and Washing Compulsions
Excessive, ritualized hand washing, showering, bathing, or tooth brushing
The unshakable feeling that household items, such as dishes, are contaminated or cannot be washed enough to be "really clean"

Compulsions about Having Things "Just Right"
The need for symmetry and total order in one's environment, for example, the need to line up canned goods in the pantry in alphabetical order, to hang clothes in exactly the same spot in the closet every day, or to wear certain clothes only on certain days
The need to keep doing something until one gets it "just right"

Hoarding or Collecting Compulsions
Minutely inspecting household trash in case some "valuable" item has been thrown out
Accumulating useless objects

Checking Compulsions
Repeatedly checking to see if a door is locked or an appliance is turned off
Checking to make certain one has not harmed someone, for example, driving around and around the block to see if anyone has been run over
Checking and rechecking for mistakes, such as when balancing a checkbook
Checking associated with bodily obsessions, such as repeatedly checking oneself for signs of a catastrophic disease

Other Compulsions
Pathological slowness in carrying out even the most routine activities
Blinking or staring rituals
Asking over and over for reassurance
Behaviors based on superstitious beliefs, such as fixed bedtime rituals to "ward off" evil or the need to avoid stepping on cracks in the sidewalk
A feeling of dread if some arbitrary act is not performed
The overpowering need to tell someone something or to ask someone something or to confess something
The need to touch, tap, or rub certain objects repeatedly
Counting compulsions: counting panes in windows or billboards along a highway, for example
Mental rituals, such as reciting silent prayers in an effort to make a bad thought go away
Excessive list making

THE FOUR STEPS

In recent years, there have been major advances in treating this condition. More than two decades of research by behavior therapists have documented the effectiveness of a technique called *exposure and response prevention*. The use of this technique involves systematic exposure to stimuli that bring on OCD symptoms, such as having a person with OCD touch a toilet seat or other objects that he or she fears are contaminated, and cause the person to have obsessions and compulsions. The therapist then enforces extended periods during which the person agrees not to respond with compulsive behaviors. These periods, in turn, cause tremendous amounts of anxiety that last an hour or more and call for a significant amount of assistance by a trained therapist. As the therapy progresses, the intensity of the anxiety decreases, and the person gains much better control over the OCD symptoms.

At UCLA School of Medicine, where we have been studying OCD for more than a decade, we have developed a simple self-directed cognitive-behavioral therapy to supplement and enhance this process. We call it the Four-Step Self-Treatment Method. It is a technique that does not require expensive professional therapy or the use of medications. By teaching people how to recognize the link between OCD symptoms and a biochemical imbalance in the brain, we were able to develop this method that very effectively treats persons with OCD solely with behavior therapy. In this book I will teach you how you can effectively become your own behavior therapist by practicing the Four Steps. This method can be used with or without a professional therapist. You will learn to fight off those urges and redirect your mind to other, more constructive behaviors.

For the first time ever for any psychiatric condition or any psychotherapy technique, **we have scientific evidence that cognitive-behavioral therapy alone actually causes chemical changes in the brains of people with OCD.** We have demonstrated that by changing your behavior, you can free yourself from Brain Lock, change your brain chemistry, and get relief from OCD's terrible symptoms. The end result: *increased self-control and enhanced self-*

command, resulting in heightened self-esteem. Knowledge, as they say, is power. There is a huge difference in the impact an obsessive thought or urge has on a trained mind compared to what it has on an untrained mind. Using the knowledge that you will gain by learning the Four Steps, you will not only have a powerful weapon in your battle against your unwanted thoughts and urges, but you will empower yourself in a much broader sense. You will take a big step toward strengthening your ability to attain your goals and improve the quality of your day-to-day life. You will develop a stronger, more stable, more insightful, calmer, and more powerful mind.

If people with OCD can do so, it is highly probable that those with a wide variety of other problems of different degrees of severity can, too. Other disorders include:

- uncontrolled eating or drinking

- nail biting

- hair pulling

- compulsive shopping and gambling

- substance abuse

- impulsive sexual behaviors

- excessive ruminating about relationships, self-image, and self-esteem

The Four Steps can be used to help you control almost any intrusive thought or behavior that you decide you want to change.

The Four-Step Self-Treatment Method is a way of organizing your mental and behavioral responses to your internal thought processes. Rather than just acting impulsively or reflexively, like a puppet, when unwanted thoughts or urges intrude, you can train yourself to respond in a goal-oriented manner and can refuse to be sidetracked by self-destructive thoughts and urges.

We call these steps the four R's:

> **Step 1. RELABEL**
>
> **Step 2. REATTRIBUTE**
>
> **Step 3. REFOCUS**
>
> **Step 4. REVALUE**

In *Step 1: Relabel,* you call the intrusive thought or urge to do a troublesome compulsive behavior exactly what it is: an obsessive thought or a compulsive urge. In this step, you are learning to clearly recognize the reality of the situation and not be tricked by the unpleasant feelings OCD symptoms cause. You develop the ability to clearly see the difference between what's OCD and what's reality. Instead of saying, "I feel like I need to wash my hands again, even though I know it doesn't make any sense," you start saying, "I am having a compulsive urge. That compulsion is bothering me. That obsessive thought is hounding me."

The question then arises, "*Why* does this keep bothering me?"

In *Step 2: Reattribute,* you answer that question. You say, "It keeps bothering me because I have a medical condition called OCD. I am having the symptoms of a medical problem. My obsessions and compulsions are related to a biochemical imbalance in my brain." Once you realize this fact, you begin to ask yourself, "What can I do about it?"

In *Step 3: Refocus,* you turn your attention to more constructive behaviors. By refusing to take the obsessions and compulsions at face value—by keeping in mind that they are not what they say they are, that they are false messages—you can learn to ignore or to work around them by Refocusing your attention on another behavior and doing something useful and positive. This is what I call *"shifting gears."* By performing an alternative, wholesome behavior, you can actually repair the gearbox in your brain. Once you learn how to Refocus in a consistent way, you will quickly come to the next step.

In *Step 4: Revalue,* you revalue those thoughts and urges when they arise. You will learn to devalue unwanted obsessive thoughts and compulsive urges as soon as they intrude. You will come to see intrusive OCD symptoms as the useless garbage they really are.

The Four Steps work together. First, you **RELABEL:** You train yourself to identify what's real and what isn't and refuse to be misled by intrusive destructive thoughts and urges. Second, you **RE-ATTRIBUTE:** You understand that those thoughts and urges are merely mental noise, false signals being sent from your brain. Third, you **REFOCUS:** You learn to respond to those false signals in a new and much more constructive way, working around the false signals by refocusing your attention on more constructive behavior to the best of your ability at that moment. This is where the hardest work is done and where the change in brain chemistry takes place. By expending the effort it takes to Refocus, you will actually be changing how your brain works in an extremely healthy and wholesome way. Finally, the real beauty of the Four-Step Method is seen in the **REVALUE** step, when the whole process becomes smooth and efficient, and the desire to act on unwanted thoughts and urges has been overcome to a significant degree. You will have learned to view those troublesome thoughts and urges as having little or no value and, therefore, your obsessions and compulsions will have much less impact on you. Things come together very quickly, resulting in an almost automatic response: "That's just a senseless obsession. It's a false message. I'm going to focus my attention on something else." At this point, the automatic transmission in your brain begins to start working properly again.

Once people learn to perform the Four Steps on a regular basis, two very positive things happen. First, they gain better control over their behavioral responses to their thoughts and feelings, which, in turn, makes day-to-day living much happier and healthier. Second, by altering their behavioral responses, they change the faulty brain chemistry that was causing the intense discomfort of their OCD symptoms. Since it has been scientifically demonstrated that the brain chemistry in this serious psychiatric condition is changed through the practice of the Four Steps, it is likely that one could also change one's brain chemistry by altering responses to any number of other behaviors or bad habits through using the Four Steps. The result could be a lessening of the intensity and intrusiveness of these unwanted habits and behaviors, making them easier to break.

WHAT'S OCD, WHAT ISN'T?

Because of the similarity in names, people tend to confuse the term *obsessive-compulsive disorder* with the far less disabling *obsessive-compulsive personality disorder* (OCPD). What sets them apart? Simply stated, when your obsessions and compulsions are bad enough to cause significant functional impairment, you have OCD. In OCPD, these "obsessions" and "compulsions" are more like personality quirks or idiosyncrasies, however unpleasant. For example, a man with OCPD may hang on to some object because he believes he may need it someday. But a man with an OCD hoarding compulsion may fill every square foot of his house with worthless trash he knows he'll never need. People with OCPD tend to have trouble "seeing the forest for the trees." Typically, they are list makers who get so hung up on details that they never get around to seeing the big picture. Their quest for perfection interferes with their getting things done. OCPD is a classic case of the "best" being the "enemy of the good." People with OCPD tend to mess up things that are good enough in their quest to make everything "perfect in every detail." They are often totally inflexible, unable to compromise. In their view, if a job is to be done right, it must be done their way. They are unwilling to delegate. It is interesting that this personality type is twice as common in males, whereas OCD does not discriminate between sexes.

The other crucial difference between OCD and OCPD is that although people with OCPD are rigid and stubborn and let their ideas run their lives, *they have no real desire to change their ways*. Either they are not aware that their behavior annoys others or they simply don't care. The person with OCD washes and washes, even though it causes him great pain and gives him no pleasure. The person with OCPD *enjoys* washing and cleaning and thinks, "If everyone cleaned as much as I do, everything would be fine. The problem is that my family is a bunch of slobs." The person with OCPD may look forward to going home at night and lining up all her pencils on her desktop like little soldiers. The person with OCD dreads going home, knowing she will give in to that false message telling her to vacuum twenty times. Unlike people with OCPD, those with OCD realize how inappropriate their behavior is, are ashamed and embarrassed by it, and are in the truest sense desperate to change their behavior. In the words of two people with OCD, "My brain had become an indescribable hell from which I could not escape," and "It's a good thing the windows in the hospital were bolted because I was ready to take the short way out."

This book is mainly about people with OCD. Most of the stories are about their struggles to overcome their disease. But millions of people with less crippling problems can take inspiration from these stories and learn a self-treatment method that can be applied to a wide variety of troublesome behaviors. Those who shared their stories are people who overcame a medical illness. The method they used can be learned and can benefit almost anyone. This book is for all those who want to change their behaviors and are seeking the tools that will help them do so.

OCD: A "DEVILISH" DISORDER

"Damned if you do. Damned if you don't." This is exactly how people with OCD feel before they learn the Four Steps for fighting back against its overpowering symptoms. They have urges to do things that lead them to act in ways that only lessen the amount of control they have over their lives. With that loss of control comes a decreased ability to manage their responses to those destructive urges, which get more and more powerful and intense as time goes by. So if they perform a compulsive behavior, they are damned in the sense that their painful feelings get worse and worse. At the same time, without proper mental training (the Four Steps), they lack the skills they need to change their disordered brain chemistry through constructive action. Furthermore, before they learn the Four Steps, very uncomfortable and anxiety-ridden feelings arise when they don't act on the compulsive urges. Thus, they are trapped in the "damned if you don't" part of this dilemma.

THE FAR SIDE   By GARY LARSON

"C'mon, c'mon—it's either one or the other."

OCD is the devil with his pitchfork at their backs. This devil knows that he has the upper hand. If people with OCD listen to him—and perform the silly rituals that the demon OCD commands them to perform—they will truly be damned because, in the long run, it will lead only to even more intense urges to perform more and more rituals. Their lives will become a living hell. But if they ignore the devil OCD's awful urges, if they refuse to perform the compulsions right now, the devil will seize the opportunity to jab them with his pitchfork over and over again, causing them great pain.

There is, however, another choice, a third door that the devil will never tell them about and, in fact, will try to hide from them. By choosing to go through this door, they can outsmart the devil. Behind this door lies the Four-Step program of self-directed behavior therapy that will enable them to change their brains, overcome these devilish urges, and free themselves from obsessive-compulsive behavior.

THE WAY WE WERE: SIX CASE STUDIES

Here are the stories of some who walked through that third door—people who were totally overwhelmed by OCD when we first met them, but have managed to beat the devil. The symptoms they describe are not rare and obscure; they are extremely common symptoms of this disease.

JACK

Jack, a 43-year-old insurance examiner, washed his hands at least fifty times a day—a hundred or more times on a bad-hands day. There was so much soap embedded in his skin that he could lather up just by wetting his hands. He knew his hands weren't dirty, just as he knew that everything he touched wasn't then magically contaminated. If there were some kind of mass contamination, he reasoned, "People would be dropping like flies." But he just couldn't get over the *feeling* that his hands were dirty, so he washed and washed, constantly worrying, "Did I really wash my hands? Did I wash them right?" His hands became so raw and red that big cracks opened between his fingers. Just a splash of water on his skin was like pouring salt in an open wound. But Jack kept on washing. He couldn't stop himself. It was his terrible secret, one he covered up with ploys that a secret agent would admire.

BARBARA

Barbara, a 33-year-old honors graduate of a prestigious Ivy League university, knew that she was an underachiever, working for a temporary agency. She was intelligent and articulate, but was plagued by intrusive thoughts that told her to check and recheck things. Had she unplugged the appliances? Locked the door? Often, she would leave early for her job, knowing she would have to turn around and come back home once or twice to check. One really bad day, she tucked the coffee machine and the iron in her book bag and took them to work. She felt very ashamed. "If you start doing these things," Barbara told herself, "you're going to lose whatever self-respect you have left." So she developed new strategies for coping with her nagging and non-sensical thoughts: Before she left for work each day, she put the coffee machine on top of the refrigerator, far from any electrical outlet, and said out loud—and very tongue in cheek—"Good-bye, Mr. Coffee!" She had come up with a mnemonic device to help her remember that she had unplugged it. She would also press the prongs of the plug on her iron into her palm, leaving deep marks that she could still see thirty minutes later to reassure herself that she had unplugged the iron.

BRIAN

Brian, a 46-year-old car salesman, lay awake in bed every night, listening for the wail of sirens. If he heard both a fire engine and a police car, he knew there'd been a traffic accident nearby. Whatever the hour, he would get up, dress, and drive around until he found the accident scene. As soon as the police had left, he'd take a bucket of water, a brush, and baking soda from his car and start scrubbing down the asphalt. He had to. Battery acid might have spilled in the collision, and Brian, who had to drive these streets every day, had a morbid fear of being contaminated by battery acid. Once he'd finished scrubbing—it might be 3 A.M.—he'd drive home, shower, put his tennis shoes in a plastic bag, and toss the bag into the trash can. He bought his shoes on sale, a dozen or more pairs at a time, knowing he could wear them only one night.

DOTTIE

Dottie, aged 52, had been battling obsessions since she was 5. One obsession was a fear of any number that included a five or a six. If, while driving with a friend, she spotted a car with a five or six on its license plate, she would have to pull over and wait for a car with a "lucky" number to pass. "We could sit there for hours," she remembers. But she just knew that otherwise something terrible was going to happen to her mother. When Dottie became a mother herself, her obsessions shifted to her son and became even more bizarre. "It was eyes," she said. "All of a sudden I got it into my head that if I did everything right, my son's eyes would be all right and mine would be all right." Neither Dottie nor her son had eye problems; still, she couldn't bear to be around anyone who did. "Just the word *ophthalmologist* would bring in very bad thoughts. I could never step where a person who couldn't see properly had walked. I'd have to throw away my shoes." As Dottie and I talked, I noticed that she had written the word *vision* four times in the palm of one hand. She explained that while watching TV that afternoon, she'd had a bad thought about eyes and had tried to exorcise it.

LARA

Lara described her obsessions this way: "They tear at my soul. One little thought, and the obsessions explode into a fireball, a monster that is out of control." It was knives that made her life hell. "It could be a butter knife, but when I picked it up I wanted to stab someone, especially someone who was close to me. It was horrible. God, I would never hurt anyone! The scariest for me was when I had these obsessions toward my husband."

ROBERTA

Roberta would drive over a bump or a pothole and suddenly panic, imagining that she'd hit someone. Once, pulling out of a shopping mall, she spotted a plastic bag in the parking lot. "In a flash, something was telling me it was a body. I stopped and stared at it, knowing that it was just a plastic bag. But the fear and panic began. I drove around to look at it again. . . ." Wherever she went, she would look in the rearview mirror, her stomach in knots. Was that just a newspaper at the side of the road? Or was it a body? Terrified to drive, she became a prisoner in her own house.

THE BALKY BRAIN

As a research psychiatrist at UCLA School of Medicine, I have treated more than one thousand people with OCD in the past decade, both one-on-one and in a unique weekly OCD therapy group. The vast majority of them are much more functional and more comfortable as a result of practicing the Four-Step Self-Treatment Method. Some of them also take modest amounts of medication, finding it improves their ability to do the work required in therapy.

Our UCLA team came to the study of OCD as an offshoot of studying depression. We had noted specific brain changes in depressed patients, and, knowing that many people with OCD also suffer from depression, we wondered if OCD patients also undergo brain changes. So, we placed an ad in a local newspaper asking, "Do you have repetitive thoughts, rituals you can't control?" We hoped to find a handful of respondents who would be willing to come to the UCLA Neuropsychiatric Institute to have a positron emission tomography (PET) scan, which measures the metabolic activity of the brain. To our astonishment, the response was overwhelming. Clearly, OCD was more prevalent than we thought. And when we did PET scans of these people's brains, we could actually see changes related to their OCD.

Over ten years, I've learned a great deal about people, their courage, their will to survive and improve, and their ability to change and control their responses to the false messages that come from their brains as a result of OCD.

Until relatively recently, there was little that doctors could do for people with OCD. Sigmund Freud and his followers believed that these obsessions and compulsions are caused by deep-seated, emotional conflicts. Patients often tell us about years of misdiagnosis by well-meaning therapists. Brian recalled one psychotherapist telling him that his fear of battery acid had sexual implications and suggesting that perhaps he had been molested by his father. That was when Brian sought help at UCLA.

WORRYING ABOUT WORRYING

From a doctor's perspective, the biggest problem that people with OCD face is how much they worry about how worried they are.

What really troubles them is how anxious they get about things they realize aren't worth worrying about. When we begin to understand the extent of this mental anguish, we can begin to understand some deep truths about the relationship between a person and his or her brain.

One way to understand this relationship is to know the difference between the *form* of obsessive-compulsive disorder and its *content.*

When a doctor first asks, "What exactly is bothering you?" most people with OCD say something like "I can't stop worrying about my hands being dirty." But a doctor who's treated a number of persons with OCD knows that this is not the real problem. The real problem is that no matter what they do in response to what's worrying them, the urge to check or to wash will not go away. This is what is meant by the *form* of OCD: Thoughts and urges that don't really make sense keep intruding into a person's mind in an unrelenting barrage. Together with many other brain scientists, our UCLA team believes that OCD is a brain disease, in essence a neurological problem. The thought does not go away because the brain is not working properly. So OCD is primarily a biological problem, tied to faulty chemical wiring in the brain. The form of OCD—the unrelenting intrusiveness and the fact that these thoughts keep reoccurring—is caused by a biochemical imbalance in the brain that may be genetically inherited.

The *content*—why one person feels something is dirty while another can't stop worrying that the door is unlocked—may well be attributable to emotional factors in a person's background and family circumstances, as traditionally understood by Freudian psychiatry. Whatever the reason, there is no biological explanation for why one person washes and another checks, but OCD is truly a neuropsychiatric disease: Its hallmark symptom—intrusive thoughts and worries—is almost certainly caused by a problem in the brain. But, of course, having a problem like that brings with it significant emotional upset and personal insecurity. And the stresses of these emotional responses can actually intensify the brain-related difficulty. In this book you'll learn to deal with both sets of problems.

TAKING CHARGE

So you have OCD. What can you and your doctor do to make those awful urges and compulsions go away?

The core message in treating OCD is this: *Do not make the mistake of waiting passively for the ideas and urges to go away.* A psychological understanding of the emotional content of the thoughts and urges will rarely make them disappear. Succumbing to the notion that you can do nothing else until the thought or the urge passes is the road to hell. Your life will degenerate into one big compulsion. Think of the analogy of the insistent car alarm that annoys you while you are trying to read a novel or magazine. No matter how annoyed you are, you are not going to sit there and say to yourself, "I'm going to make that alarm turn off and I'm not even going to try to read this until it does." Rather, you're going to do your best to ignore it, work around it. You're going to put your mind back where you want it and do your reading as well as you can. You'll become so absorbed in what you're doing that you hardly notice the alarm. So by focusing your attention on a new task, what would otherwise be extremely annoying and bothersome can be worked around and ignored.

Because OCD is a medical condition—albeit a fascinating one—and is related to the inner workings of the brain, only a change in the brain itself, or at least in brain chemistry, will bring about lasting improvement. You can make these changes through behavior therapy alone or, in some cases, behavior therapy in combination with medication. However, medication is only a "waterwings" approach to OCD therapy; it will help you stay afloat while you learn to swim through the rough waters of OCD. At UCLA, medication is used only to help people help themselves. But the underlying principle is: *The more behavior therapy you do and the more you apply the Four-Step Method the less medication you'll need.* This is especially true over the long haul. (Behavior therapy is discussed in detail in Chapter Eight and medication in Chapter Nine.)

In developing a new approach to treating people with OCD, our research team thought that if we could make patients understand that a biochemical imbalance in the brain was causing their intrusive urges, they might take a different look at their need to act on those urges and strengthen their resolve to fight them. A new method of behavior therapy might result.

To help patients understand this chemical imbalance, we showed them pictures of their brains at work. During a study of brain energy activity in people with OCD, my colleague, Dr. Lew Baxter, and I took some high-tech pictures using positron emission tomography, or PET scanning, in which a very small amount of a chemically labeled glucoselike substance is injected into a person and traced in the brain. The resulting pictures clearly indicated that in people with OCD, the use of energy is consistently higher than is normal in the orbital cortex—the underside of the front of the brain. Thus, the orbital cortex is, in essence, working overtime, literally heating up. (Figure 1, opposite, shows a PET scan—presented in color on the cover of this book—of a typical OCD patient. Note the high energy use in the orbital cortex, compared to that in a person who does not have OCD.)

We already knew that by using behavior therapy we could make real and significant changes in how people cope with their urges. Perhaps, we reasoned, we could use these visually striking pictures of the brain to help inspire people with OCD. Since a brain problem appeared to be causing their intrusive urges, strengthening their will to resist the urges might actually change their brain chemistry, in addition to improving their clinical condition.

Benjamin, a 41-year-old administrator in a large school district whose brain photos are pictured later, in Figure 3, suffered from a compulsive, time-consuming need to have everything in his environment clean and orderly to an abnormal degree. He recalls vividly having his brain photographed and then being shown proof that it was overheating. "Boy, was that a real jolt!" he said. "It was very distressing to learn that I had a brain disorder, that I wasn't perfect. Initially, it was very difficult to accept." At the same time, seeing the picture was critical to his understanding that he had OCD, in his words, "incontrovertible evidence that I had a brain disorder." In our program at UCLA, Benjamin mastered the Four Steps of cognitive-biobehavioral self-treatment, and today, six years later, his symptoms are largely under control and he is functioning well, both professionally and in his personal relationships.

Figure 1. PET scan showing increased energy use in the orbital cortex, the underside of the front of the brain, in a person with OCD. The drawings show where the orbital cortex is located inside the head. The arrows point at the orbital cortex.

location where brain slice is taken

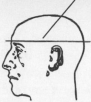

ORBITAL CORTEX   ORBITAL CORTEX

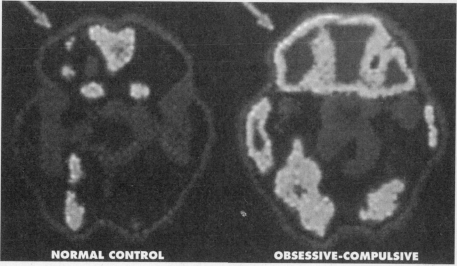

NORMAL CONTROL   OBSESSIVE-COMPULSIVE

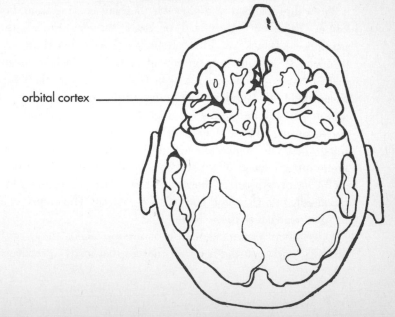

orbital cortex

Understanding the difference between the form of OCD urges and their content is the first step toward understanding that brain malfunction is the main culprit in these urges. Remember Barbara and her obsessive worry about Mr. Coffee? She was being driven to distraction, worrying whether she'd turned off that machine. That was the content of her obsession. Superficially, that was her problem. But in treatment, it soon became obvious to her, and to us, that the real problem was that she couldn't rid herself of the *feeling* that Mr. Coffee might still be on. That she was plagued by that worry hundreds, even thousands, of times a day gave us an important clue to the mystery of OCD: She could have that all-consuming worry even while holding the unplugged cord from Mr. Coffee in her hand!

Likewise, Brian knew that a brand-new battery was not going to leak acid. Still, if someone placed a battery on his desk, he freaked out: "The kid who worked with me said he saw guys under fire in Vietnam who didn't have the fear in their faces that I had."

And Dottie knew that her son was not going to go blind if she didn't perform a certain compulsion. But if she happened to see a TV show about a person who was blind, she'd have to jump in the shower, clothes and all.

What really worried Barbara, Brian, and Dottie was how they could be so worried about something so ridiculous.

We will probably never know why Barbara became fixated on Mr. Coffee, Brian on battery acid, or Dottie on eyes. Freud's theories may provide clues, yet Freud himself believed that these types of problems stem from "constitutional factors," by which he meant biological causes. Today, most psychiatrists in the Freudian tradition acknowledge that understanding the psychological content of these symptoms—the deep inner conflicts that lead one person to worry about causing a fire and another to fear that he or she will do something violent to someone—will do little, if anything, to make the symptoms go away. Why not? Because the core of the problem in OCD lies in its form, in the fact that the worrisome feeling intrudes repeatedly into the mind and will not go away. The culprit is a neurological imbalance in the brain.

Once people understand the nature of OCD, they are better armed to carry out the behavior therapy that leads to recovery. Just knowing, "It's not me—it's my OCD" is a stress reliever that enables them to focus more effectively on getting well. From time to time, we remind them that they are not just pushing a rock to the top of a hill only to have it roll back down again and again. They are actually *changing* the hill. They are changing their brains.

IT'S WHAT YOU *DO* THAT COUNTS

The brain is an incredibly complicated *machine* whose function is to generate feelings and sensations that help us communicate with the world. When it works correctly, it's easy to assume that "it is me." But when the brain starts sending false messages that you cannot readily recognize as false, as happens with OCD, havoc can ensue.

This is where **mindful awareness,** the ability to recognize these messages as false, can help. We learned from OCD patients that everyone has the capacity to use the power of observation to make behavioral corrections in the face of the brain's false and misleading messages. It's like listening to a radio station that's jammed with static. If you don't listen closely, you may hear things that are misleading or make no sense. But if you make an effort to listen closely, you'll hear things the casual listener misses entirely—especially if you've been trained to listen. Properly instructed in what to do in the face of confusing messages, you can find reality in the midst of chaos.

I like to say, *"It's not how you feel, but what you do, that counts."* Because when you do the right things, feelings tend to improve as a matter of course. But spend too much time being overly concerned about uncomfortable feelings, and you may never get around to doing what it takes to actually improve. Focus your attention on the mental and physical actions that will improve your life—that's the working philosophy of this book, and the path to overcoming Brain Lock.

The Four Steps are not a magic formula. By calling an urge what it is—by Relabeling it—you cannot immediately make it go away. Excessive wishful thinking about immediate recovery is one of the biggest causes of failure, especially at the start of treatment. The goal here is not to make obsessive thoughts simply disappear—they won't, in the short run—but, rather, to be in control of your responses to them. The behavior therapy guidelines you will learn while doing the Four Steps will help you remember this crucial principle. You will gain control and change your brain mainly by using your new knowledge to mentally organize your behavioral responses and by learning to say, "That's not me—that's my OCD."

The key to remember is this: **Change the behavior, unlock your brain!**

KEY POINTS TO REMEMBER

•OCD is a medical condition that is related to a biochemical imbalance in the brain.

•Obsessions are intrusive, unwanted thoughts and urges that don't go away.

•Compulsions are the repetitive behaviors that people perform in a vain attempt to rid themselves of the very uncomfortable feelings that the obsessions cause.

•Doing compulsions tends to make the obsessions *worse,* especially over the long run.

•The Four Steps teach a method of reorganizing your thinking in response to unwanted thoughts and urges: They help you to *change your behavior* to something useful and constructive.

•Changing your behavior changes your brain. When you change your behavior in constructive ways, the uncomfortable feelings your brain is sending you begin to fade over time. This makes your responses easier to manage and control.

•It's not how you feel, but what you *do* that counts.

PART I

The Four Steps

WORDS OF WISDOM TO GUIDE YOU ON YOUR JOURNEY
(in chronological order)

One who is slow to anger is better than a warrior, and one who rules his spirit is better than one who takes a city.

—King Solomon, *Proverbs 16:32*

You yourself must do the strenuous work. Enlightened Ones can only show the way.

—Gotama Buddha, *Dhammapada 276*

Be not deceived; God is not mocked: For whatever you may sow, that you will also reap.

—St. Paul the Apostle, *Galatians 6:7*

God helps those who help themselves.

—Benjamin Franklin, *Poor Richard's Almanac*, 1736

1

Step 1: Relabel

"It's Not Me—It's My OCD"

Step 1. RELABEL

Step 2. Reattribute

Step 3. Refocus

Step 4. Revalue

Step 1: **Relabel** answers the question, "**What are these bothersome, intrusive thoughts?**" The important point to keep in mind is that you must **Relabel these unwanted thoughts, urges, and behaviors.** You must **call them what they really are: They are obsessions and compulsions.** You must make a conscious effort to keep firmly grounded in reality. You must strive to avoid being tricked into thinking that the feeling that you need to check or to count or to wash, for example, is a real need. It is not.

Your thoughts and urges are symptoms of obsessive-compulsive disorder (OCD), a medical disease.

**Professor Gallagher and his controversial
technique of simultaneously confronting
the fear of heights, snakes and the dark.**

Professor Gallagher, as you see, has his own ideas about "curing" patients who suffer from frightening and intrusive thoughts or obsessions.

He is actually performing a cartoon variation on what is known in the language of traditional behavior therapy as "flooding." Unfortunately, this poor patient more than likely ended up crazed rather than cured.

In working with patients with OCD, our UCLA team has had excellent results using behavior therapy, sometimes in conjunction with medication. Ours is not Gallagher's sink-or-swim approach but, rather, a long-term self-directed therapy we call cognitive-biobehavioral self-treatment.

Typically, our first consultation with a person with OCD begins with the person explaining with a considerable amount of embarrassment, "Doctor, I know this sounds kind of crazy, but . . . "

The person then describes one or more from a checklist of classic OCD symptoms: compulsive washing or checking, irrational violent or blasphemous thoughts, or feelings of impending doom or catastrophe unless some bizarre or senseless ritual is performed.

These people usually know that no one is supposed to think such weird thoughts. As a consequence, they feel humiliated and at their wit's end. Their self-esteem has plummeted, their OCD may well have affected their ability to perform on the job, and they may even have become socially dysfunctional, withdrawing from family and friends in an attempt to hide these awful behaviors.

IT'S NOT INSANITY, IT'S BRAIN LOCK

In treatment, the person is first assured that the diagnosis is just OCD. It is just the brain sending false messages. We show pictures of the brains of people with OCD that prove conclusively that OCD is associated with a biochemical problem that causes the underside of the front part of the brain to overheat.

In short, the person is suffering from Brain Lock. The brain has become stuck in an inappropriate groove. The key to unlocking the brain is behavior therapy, and that begins with the Relabeling step.

Relabeling simply means calling the unwanted thoughts and urges by their real names—*obsessive* thoughts and *compulsive* urges. These are not just uncomfortable feelings like "maybe it's dirty," but gnawing and unremitting obsessions. Not just bothersome urges to check for the fourth or the fifth time, but brutal, compulsive urges.

This is war, and the enemy is OCD. In fighting back, it is critical to keep in mind what that enemy really is. The person with OCD has a powerful weapon: the knowledge that "It's not me—it's OCD." He or she works constantly to prevent confusing the true self with the voice of OCD.

All well and good, you may say, but OCD has a mind of its own. It won't shut up. To this I reply, "Yes it will, but it takes time." Praying for OCD to go away won't instantly make it happen, nor will idle and futile cursing.

If you wish to pray, what you should pray for is the strength to help yourself. God helps those who help themselves, and it's only reasonable to believe that God would help someone engaged in such a worthwhile struggle. In this case, it means concentrating on doing the right thing, while letting go of an excessive concern with feelings and comfort level. This is, in the best sense, performing a good work!

At the same time, it is medical self-treatment that begins with accepting what you cannot change—at least in the short term.

Right off, it is vital to understand that the simple act of Relabeling will not make your OCD disappear. But when you see this enemy for what it is, OCD, you sap its strength and you, in turn, become stronger.

In time, it won't matter that much to you whether the bothersome thoughts totally go away because you are not going to act on them. Furthermore, the more you are able to dismiss the importance of your OCD, the more you will feel in control and the more it *will* go away. On the other hand, the more you focus on it, wishing and hoping and begging for it to leave you alone, the more intense and bothersome the feelings will become.

TALKING BACK TO OCD

Because OCD can be a fiendishly clever opponent and a demonically self-protective one, it will deny that it is simply a false message from your brain. You may say, "A plane is *not* going to crash because I didn't wash my hands again." But OCD will say, "Oh, yes it will, and many people will die." That's the time to show some faith and strength because *you* know what the truth is.

You can't afford to listen. If you sit and fret about whether OCD is going to invade your life on a given day, you're only assuring yourself more dread and pain. You must say, "Go ahead, make my day. Just *try* to make me wash my hands one more time."

Then you must deal with the ever-present uncertainty, "How can I be *sure* that this is not me, just my OCD?" Well, perhaps there are no metaphysical guarantees that there is no possible relationship between hand washing and a plane crash, but I *can* guarantee that if you give in and wash your hands again, things will only get worse and the OCD will only get stronger. On the other hand, within a few minutes of Refocusing on another behavior and not responding to the OCD, the fear of some dreadful consequence will begin to fade, and you will begin to see the OCD compulsion as the ridiculous nonsense it is.

The decision is clear-cut: Listen to your OCD and have your life disrupted and ultimately destroyed, or fight back, secure in the knowledge that within a few minutes you will begin to feel more and more certain that planes aren't going to fly into mountains and cars aren't going to crash just because you didn't wash your hands or check the lock again.

It is a matter of exerting effort so that good triumphs over evil.

IT'S JUST A CHEMICAL

At UCLA, our patients have come up with amazingly creative ways of applying the Four Steps—Relabel, Reattribute, Refocus, Revalue.

Chet, who has since successfully controlled his OCD through behavior therapy and is now in dental school, was obsessed by violent thoughts. If he saw a fire, he thought he had started it. If he heard that someone had been fatally shot across town, he obsessed that he had done it. He would walk around saying to himself, "Man, you're just one messed-up guy. You're a bad person." He was in a dead-end job that he hated and was dealing with debt. These factors made his stress level escalate and his OCD symptoms worsen. Stress commonly heightens OCD anxieties.

At first, when Chet began Relabeling, telling himself that his violent thoughts were just OCD, his OCD would talk back, "Oh, is this upsetting you? Why? Maybe because you really will do it." By gaining the knowledge that OCD is a biochemical imbalance in the brain, Chet was eventually able to use this phrase with his OCD: "Don't be polemical—it's just a chemical."

Anticipation is an important substep in Relabeling, and Chet understood it perfectly. Watching a movie in which he knew a violent scene was coming, he would tell himself, "Okay, here comes my obsessive thought." When he did that, it didn't hurt as much.

In combating his OCD, Chet was both pragmatic and philosophical. He had always wished that he were six inches taller, he reasoned, but he knew that wishing wasn't going to make him grow and he could deal with being short. He realized it was the same with OCD: Wishing wouldn't make it go away, but he could learn to deal with it.

Chet found another way to best the OCD: Every time he had an OCD thought, he would do something nice for his fiancée—buy her roses, perhaps, or cook her dinner. Whenever the OCD wanted to make him miserable, he would make himself happy by making his fiancée happy.

A deeply religious man, Chet also turned to the Scriptures for inspiration and found comfort in the passage "The Lord searcheth all hearts and He understands all the imaginations of the mind" (I Chronicles 28:9). Chet clearly understood how this passage applied to him: God understands my heart and knows that my mind is messed up. I must work to stop beating myself up over it.

It's interesting to note that there is a centuries-old precedent for this. John Bunyan, the seventeenth-century British author of *The Pilgrim's Progress*, suffered from what we now know was OCD. Because Bunyan was an intensely religious man (an itinerant preacher who was imprisoned for preaching without a license), he agonized over his OCD-induced blasphemous thoughts. He dealt with his guilt—as does Chet—through a conviction that God would be upset with him for punishing himself for having false and meaningless thoughts. For this brilliant insight, I consider Bunyan the father of cognitive-behavior therapy for OCD.

THE IMPARTIAL SPECTATOR

In learning to Relabel, it is not enough to shrug and say, "It's not me—it's my OCD" in an automaton-like manner. Mindful awareness is essential. Mindful awareness differs from simple, superficial awareness in that it requires you to consciously recognize and make a mental note of that unpleasant feeling, Relabeling it as an OCD symptom caused by a false message from the brain. As the feeling sweeps over you, you must say to yourself, "I don't *think* or *feel* that my hands are dirty; rather, I'm having an *obsession* that my hands are dirty." "I don't feel the *need* to check that lock; rather, I'm having a *compulsive urge* to check that lock." This will not make the urge go away, but it will set the stage for actively resisting the OCD thoughts and urges.

We can learn from the writings of the eighteenth-century Scottish philosopher Adam Smith, who developed the concept of "the impartial and well-informed spectator," which is nothing more or less than "the person within." Each of us has access to this person inside us who, while fully aware of our feelings and circumstances, is nonetheless capable of taking on the role of spectator or impartial observer. This is simply another way of understanding mindful awareness: It enhances our ability to make mental notes, such as "That's just OCD."

In Relabeling, you bring into play the Impartial Spectator, a concept that Adam Smith used as the central feature of his book *The Theory of Moral Sentiments*. He defined the Impartial Spectator as the capacity to stand outside yourself and watch yourself in action, which is essentially the same mental action as the ancient Buddhist concept of mindful awareness. People with OCD use the Impartial Spectator when they step back and say to themselves, "This is just my brain sending me a false message. If I change my behavior, I'll actually be changing how my brain works." It is inspirational to watch people with OCD shift from a superficial understanding of their disorder to a deep mindfulness that allows them to overcome their fears and anxieties, to mentally organize their responses, to shift gears, and to change their behavior. This process is the basis for overcoming OCD.

Once a person with OCD learns behavior therapy and resolves to change his or her response to an intrusive, painful thought by not performing some pathological behavior, a willful resolve kicks in: "I'm not going to wash my hands. I'm going to practice the violin instead." But, in the beginning, the person is beset with fear and dread and may very well have catastrophic thoughts, such as, "But then my violin will get contaminated. . . ."

Adam Smith understood that keeping the perspective of the Impartial Spectator under painful circumstances is hard work, requiring, in his words, the "utmost and most fatiguing exertions." Why? Because focusing on a useful behavior when your brain is bombarding you with distracting doubts and disturbing mental aberrations takes a great deal of work.

Of course, performing a compulsive behavior repetitively, ad nauseum, is also exhausting. But it is exhaustion with no positive payoff. When the Impartial Spectator is attended to, when an action is done mindfully, it makes a significant difference in how the brain functions. And that is the key to overcoming Brain Lock. This is what our scientific research at UCLA has shown.

WHO'S IN CHARGE HERE?

There will be times when the pain is too great and the effort required too debilitating, and you will give in and do a compulsion. Think of it as a tiny backward step. Tell yourself that you'll win next time. As Jeremy, a man with OCD, put it, "Even when you fail, you succeed—so long as you persevere. So long as you take on this enemy, OCD, with mindful awareness."

Anna, a philosophy student, described how she used the Relabel step in battling an obsession that her boyfriend (now her husband) was unfaithful to her. Although she knew her fears had no basis in fact, she would bombard him with questions about past romances, about whether he had ever looked at pornographic magazines, about what he drank and how much, what he ate, and where he was every minute of the day. Her relentless interrogations almost led to the breakup of their relationship. Anna recalls, "The first step in beginning to conquer my OCD was to learn to Relabel my thoughts and urges. The second step was to Reattribute them to OCD. In my treatment, these went hand in hand. On an intellectual level, I knew that OCD was a chemical problem in my brain and that the sensations this problem produced were more or less meaningless side effects of the chemical problem. Still, it is one thing to know this intellectually and another to be able to say while in the midst of an OCD attack that what you are feeling really isn't important per se.

The irritating thing about OCD is that when you have it, your worries, urges, and obsessions seem like the most important things in the world. Stepping back from them long enough to identify them as OCD-generated is thus no mean feat."

In the early stages of Anna's learning to Relabel, her boyfriend, Guy, kept reminding her that her obsessions were "just OCD," but he could not always convince her. Over time—and with practice—she became, in her words, "pretty good at recognizing what is OCD and what is a 'real' worry or anxiety. As a result, I can frequently avoid buying into OCD when it strikes. I no longer become mentally distressed each and every time an obsessive-type thought enters my mind. Often, I can look beyond it and say to myself, 'You know, it won't do any good to get all upset about this thought. I've been through all this before, and it doesn't accomplish anything to allow myself to be sucked into OCD's tricks.' Doing this allows a certain calm and satisfying detachment." Anna found that the intrusive thought—or at least the intense anxiety surrounding it—dissipates, usually within fifteen to thirty minutes.

For Dottie, who had the obsession about her son losing his eyesight and who coined the phrase "It's not me—it's my OCD," Relabeling was the biggest help in combating her compulsion. "It was not dwelling on it, recognizing it, and saying, 'It's okay, it's just a thought and that's all it is.' Most days, that works for me. Some days it's a struggle. I say people with OCD will always have OCD unless they find some magical pill." But, as you'll learn from the stories throughout this book, the mental strength and power you gain while fighting OCD can never be gained from any "magic pill."

Jack, the hand washer, had been looking for that magical pill. "That's America. You take a pill and your life will be wonderful; you'll be a whole new person, more aggressive or nicer or thinner or whatever." But when medication did not make his OCD symptoms abate and the side effects of medication grew too bothersome, he turned to cognitive-biobehavioral therapy. For him, the first step in Relabeling was to recognize the absurdity of his hand washing and to convince himself that it was not logical. When he was at home, he washed almost continuously, but when he was out, it didn't seem so important to wash. "In behavior therapy, I thought, 'Wait a minute.

You go out to fast-food places and you don't wash your hands, then you handle money or they handle money, and nothing bad has happened to you yet, you know. And even if you use their rest rooms to wash your hands, it's hard to get out without touching a doorknob." Jack didn't have dirty hands; he had OCD, and he was beginning to use his rational mind to overcome it.

Barbara, who had obsessions about Mr. Coffee, spoke of mindful awareness as a tool that helped her to Relabel. "By putting myself into a deliberately aware or conscious state when checking, I could walk away from the site of the compulsion with, if not the certainty that the appliance was off, at least with the real, firm knowledge that the check had been performed. I also learned to say to myself when feeling the horrible uncertainty that, say, the stove was not off, 'This is not me—this is my OCD. It is the disease that is making me feel uncertain. Although I *feel* the stove is not off, I have checked it mindfully and should now walk away. The anxiety will lessen eventually, and fifteen minutes down the line I'll feel even more certain that the stove is off.'" If you have problems with checking compulsions, take particular note of Barbara's description. It's excellent advice on how to perform checking behaviors in a way that prepares you to deal with compulsive urges.

Lara, who has the terrifying obsession about knives, learned to tell herself, "Lara, it's only an obsession. It's not reality. You're frightened because it seems so horrific and unbelievable. This is a disorder, just like any other disorder." Understanding that OCD is a medical condition and that obsessions are false messages with no real power or meaning "lessens their power and punch," Lara learned. Obsessions *don't* take over your will. You can *always* control—or at least modify—your responses to them.

Jenny developed a lingering obsession about nuclear contamination while working in the Soviet Union. Learning that she had a biochemical problem in her brain "lifted some of the burden," she said. "I'd always been so angry with myself. 'How can you be so strong and successful in so many areas of your life and still have this problem?' I'd always felt that I was entirely at fault because I was not able to psychoanalyze myself. I could never get in there and find out what was bothering me or find the right mantra, the right shrink, whatever." Now, when OCD attacks strike, she talks to herself, telling herself, "Well, I know what *that* is." And, usually, she manages to move on.

Roberta, who has the obsession that she has hit someone while driving, said, "I still have the unwanted thought, but it is now controllable. Now, when I go over a bump in the road, I tell myself that it is just a bump. The thought that I hit someone is just a wrong message. It's OCD—not me! I try not to look back or to retrace my route. I force myself to keep going forward. I am no longer afraid to drive. I understand that if the obsessive thought comes, I know that I can deal with it. When I'm getting frustrated, I even say out loud, 'It's not me—it's the OCD.' And then I'll say, 'Okay, Roberta, just keep going straight ahead.'"

Jeremy, an aspiring young screenwriter, is largely free of OCD after eight months of behavior therapy. Today, he says, "I still feel the anxiety of freedom. It hurts, but it is the price to pay to be a free man."

From childhood, Jeremy had been overwhelmed by touching and checking compulsions that he performed without fail, fearing that a family member would die "and God would damn me to hell for it." Home became a "torture chamber" of rituals. By his teens, Jeremy was seeking escape in alcohol and drugs. As a young adult, he kicked his drinking habit with the help of Alcoholics Anonymous, but he began to obsess that something he had eaten contained alcohol. It could be Rice-a-Roni or something equally nonsensical. Logic played no role here.

At his gym, Jeremy imagined that someone had used drugs or alcohol before touching the bars and weights and that he would somehow absorb it. In a public bathroom, he would be seized by the thought that a drunk had vomited in the toilet just before he used it and, through some kind of magical transference, the alcohol was going to get into his system. Mentally and emotionally, Jeremy was exhausted from dealing with his obsessions and compulsions. When he first came to UCLA seeking help, he said, "I feel like I have been through the jungle in Vietnam."

During treatment, Jeremy kept with him a small spiral notepad on which he'd written CAUDATE NUCLEUS. That's the part of the brain that's not filtering out the OCD thoughts properly. This was his constant reminder that he had a brain-wiring problem, that he had OCD. It helped him to be mindful that he had to screen the OCD thoughts through his own mental power. "Once the pain had a name," he says, "the pain wasn't as bad." Making mental notes eventually made his brain's filtering system begin to work better.

Earlier, I mentioned the Relabeling substep, Anticipation. The other substep in Relabeling is Acceptance. Jeremy became adept at both. Before treatment, he had lived in fear of being caught in some imaginary dastardly act and being fired from his job as a night watchman. With behavior therapy, he was able to say, "Big deal. Nobody's perfect. Let them fire me; I'll get another job. Worst-case scenario? I'll eat at soup kitchens. Hey, George Orwell did it and wrote a great book about it," *Down and Out in Paris and London.* And if there really was forbidden alcohol in something he'd eaten, Jeremy would say, "Just a slip. Not intentional." No guilt. No recriminations.

Once free of OCD symptoms, Jeremy had a reaction that is not uncommon. "For years, OCD had run—and been—my life. I thought of little else. I actually mourned my OCD." But this mourning period was short, and soon Jeremy began to fill the vacuum with positive, wholesome activities.

RX: ACTION

Learning to overcome OCD is like learning to ride a bicycle. Once you learn, you never forget, but getting good at it takes practice. You'll fall off, but you must get back on. If you give up, you'll never learn. Most patients find that it helps at first to have training wheels for the bike. That's where the medication comes in. In combination with behavior therapy, medication has been shown to produce an 80 percent success rate.

The vast majority of those who fail to respond to this treatment combination do so because they become demoralized and throw in the towel. It is essential that you never do the compulsion and tell yourself, "I can't avoid doing it. It's bigger than I am." It's okay to feel overwhelmed by the compulsion, and even to act on it if you must, as long as you remind yourself, "This is a compulsion. Next time, I'm going to fight it."

Passivity is your enemy. Activity is your friend. The biggest enemy is boredom. Having something else you really need to do—something much more important than that nonsensical ritual—is a great motivator. People with nothing to do may not develop the mental and emotional strength to shift those gears in the brain and move on to a positive behavior. If you have a job, you're apt to lose it if you go home to check that lock once more, so you'll be much more motivated to pull yourself away. When you pull yourself away, you're treating your OCD. Idleness is indeed the devil's workshop. If you're not up to working, you can get a volunteer job, but the important thing is to **stay busy.** Make sure you have something useful to do. Being useful will increase your self-confidence and motivate you to get better because others need you. It's also a tremendous aid to the Refocus step.

Some people are too depressed to work. Depression often, but not always, goes hand in hand with OCD. If your sleep pattern is radically altered, with repeated waking during the night; if you're not eating properly and are losing weight; if you have poor energy and serious suicidal thoughts, you may have a severe depression. If that is the case, you must see a doctor.

As you have learned, acting on a compulsion brings only momentary relief, followed very quickly by an increased intensity in the intrusive urge or thought—a true vicious cycle.

After treating about a thousand people with OCD, I find that one of the most amazing things about OCD is that people continue to be shocked by their internal feeling that something is dreadfully wrong—that the stove is not turned off, or whatever—no matter how many times a day that thought intrudes. They would get used to, say, an electric shock after a while, but they never seem to get used to these OCD fears and urges. That is why mindful awareness, mental note taking, is so important. In step one, Relabel, you increase your insight. You call an obsession an obsession and a compulsion a compulsion.

HANGING TOUGH

After Relabeling, many patients ask, "Why the hell does this thing keep bothering me?" It does so because of a brain-wiring problem. The struggle is not to make the feeling go away; the struggle is *not to give in to the feeling.* Emotional understanding will not make the OCD symptoms magically disappear, but cognitive-biobehavioral therapy will help you manage your fears. If you can hang in through the first few weeks of self-directed therapy, you will have acquired the tools you need. You will have become stronger than your OCD. Mastering these therapy skills is like having exercise equipment in your head. It makes you strong. OCD is a chronic disease. You can't run from it, and you can't buy your way out of it, but you *can* fight back.

Patients often say to me, "Oh, if only I could have someone wash my clothes whenever I feel that they need to be washed over and over. . . ." They think that would take care of the OCD. They're dead wrong. Remember Howard Hughes? That's precisely what he did— and look where he wound up. OCD is insatiable. You cannot do a compulsion enough times—or have someone else do it for you—to get a feeling of "That's enough." The more you do it, the worse it gets. It doesn't matter whether you wash your clothes or hire someone to wash them. Giving in to OCD is giving in to OCD. It makes things worse!

In *Howard Hughes: The Untold Story,* Peter H. Brown and Pat Broeske provide more evidence that Hughes's obsession about germs and contamination caused him to act in irrational ways. We now know that his actions only served to make his symptoms worse. For a period of time, Hughes weekly invited his friends, underworld figures Lucky Luciano and Bugsy Siegel, to dinner. Because he was obsessed with the idea that gangsters had germs, he kept in a cabinet a set of special china for these occasions. This china could be used only once. At one time, Hughes shared a house in Los Angeles with Katharine Hepburn and Cary Grant. One evening, having come upon the housekeeper smashing the dinner plates, Hepburn confronted Hughes: "This is stupid! People can't spread germs like this." Hughes was not convinced. Furthermore, he told Hepburn,

"As a woman who takes eighteen showers a day, I don't think you're in a position to argue with me."

It is possible that Hepburn, too, was afflicted with OCD. We do know that it is not unusual for people with OCD to be attracted to one another. First of all, it's comforting to find another who understands the agony, who hears the inner voice asking, "Why do I do all these weird things?" People with OCD know that they do things that are a little strange. So, it can be comforting to know others who also do these things. At UCLA, we started the first OCD behavior therapy group in the country. This group still meets weekly at UCLA; it's a place where people with OCD feel free to divulge their most bizarre thoughts and behaviors and to exchange self-therapy techniques they may have developed on their own. (The Four-Step Method allows for a lot of personal creativity.) At first, there was some concern that these sessions might prove counterproductive, since in some well-intentioned victim-support groups, participants get into a sort of sick competition about who has suffered the most. Also, several patients expressed to me their fear that, through the power of suggestion, they might develop new symptoms to pile onto their existing ones. Neither of these fears has proved true in the nearly ten years the group has been meeting.

One of the many success stories in the OCD group is Domingo, a onetime plumber who is now a self-taught art dealer. Domingo, who was diagnosed with OCD in his native Mexico, was "all the way at the bottom" of the OCD heap when he came to UCLA for treatment. Over a fifteen-year period, his symptoms have included showering five or more hours a day, the fear of showering, checking and eating rituals, and—what is the most bizarre—an obsession that he had razor blades attached to his fingernails. This last obsession led to his reluctance to wear certain clothes, including a favorite vintage motorcycle jacket, for fear that he would rip them to shreds with his imagined nail-blades. "I can't touch babies," he says. "They're too delicate. My dog, I play with him but I cannot touch his face, his eyes, for fear I'll cut him." At times when Domingo and his wife made love, he drew back from touching her, especially her chest. As he said at the time, "I think I'm going to cut her. I keep thinking I've got blades on me, and my hand begins to shake, my muscles get real tight, and I have to pull back. My eyes see there are no blades, but my mind won't believe. And I have to ask her, 'Are you okay? Did I hurt you?'"

Through therapy, he has learned a basic truth: "You have to be stronger than OCD, physically and mentally. If you're not, it will eat you alive. It will put you in bed, and you will rot like a vegetable." Most days, when seized by a compulsion to wash or check, he is able to say to himself, "This is not real. You have to stop. You have things to do."

Domingo makes himself choose: "Am I going to listen to this OCD or go and do my laundry? I tell myself, 'It's going to hurt really bad, but I have to go on.' I close my eyes, take a deep breath, and just go through it—just push as hard as I can."

Because he is capable of seeing quite clearly the difference between normal behavior and OCD behavior, he is able to bring himself around by zeroing in on reality. He reminds himself that a beautiful woman has chosen to be his wife and that she sees something special in him. "Look at all you've done," he tells himself. "This is the reality you have to grab onto. You have to stop this thought right now. You must. If you don't stop this, it will take over—and then what?" Domingo knows that if he gives in to the compulsion or the thought, it will keep going around and around in his brain, sapping his energy and wasting his time. He calls this "brain loop."

He also knows that even if his OCD is never cured, he now has the upper hand. "Before, I couldn't count the compulsions. One would go, and another would take its place. Now I know how many I'm fighting. Before, they were coming from right and left. I was overwhelmed. Now I know where it's going to get me. I'm ready. I don't listen to my OCD because I know it's fake. I let it go quickly."

TELL IT TO YOUR TAPE RECORDER

Another regular in the OCD group is Christopher, a devout young Roman Catholic who for more than five years has been battling OCD-induced blasphemous thoughts. Christopher's disease reached a crisis point during a pilgrimage to a European shrine well known as a site where numerous apparitions of the Virgin Mary have been reported. Though he had gone seeking spiritual enrichment, to his horror, he found himself in the little church one day thinking, "The Virgin Mary is a bitch." Profoundly sad and ashamed, he broke down and cried. Back home, these blasphemous thoughts piled one on another. He began having thoughts that the holy water is "shit water," the Bible a "shit book," the churches "shit houses." In Mass, he would imagine the holy statues naked. In his OCD-invaded brain, priests had become "scoundrels." The mere sight of a church made him cringe.

In desperation, Christopher checked himself into a psychiatric hospital, where he was diagnosed as paranoid psychotic and questioned about being "demonically possessed." It would be two years before he was correctly diagnosed as having OCD.

Christopher is one of the patients who has found the use of tape-recorded loops a useful tool in performing the Relabel step. This simple and effective technique was developed by Dr. Paul Salkovskis and Dr. Isaac Marks in England. Anyone can practice it at home. All you need are answering machine tape loops—thirty seconds, sixty seconds, and three minutes—a cassette player, and headphones. The idea is to record the obsession, repeating the thought over and over, and then to listen to it repeatedly, perhaps forty-five minutes at a time. The tape will keep relooping over itself, so there is no need to rewind.

Christopher suggests writing complex obsessions down in short-story form before taping, creating a scenario in which the dreaded consequences actually come true. For example, "If you have scrupulosity and religious obsessions, have God strike you dead and throw you into the fire at the end. If you obsess about committing a crime, have the police arrest you and make you spend the rest of your life in jail. If you fear dirt and germs, make yourself look like you fell in a pool of mud or came down with a deadly germ-spread disease and died. The important thing is to make the obsession look as stupid and ridiculous as possible." On a scale of one to ten, playing the tapes should cause anxiety in the five or six range at the beginning of a forty-five-minute session.

Another tip from Christopher: "I prefer using one of those big boom boxes. I found that, with the small players, I would often be tempted to get up and do things because it's very easy to carry those things around. That's not very effective for behavior therapy. A big boom box kind of makes you sit there." When privacy is important, of course, you can use headphones.

The idea of the tape loops is to create anxiety that will peak and then ebb. The person listens to the tape perhaps twice a day for several days, perhaps as long as a week. "Eventually," Christopher promises, "you'll get to the point where you can't stand even listening to it, not because it's too anxiety-provoking but because it's too boring. That's why it works." It's also helpful, he believes, to keep a chart of your anxiety levels at ten- or fifteen-minute intervals. After some days have passed and the anxiety level is at zero, it's time to rerecord the tape, this time in more anxiety-provoking language, and then do another tape, working toward recording the most anxiety-provoking aspects of the obsession.

Christopher cautions, "Don't expect that after these sessions you will no longer have the obsessive thought. It's just that you will more easily dismiss it from your mind and, eventually, it should decrease."

Before behavior therapy, Christopher had literally dozens of obsessions, including violent thoughts about flying knives. "I used to have these horrible, wild fits where I would take a pillow and hit my face into it really hard and scream at the top of my lungs, punching the pillow or punching the couch. The OCD was so bad. It was terrible." At first, working out his anxieties with the tape loop was no picnic. "There were times when the anxiety shot through my body so bad that I felt like a woman giving birth . . . that much pain. I would be sweating, and my arms and hands would be tingling. That doesn't happen anymore."

"DEAR DIARY"

As part of cognitive-biobehavioral self-treatment, I urge patients to keep a journal of their progress. Christopher, a faithful journal keeper, says, "I've found that whenever I recover from an OCD symptom, the natural tendency is for that symptom to become relegated to the back of my mind or forgotten. That's the goal, of course, but as you forget each symptom, you tend to forget your progress." Without this written record, he believes, the road to recovery is "like taking a journey across a desert and only walking backwards, while wiping away your footprints with your hand. It looks like you're always at the starting point." The critical point is to chart your progress, to keep a record of your behavior therapy efforts. It can be short and simple. It doesn't have to be fancy or complicated.

Christopher also uses the Impartial Spectator in Relabeling. He prefers to call it "my rational mind," as in, "My rational mind says this isn't true. This is reality. This isn't. I'm going to follow the advice of my rational mind." This is a perfectly legitimate and accurate alternative term. It's the action of making mental notes that's important, not what you call the process of mental observation.

Think of the Impartial Spectator as a vehicle for distancing your will from your OCD. In other words, create a safety zone between your internal spirit and the unwanted compulsive urge. Rather than respond to the urge in a mechanical, unthinking fashion, you present yourself with alternatives. As you'll learn later, it's good to have some alternative behaviors up your sleeve, so you'll be ready when the intense pain occurs. As Domingo said, "This thing, OCD, is damned clever. You have to keep your wits about you to beat it."

Frequently, patients find that one symptom disappears, only to be supplanted by another. However, a new symptom is always easier to control than one that has been long entrenched. Without treatment, OCD will just beat you into submission. Anticipate—be ready to resist this thing early on—and it will be far less painful.

HUGHES: BEYOND BIZARRE

This disease, OCD, manifests itself in ways that give new meaning to the word *bizarre*. Consider, once again, Howard Hughes. He went so far as to come up with a theory he called the "backflow of germs." When his closest friend died of the complications of hepatitis, Hughes could not bring himself to send flowers to the funeral, fearing in his OCD-controlled mind that if he did, the hepatitis germs would somehow find their way back to him. Hughes was also a compulsive toilet sitter, once sitting for forty-two hours, unable to convince himself that he had finished the business at hand. This is not a rare OCD symptom, and I've treated a number of people for it. When they're ready to get better, they'll say, "I'd rather soil my trousers than sit here another minute." Of course, no one has ever soiled his or her clothing.

Senseless repetition was another common symptom that Hughes was observed to have. Hughes, a cross-country pilot, once called an assistant to get the Kansas City weather tables before he took off. He didn't ask for those tables just once. Although he got the information he needed for his flight the first time, he asked thirty-three times, repeating the same question. He then denied having repeated himself.

Interviewing me for his book on Hughes, Peter Brown asked, "Why couldn't he stop it, someone as brilliant as he was?" Brilliance has nothing to do with it. Hughes had the feeling that something really bad was going to happen if he didn't repeat that question 33 times. In this case, the catastrophic thought may have been that the plane would crash. Maybe he'd planned to ask the question only 3 times—to quell his OCD-induced anxiety—but didn't put the accent on the right syllable, or something equally ludicrous, the third time, and thus felt compelled to ask it 33 times. Had he not gotten it right then, he might have had to ask it 333 times. These kinds of symptoms are common with severe OCD. The fact that he denied repeating himself indicates that he felt humiliated by having done the compulsion.

While testing an amphibian plane, Hughes insisted on landing in choppy water 5,116 times, although the aircraft had long since proved its seaworthiness. He just kept on and on, and no one could stop him. When this incident was reported in earlier biographies of Hughes, it was explained by Hughes's need to be in control. Other things in his life were slipping out of control at that time, among them his fortune. That may be part of the explanation for his behavior, but I believe that the answer is less related to deep emotional factors and that Hughes wouldn't have behaved this way had he not had OCD.

THE CASE OF THE FLYING PAPER CLIPS

Josh had a whole range of bizarre OCD symptoms. One was a fear that he had brushed against someone's desk at the office, thus causing a paper clip to flip into that hapless person's coffee cup. In Josh's worst-case scenario, the person would then drink the coffee and choke on the paper clip. Now, Josh knew there was a one-in-a-million chance that a paper clip would flip into someone's coffee cup, yet he couldn't get the idea out of his mind.

Josh then developed an obsession that he had grazed a parked car while driving and, in doing so, had knocked loose the hood ornament or a chrome strip. Then he imagined, "That guy's driving along the freeway, and the part falls off and kills six people." Josh went so far as to memorize the license plates of all the cars that regularly parked on the street where he lived so he could check each day to make certain they were there, intact, and everything was fine. But he was constantly plagued by worry about cars that he might have come in contact with during the day and would not be able to trace. Once, he drove two hours in a vain effort to track down a car on which he had inflicted imaginary damage.

Another time, Josh flew to St. Louis on business, flew home to Los Angeles, then turned right around and flew back to St. Louis, intent on finding the car on which he imagined he had loosened the hood ornament.

Josh knew that none of his actions made sense, but he also mentioned—and this shows a deep insight into OCD—that sometimes when dealing with a particularly vexing business problem, he found that his compulsions, unpleasant as they were, had the power to divert him. During a very stressful time, he would literally prefer to be doing the compulsion to thinking about what he was supposed to be doing at work. In the same way, Howard Hughes might have been using a compulsion as an outlet. First, there was just the thrill of that amphibious landing, but he soon developed a compulsion around it. Without behavior therapy, which teaches you how to resist those urges, the urges can escalate into an unstoppable cycle. The lesson is: *If you let your emotions cling to an OCD behavior, the behavior can easily get out of control.*

In a similar way, Josh tended to have relapses during treatment because, by his own admission, he would let his guard down when his OCD symptoms were, say, 80 percent gone. As a consequence, he's been dealing with the same symptoms for a number of years, never quite dispatching this devil OCD, doing the Four-Step method just enough to give him a livable comfort level. Then, in times of stress, his OCD flares up badly. Josh had the insight to realize that, in effect, his brain was looking for something mischievous to do all the time he'd put it in neutral. Mentally, he was allowing the OCD to lie in wait and not attacking it aggressively enough.

What he should have been telling himself was that by doing the compulsion, he was only assuring himself that another compulsion would follow, that his ability to function effectively would decrease and his stress level would soar. He needed to be brave, to confront his OCD and work past it. It's true, in this case, that a coward dies a thousand times before his death, but the valiant fight off OCD right now!

Howard Hughes's germ-backflow theory is similar to an obsession described by Jenny, a professional woman in her early 30s with a longtime involvement in ecological and environmental issues. While working for a U.S. government agency in Moscow, she developed the obsession that radiation could spread and attach itself to things. This was only a few years after the Chernobyl nuclear disaster, so, as is true with many OCD thoughts, there was a small element of logic. However, Jenny's reasoning was totally illogical. "When people would come in from Kiev or Chernobyl, I'd worry that radiation would just come off of them and contaminate my things. Any logic that I tried to infuse about the physics of radiation was not working. It was kind of a basic contamination fear."

Always, what she really worried about was that she, in turn, was going to contaminate others. She began to keep separate in her closet those clothes that were still okay to wear when she was around friends. These were the clothes that she'd never worn when around someone who'd been near Chernobyl. Certain books and papers had to be disposed of. "I threw away perfectly good things because I thought they were contaminated. I didn't want people getting them out of the trash, so I would rip them up to make them unusable." She became afraid to phone home, in fear that the "radiation" would somehow travel over the telephone lines.

ONE HOARDS, ANOTHER SCRUBS

With regard to the form of OCD and the content of OCD, it is certainly possible that a person's life experience plays a role, especially in the content of that person's irrational fears. Many of my patients believe this. Jenny, for example, wonders whether she might have been subliminally affected by a film on the bombing of Hiroshima that she saw on television when she was 12. She still recalls it vividly: "I couldn't sleep. I kept thinking of burnt hands reaching up from behind my pillow and of faces with burnt skin sagging, faces staring at me."

Jenny's first OCD thoughts—of feeling compelled to tell people inappropriate things—date from early childhood. By her teenage years, OCD was a monster that had a real stranglehold on her. This moving diary entry was written when she was 18:

> You are the awful . . . the awful. It has gone too far. There is no message, no inspiration, just pain. So that all else that is so fine is dulled. You are the duller, the awful . . . what fault mine? Possibly that I let you do this to me? No, I had no control. You took power of me, the fear holds me. Take your awful fingers from my mind . . . you awful . . . you be damned in heaven, hell the better. I hate it. I hate it. I hate it. I want to be free.

Using Four-Step self-directed therapy in combination with Prozac to make it a little easier, Jenny is now able to control her OCD. She is no longer afraid to mail letters because of some wild idea that they are contaminated. She forces herself to wear all the clothes in her closet. She says she would have no qualms about driving past a nuclear power plant or working near a nuclear reactor. One day recently, while cleaning out her office at a medical complex, Jenny came across a box in which were stored old cardboard covers for lab slides. "I had an idea that there were diseases in there. Well, I brought them out and put them on my desk and touched them and said, 'This is ridiculous. Pathogens die within seconds. It's not me—it's my OCD.'" She was able to put the absurd thought aside.

At UCLA, we have provided scientific evidence that OCD is related to a chemical imbalance in the brain, that critical parts of the brains of people with OCD use too much energy because the brain circuitry is out of whack. This is true across the spectrum of people with OCD. But OCD presents itself in a huge variety of ways, some outrageous, some ludicrous. In my behavior therapy group, patients sometimes can't help but laugh at themselves, but the disease is so painful that I have long since learned never to make light of any symptoms.

Let me share a few more of our case histories from UCLA:

OLIVIA
Olivia, a middle-aged homemaker, developed an obsession soon after the 1994 Los Angeles earthquake that the water in her washing machine was contaminated. She even imagined that water from the toilet was somehow pouring into the washer.

LISA
Lisa, an X-ray technician, developed an irrational fear of lead. Because she worked around lead, it became a terrible problem. First, she imagined that her hands were contaminated, then her shoes, then anywhere that she had stepped. She began to designate "clean zones" in her home. She would warn people that she worked around lead, so they could get away from her. Washing became a time-consuming compulsion.

LYNN
Lynn, an attractive college student, became obsessed with picking at her face, trying to rid it of imaginary flaws. She had a condition called body dysmorphic disorder, which may be related to OCD. Ultimately, she had to lower all the lights in her apartment and tape sheets of paper over the mirrors. (A similar disorder, trichotillomania, or compulsive hair pulling, may also be related to OCD.)

KAREN

Far more typical is the case of Karen, a homemaker and former dental assistant in her early 50s. Karen is a hoarder. Her problem began as a harmless hobby early in her marriage, when she and her husband, Rob, would haunt yard sales for inexpensive treasures for their new home. Before long, Karen was bringing home useless curbside castoffs. In time, every room in their house was crammed so full of junk that it was impossible to open the doors. Even the bathtub became a dumping ground for this rubbish. So much stuff was heaped on the stove that only a single burner was usable. Only a narrow path was navigable through the living room, between trash bags and boxes stuffed to overflowing. With their sixteen cats and four dogs sometimes relieving themselves behind those piles of trash, the stench became gagging.

Karen recalls, "We were too embarrassed to invite anyone in." There was no heat in the house because they were afraid that they would start a fire if they lit the pilot on the floor furnace. Throughout the house, there were only two sittable chairs. Appliances would break down, but Karen and Rob couldn't get them fixed because they were terrified that a repairman might report them to the health department. They shuttered the bottoms of their windows and let the shrubs grow so no one could peek inside. Rob had lived with this mess for so long that he no longer viewed the situation as wildly bizarre. "Our home was no longer a refuge," Karen says. "It had become a prison. We were foundering, like a sailing ship that is depending on winds that don't come."

For them, help came inadvertently from one of Karen's former colleagues who dropped by unexpectedly. Karen was so humiliated that she gave up yard sales cold turkey, only to begin haunting book sales. Now Rob had to build library stacks to house all the books she brought home. Still, Karen did not seek help, fearing that she'd be committed to a psychiatric hospital. Finally, in desperation, she saw a psychiatrist who suggested that she just set up a dumpster in the driveway and purge the house. Karen wasn't about to do that. "I could just see myself running out into the yard, screaming and throwing myself on the dumpster and being forcibly removed to a psychiatric hospital—all in full view of my neighbors."

Finally, after ten years of hoarding, she joined Obsessive-Compulsives Anonymous, a twelve-step program based on Alcoholics Anonymous. There she met someone who persuaded her to begin the long, hard process of cleaning out that would take years.

"My big mistake," Karen says, "was that I thought I had to fix my problem myself. I had false pride. I did not want anyone to see my shame."

At UCLA, we taught Karen the Four Steps, which she keeps pasted on her bathroom mirror and consciously invokes whenever she spots a tempting yard sale or an attractive item poking from a trash can. When Karen Relabels an obsession and says to herself, "Let it go!" she means letting go of both the obsessive thought and the fleeting wish to hang onto another piece of junk. "If I make the right choice," she says, "I get to feel good about myself. I get to be that much closer to a rubbish-free, hassle-free environment. I get to be healthy. I get to have friends. I get to have a life!" One technique she uses is to get angry at all that stuff and how it's wrecked her life. "I don't just toss things into garbage cans. I throw them in with a vengeance, as if to kill them, as if our lives depended on it, and—in a deep sense—they do."

BLAME IT ON YOUR GENES?

In telling her story, Karen mentions that she grew up in a rigidly perfectionist household with an eccentric father who would rant constantly against waste. She wonders if this experience mandated the content of her OCD, which is possible, especially since as yet there is no biological explanation as to why one person washes, while another hoards.

Other patients also reflect on their childhoods and their genetic legacies in attempting to find answers to why they developed OCD. Certainly, genetics does seem to play a role. Again and again, patients have told me of mothers or sisters or grandparents who certainly had OCD tendencies long before the disease was given a label. Formal studies show the same thing: OCD tends to run in families. Frequently, parents of people with OCD were rigid and inflexible and became very uncomfortable if things weren't done in a certain way. For example, at five on the dot each day, Howard Hughes's grandparents went out on the porch of their summer house. As a child, Howard had to be there precisely at five, or there was hell to pay. One can think of this kind of rigidity as low-grade OCD. These traits can be highly advantageous if you are, say, a surgeon or an accountant, but they can become pathological if they are amplified. Thus, it's not surprising to see that a precursor of an OCD biochemical imbalance is this much less disruptive habit-based brain function.

Childhood-onset illnesses have also been linked to OCD. Dr. Susan Swedo's group at the National Institutes of Health has established a link between OCD and Sydenham's chorea, a variant of rheumatic fever that involves an autoimmune attack on the brain. Her work implicated Sydenham's chorea in both the onset and exacerbation of OCD. The fact that there is a strong relationship between Tourette's syndrome, a motor tic disease, and OCD is also intriguing. The link between childhood psychological experiences, especially traumatic ones, and classic OCD is less clear, but some of my patients are convinced there is one.

Michael, a stenographer, feels strongly that his OCD stems from growing up in a household with a father who would dwell for days on minutiae and a mother he describes as an "anal-retentive" compulsive cleaner. He recalled: "My mother tended to be very overpossessive. But, though she smothered me, she didn't nourish me in other ways. Which is the same thing my OCD does. You know, you have all this potential that is smothered. I remember other kids taking piano lessons, whatever, but she never allowed me to do those things. She just did the smothering. With OCD, you might have the potential, but it smothers you and does not allow you to get it out."

Michael describes himself as having a "Dr. Jekyll and Mr. Hyde brain," with a good side and a bad side—the OCD side. He has had counting and touching compulsions, compulsions about "good" numbers and "bad" numbers, and compulsions to repeat sentences over and over again in his head. But his most bizarre compulsion—one with which he still struggles—began in fifth grade. "I would be sitting in class and suddenly I would feel my pants were too tight." He was unhappy in school, partly because his OCD made it difficult for him to concentrate, and he now wonders if this feeling of creeping pants was some sort of subconscious distraction technique.

Although Michael has overcome most of his other obsessions, he says his OCD "seems determined to dig in for all it's worth and win the final battle," the battle of the too-tight pants. Or, as Michael somewhat inelegantly puts it, the fear that "my jockey shorts are going up my butt and are going to come through my mouth, they're shrinking so much." Before behavior therapy, he would sometimes shed his clothes in an attempt to shed the feeling. Now, he realizes that giving in to a ridiculous thought is the worst thing he could do.

Michael finally overcame his obsession about pesticide contamination, an obsession so severe that "just seeing a can of Raid at the supermarket" traumatized him. "If I'd put my things down for the cashier and somebody ahead of me had a can of Raid, I'd have to take all my food, everything, and put it back on the shelves and restock my basket. I thought everything had been contaminated. Of course, I'd have to go to a different checker because I didn't know if the conveyor belt was contaminated. Sometimes it would take so long that I would just have to forget about getting food." If Michael saw an exterminator's truck on the road, he would have to go home, wash his clothes, and shower. Always, he says, "I felt like this shroud of poison was kind of draped over me."

The moment of truth came when he was informed that the apartment house where he was living had been sold and the building was to be tented for termite treatment. Michael panicked. Should he protest at city hall? Get a psychiatrist's note saying that the exterminators couldn't be allowed in because he was mentally ill? Then he got hold of himself. "I thought, 'Wait a minute. Just let them do it because maybe I'll get better.' I had resolved that this had to be done and that I wasn't going to die. This was a really big thing for me." One moment of clarity, after twenty years of suffering from this obsession. The work of using mindful awareness to know what obsessions really are began to pay off for him in a big way. Michael then went one step further. When the exterminator came, Michael asked him for his business card. He took to carrying the card around as a reminder that he wasn't going to die. By purposely exposing himself to what once had terrified him, he knew he was making himself better.

Through practicing the Four Steps, Michael has learned to think of OCD as "this bad guy in my brain that can't fool me anymore. I know I'm not going to die from pesticides. I know I can touch a table twice without touching it a third time" and nothing disastrous is going to happen. But those creeping pants still nag at him. "That's part of my body. They're on my skin. They're there all the time, something I can't escape." Although Michael still has a modest amount of residual OCD, he's well aware of the tremendous amount of improvement he's made and of how much he has increased his ability to function.

In the battle against OCD, he has learned, "You just do anything you can to sabotage yourself. It takes incredible drive, total effort, to resist it. It's just intense pain, as bad as any physical pain." He has learned, too, that robotlike performance of the Four Steps, without mindful awareness, does not work. This is Michael's description of himself locked in combat with his OCD, practicing self-directed exposure therapy: "You're thinking, 'Well, if I touch this, my father's going to die, but I'm going to do it anyway.' So you touch it and you *still* feel your father's going to die. You just have to say to yourself, 'Okay, whatever happens, it's better than living this life.' Just do the Four Steps and keep the faith." What a deep insight that is! Today, Michael says, he's "down in the dirt with my OCD." The smart money won't bet against someone who can fight like that.

At UCLA, we have many case histories of OCD-related contamination fears. In the case of Jack, a temporary worker, actual physical pain was the impetus for him to seek help for his compulsive hand washing. He couldn't face another winter with red, raw, cracked hands. He washed his hands so much that his young daughter called them his "soap popsicles"—icy cold with the smell of embedded soap that he could never quite wash away. In treatment, he learned that when he refuses to give in to the urges to wash his hands, nothing catastrophic happens. "I know if I don't do it that it's not going to be the end of the world." Before, he always felt as though "catastrophe was just around the corner. My safe places—my car, my home— were all going to be invaded if I didn't do those compulsions."

It is not vital that Jack, and other patients, successfully Relabel every time an urge to do a compulsion arises. But if they give in and perform the compulsion, it *is* vital that they recognize mindfully that it is a compulsion and that, this time, they were unable to resist it. *This is much more useful than Relabeling in an offhanded automatic manner.* When you Relabel automatically, it becomes a ritual in itself and has no meaning. There is nothing magical about saying to yourself, "Oh, that's an obsession." Following doctor's orders in that fashion—mechanically, without thinking about what you are doing—is not helpful. Mindful awareness is. So you say, "The feeling is too strong. I don't have the strength to fight it this time, so I'll look to see if I locked the door." Then, when you do check the door, do it carefully, with mindful awareness, so you'll be ready to fend off the urge next time. You don't say, "Let me just make sure the door is locked." That's a sure prescription for endless compulsive checking.

ASSERTIVE RELABELING

At UCLA, patients are asked to write essays in which they describe their symptoms and how they respond to them—another type of self-directed therapy. These essays have also provided us with an extraordinary library of knowledge on OCD. Since OCD patients tend to be bright, creative people, their ways of expressing what they go through in battling their disease make for fascinating reading.

Joanne, who'd suffered for years from a small voice in her head repeating negative thoughts over and over like a broken record, told of seeking a cure in a self-help book. The author suggested she snap a rubber band on her wrist as a distraction technique whenever her mind started playing its OCD tricks. Joanne wrote, "All I got was a sore wrist the first day." What eventually made her better was not a rubber band, but the Four Steps. She first began to feel that she had some control over her life when she told herself, "If I don't want to get hit by the train [the negative obsessive thoughts], I have to get off the track and let the train go by." She was applying a technique we call "working around" her OCD. Today, with the help of behavioral therapy and medication, Joanne is able to say, "The sun shines on my soul."

Mark, a young artist, described a true-life OCD experience that reads like a pilot for a horror film. His OCD started in childhood with prayer rituals and, by his early 20s, had shifted focus to a cleaning compulsion. He would have to clean his apartment twelve times (twelve was a "good" number) and then "find some girl and have sex in order to cosmically sort of switch the energies back the right way," so a member of his family would not die. Using a woman in that way made him feel bad, so he would clean one more time as a sort of purification ritual. Then, one day, after the thirteenth cleaning of his apartment, he was walking down the street and "a pigeon literally dropped out of the sky, dead at my feet, with blood gurgling out of its beak." Clearly, this was an evil omen. Thirteen was a bad number; he had to clean a few more times. Having done so, Mark went to a coffee shop for lunch but, as luck would have it, the man in the next booth was reading a newspaper with the headline WHERE PIGEONS GO TO DIE. Okay, he thought, let's clean some more. Finally, after he had cleaned his apartment twenty-one times, he was able to rest easy.

For a time, Mark thought he could fool his OCD by turning the tables on it, saying that if he *did* his compulsions, a family member would die. "I thought, okay, Mr. Smarty Pants. I've solved this thing. There you go." It didn't work. New compulsions took over. "I hadn't learned my lesson, which is that you can't use this shortcut and get to the finish line. It doesn't work, and it always backfires." It would be years before he would rid himself of his cleaning compulsion: "There was actually one time when I had to clean my apartment 144 times. It took months."

For Mark, the breakthrough during behavior therapy came when he found an apartment he wanted but was warned by his inner OCD voice, "No, you shouldn't move in there." The numbers in the address were not "good" numbers. Mark took a stand. "Damn it, I can't believe I'm going to let a choice in my life that's this major be dictated by OCD." This is assertive Relabeling. Right after Mark moved in, his thoughts about "bad numbers" went away. He told himself, as he always does now when OCD thoughts intrude, "I don't have to do it. I don't have to do anything about it."

OCD: A TUMBLEWEED

Lara, who suffers from Tourette's syndrome as well as classic OCD, describes a plethora of symptoms, ranging from violent thoughts about knives to compulsive shopping sprees. Once, she sought help at Shoppers Anonymous, but quickly learned a basic fact of OCD: Whereas the anonymous compulsive shoppers described getting a rush, a high, from shopping, Lara gains no pleasure from her repeated trips to the mall. She says, "My obsessions are painful. They're not nice. I'll buy something I don't need, and then I'll return it. I almost get more charge out of returning it than buying it." Lara's statement helps to clarify an important difference between OCD and problems with impulse control. As a behavior, OCD in itself is essentially *never* enjoyable.

Lara is also driven crazy by obsessions—the fear of harming herself or someone else, of doing something embarrassing, of planes crashing into her house, or of freeway overpasses toppling on her. "It's like one obsession propels another that propels another. If you've seen the rat on the wheel, that's what it's like. Or the teacup ride at Disneyland that spins unforgivingly fast."

Lara has never acted out a violent thought. People with OCD never do. Through behavior therapy, she has learned to Relabel her thoughts as irrational, to tell herself, "It's not reality. You're frightened because it seems so horrific and unbelievable." She now knows that she can control those thoughts and urges, no matter how strong or disruptive they become. She still battles the obsessions, which she describes as her "added baggage" that she takes everywhere with her and cannot walk away from.

Carla, a beautician, became so obsessed with the idea that she was going to harm her infant daughter that she considered giving up for adoption this child she had wanted so much, for so long. (She was 40 and had been married for fourteen years when her daughter was born.) Carla, who was at first misdiagnosed as having severe postpartum depression, would suffer panic attacks—thoughts that she was going to kill the baby—that were so severe that she couldn't look at a knife or a pair of scissors. "It was like watching a movie where you almost put yourself into that screen and you think, 'Oh, God, am I capable of committing such an act?' I was fighting this every day, all day." Only her determination to take care of her baby's needs kept her going. She would literally crawl on her hands and knees into the nursery to change the baby's diapers.

Her daughter is now 6, and Carla thanks God every day that she is around to watch her grow up. There was a long time when her OCD thoughts were so bad that she wanted to be committed, so bad that she thought of taking her own life to spare her daughter's life. Carla describes OCD as a "tumbleweed" that picks up more and more non-sensical thoughts as it rolls along. But in treatment, she has learned to separate herself from those thoughts. When an OCD thought intrudes, Carla says to herself, "First, my name is Carla and, second, I have OCD. My life is not OCD." It's so automatic now, she says, that it's like writing her name or taking a drink of water. Click! A lightbulb goes off in her head. Her defenses are ready. Mindful awareness and the ability to Relabel arise in a flash to the prepared mind.

Although many people with OCD are loath to tell others they have this problem—either out of embarrassment or of fear of losing their jobs or perhaps because they've learned that people just don't want to hear about it—Carla finds a great sense of relief in sharing her secret with others. She does a great deal of volunteer work, some of it helping people with physical problems. "For me to say, 'Hey, I have OCD. How can I help you?'—it's almost like coming out of the closet." Training your mind to think, "How can I help you?"—that's behavior therapy with a capital B.

"Of course," Carla says, "I wish there were some super-remedy where I could commit myself to a hospital, have surgery, and come out healthy. But that's not fact." Behavior therapy is the next best option, and in some ways it's even better when it results in a person's development of mindful awareness.

Now that you have an understanding of Step 1: Relabeling—calling OCD what it really is—I will introduce you to the Reattributing step. In essence, Reattributing is nothing more than placing the blame for OCD symptoms squarely where it belongs—with your sticky brain.

Reattributing answers those nagging questions, *"Why is this thing bothering me so much? Why doesn't it go away?"*

OCD doesn't go away because it is a medical condition. Someone with Parkinson's disease may decide, "Oh, I'm no damned good. Why can't I move at the same speed as everybody else?" The person with Parkinson's has to regroup, to say, "Because I have a medical condition. I must adjust to this condition." You must adjust to the condition called OCD and maximize your function. You're not a victim. You're working on a problem.

KEY POINTS TO REMEMBER

•Step 1 is the Relabel step.

•Relabel means calling the intrusive unwanted thoughts and behaviors what they *really are:* obsessions and compulsions.

•Relabeling won't make unwanted thoughts and urges go away immediately, but it will prepare you to change your behavioral responses.

•When you change your behavior, you change your brain.

•The *key to success* is to strengthen your Impartial Spectator, your ability to stand outside yourself and observe your actions with mindful awareness.

2

Step 2: Reattribute

"Unlocking Your Brain"

> **Step 1. Relabel**
>
> **Step 2. REATTRIBUTE**
>
> **Step 3. Refocus**
>
> **Step 4. Revalue**

Step 2: **Reattribute** answers the questions, **"Why don't these bothersome thoughts, urges, and behaviors go away?" "Why do they keep bothering me?" "What should I attribute them to?"**

The answer is that they persist because they are symptoms of obsessive-compulsive disorder (OCD), a condition that has been scientifically demonstrated to be related to a biochemical imbalance in the brain that causes your brain to misfire. There is now strong scientific evidence that in OCD a part of your brain that works much like a gearshift in a car is not working properly. Therefore, **your brain gets "stuck in gear."** As a result, it's hard for you to shift behaviors. Your goal in the Reattribute step is to realize that the sticky thoughts and urges are due to your balky brain. (See Figure 1 on page xxxiii.)

THE FAR SIDE   By GARY LARSON

Professor Lundquist, in a seminar on compulsive thinkers, illustrates his brain-stapling technique.

With a bow to Professor Lundquist, in this chapter you will learn about *our* "brain-stapling technique" for overcoming the symptoms of OCD.

Our method, I hasten to add, has nothing to do with little metal clips. At UCLA, we use self-directed behavior therapy as a brain-stapling technique. In other words, we use the mind's own power to actually change the chemistry in the brain. That's what you accomplish when you get around those intrusive thoughts that get stuck in your brain and won't go away. Our tools are the Four Steps—Relabel, Reattribute, Refocus, Revalue. In time, with persistence, they will enable you to "staple off" that hyperactive orbital cortex. No neurosurgery is needed. You can do it with your mind.

When I talk about self-directed behavior therapy, I mean an active response to OCD symptoms in which you recognize this intruder for what it is and you fight back, using the Four Steps to shift those sticky gears in your brain.

In Step 1: Relabel, you learned the importance of calling an obsession an obsession, a compulsion a compulsion. But Relabeling alone does not make those painful thoughts and urges go away. You wonder, "Why the hell does this thing keep bothering me?" It keeps bothering you because you have a glitch in your brain—the sticky automatic transmission that you learned about in the Introduction.

Now it's time to bring into play Step 2: Reattribute. You have already identified your problem as OCD. In Reattribute, you learn to place a lot of the blame squarely on your brain: This is my brain sending me a false message. I have a medical condition in which my brain does not adequately filter my thoughts and experiences, and I react inappropriately to things that I know make no sense. But if I change the way I react to the false message, I can make my brain work better, which will improve the bad thoughts and feelings.

"IT'S NOT ME—IT'S MY BRAIN"

Because these thoughts and urges make your life unbearable, you must devise active, positive strategies for working around them. You need to adapt, to keep telling yourself, "It's not me—it's just my brain."

I would never tell a person with Parkinson's disease, "Stop that tremor! Don't move until you stop that tremor." That person cannot wish the shakes away, just as the person with OCD cannot wish away the false messages that the brain is bombarding him or her with. Both have a medical condition to which they must adjust. (It is interesting to note that both Parkinson's disease and OCD are caused by disturbances in a brain structure called the striatum.) It's futile and counterproductive for the person with Parkinson's disease to decide, "Oh, I'm no damn good. I can't move as fast as everybody else," and it is equally counterproductive for a person with OCD to give in, to say, "This thing's too monstrous, too powerful. I can't fight it, so I'll do as it tells me."

Earlier, I introduced the concept of the Impartial Spectator, or mindful awareness. Using the Impartial Spectator, you can distance yourself from your OCD, create a gap or safety zone between your will—your wholly internal spirit—and your unwanted, intrusive urges. Rather than respond to urges in an unthinking, mechanical fashion, you present yourself with alternatives. *Early in therapy, it's good to think of some alternative behaviors to have ready when the pain of OCD seizes you.* Any pleasant and constructive activities will do. Hobbies are especially good.

The Reattribute step intensifies the mindful-awareness process. Once you realize this thing is OCD, the next step is to gain a deep understanding of why it's so bothersome and why it won't go away. We now know beyond a reasonable doubt that it doesn't go away because it's due to a medical condition, a biochemical imbalance in the brain. By Reattributing the pain to this medical condition, you strengthen your certainty that it is not your will, not you, and that it won't take over your spirit. You are still intact and able to make conscious, considered decisions in response to your pain.

FALSE ALARM!

A woman in my weekly OCD therapy group said it so well: "Behavior therapy breaks the lie of what the anxiety is saying." In other words, the intensity and pervasiveness of these thoughts or urges is not a personal weakness or a psychological problem. It is simply a false alarm caused by a short circuit in the brain. Thinking of this analogy should help you understand the proper response to these urges: In the middle of the night, a car alarm goes off. It wakes you, and you become agitated and annoyed. But only a fool would lie in bed tossing and turning, trying to will that alarm to cease. It won't. In all probability, it is responding to a short circuit that has caused a false message. So the sensible person tries to ignore the alarm, think about something else, and go back to sleep. When OCD sends a false message to your brain, you can't make it go away, but you don't have to act on it. First, you Relabel it; then you Reattribute it. You tell yourself, "I will not do this. I do not want to do this. It's not me—it's just OCD."

In combating compulsions, we have had success using the fifteen-minute rule: When you are overtaken by the urge to perform a compulsion, you try to wait fifteen minutes. But this is not just passive waiting. It's a waiting period during which you actively keep telling yourself, "These are not real thoughts. These are faulty messages from my brain." If, within fifteen minutes, the urge begins to fade—and it frequently does—you begin to see that you have a sense of control over your OCD. You are no longer a passive victim.

It is pointless to sit and ruminate about how dreadful your life is going to be if you act on a fearsome, violent, obsessive thought. You are not going to do it. Why not? Because the real you doesn't want to do it. Think of heavy smokers who have to quit for their health's sake: They may never be free from the urge to smoke a cigarette, but they can stop smoking by changing their behavior in response to that urge to smoke. Over time, the urge to smoke fades.

Remember: OCD is not some hidden wish fulfillment. It is simply a broken machine. *OCD may mimic the feeling of reality, but reality never mimics the feeling of OCD.* This fact leads to a very important principle: If it feels like it *might* be OCD, it *is* OCD! If it were reality, it wouldn't feel like it even might be OCD.

THIS IS WAR

The Relabel and Reattribute steps are often done together because they reinforce one another; that is, mindful awareness (the Impartial Spectator) and a cognitive understanding that this is a blip of misinformation coming from the brain are working together. These techniques are the foundation for building a powerful defense system against this enemy, OCD. You may want to think of it as creating a platform on which to stand to observe the ridiculous nature of OCD and from which to plot your counterattack. No matter how uncomfortable the feelings, when you stand on that platform, you're in charge. Truth is on your side.

There was a time when Barbara, who obsessed about checking things and locking things (Remember Mr. Coffee?) would come home from work each day so stressed out from her obsessive thoughts—Had she hit someone while driving? Had she put a business contract in the wrong envelope? Had that letter she dropped in the mailbox really gone down?—that she would have to go right to bed. But she wouldn't let herself go to sleep "because that brought the next day's OCD on that much sooner. I would lie in bed like a convalescent and just decompress. My life was getting through the day and then recovering from it. And dreading the next day."

Today, ten years after the onset of OCD and six years after starting self-directed behavior therapy, Barbara is able to say that her few remaining OCD rituals are "just a minor nuisance, like having to floss my teeth every day."

After four years of suffering, she felt she was losing the fight. Several things had conspired to contribute to her sense of defeat. Once, while out of town for a weekend, she was overcome by the fear that she had failed to lock her apartment door although, of course, she had locked it. So Barbara called her landlady, told her the door was not locked, and asked her to lock it. Naturally, she didn't say she wasn't *sure* she had locked it—"I didn't want her to think I was bizarre or unstable." The inevitable happened. The landlady *unlocked* the door. When Barbara returned home to find the door unlocked, she realized, "I can't even enlist people unwittingly to help me because I end up sabotaging myself." For the first time, she felt truly defeated.

About that time, her mnemonic (memory) devices were losing their novelty. At first, Barbara could say, "Okay, I'm locking the door now. I'm wearing a blue shirt. It's Tuesday." Then when she got to work, she could tell herself, "Okay. Blue shirt. Tuesday. The door must be locked." But that technique no longer worked. Her brain had begun to tell her, "Aha! Maybe you also wore a blue shirt on *Monday.*"

It was at this point that she succumbed one day to hiding the coffee machine and the iron in her book bag and taking them to work. She was mortified. "I had self-esteem problems connected with the OCD and what I was doing professionally [she was a perennial underachiever]. I didn't also need for it to be found out that I had an iron in my purse."

Once she learned that she had a biochemical disorder of the brain—and that she could help herself through therapy—she began to improve. Looking back, Barbara says, "Your brain can get into such bad things. You say, 'Is the stove off? Is the stove off?' And then you get to the point of saying, 'Well, what's *off*? When I turn the knob up to the off position, how do I know that's really the off position?'"

When her OCD was at its worst, she couldn't escape it even on vacation. She'd check other people's stoves. If she didn't, her brain was telling her, some terrible catastrophe was going to take place.

By using mindful awareness whenever she checks something, Barbara can now ignore her OCD urges, knowing she has turned off the stove or locked the door. She tells herself, "It is the disease that is making me feel uncertain. And while I feel the stove is not off, I have checked it mindfully and should now walk away." Her OCD is no longer severely disruptive. It is, rather, "a presence in my life as real and insistent in its own way as a fussing infant." She knows what to do when her toddler cries. She also knows what to do when her OCD kicks up a fuss.

Incidentally, Barbara became pregnant while in therapy and credits her pregnancy with accelerating her healing process. Stress, we know, exacerbates OCD symptoms. When Barbara became pregnant, her priorities changed. "I no longer cared so much about my job as I cared about remaining stress-free through the pregnancy. I just decided, 'Well, if a letter goes out riddled with mistakes, who cares?' I knew I wasn't going back to that job. And then the OCD symptoms would be greatly lessened." What's more, her number of mistakes did not increase.

Anyone who has OCD will tell you that refusing to give in to urges or compulsions is hard to do. *Painful* is the word I hear most frequently.

Dottie, who performed all manner of bizarre rituals out of an unfounded fear that something terrible was going to happen to her son's eyes, describes not giving in to doing the behaviors as "like losing an old friend. I always say OCD is like a friendly enemy. It's something you want to get rid of, but it's also like a part of you that you don't want to give up." It's easier to take comfort in doing the ritual than to fight off the feeling. And sometimes we can use compulsions to avoid someone or something we don't want to deal with. But, as we now know, that is a prescription for lifelong pain.

One person with OCD described so well what happens to those who don't resist: "Bad habits make a groove in your brain." And those horrible, intrusive thoughts get stuck right in that groove.

IT'S ALL IN YOUR HEAD

The human brain, which weighs about three pounds and is roughly the size of two fists pressed tightly together, is the most complex and fascinating of all our organs, with its network of about ten billion interconnected nerve cells, or neurons.

Our research on people with OCD at UCLA led us to find that, without question, OCD is a neuropsychiatric illness resulting from a malfunction in the circuitry of the brain. But first, let's take a look inside a human brain and learn a little more about those parts with their mysterious-sounding names, about their functions, and what goes awry to allow OCD to intrude.

This miniglossary should be helpful. (The key structures are illustrated in Figure 2, opposite.)

• STRIATUM: The stratum is composed of two parts, the putamen and the caudate nucleus, which sit next to one another in the core of the brain, deep in the center. The putamen is the automatic transmission for that part of the brain that regulates motor or physical movement, and the caudate nucleus is the automatic transmission and filtering station for the front part of the brain that controls thought.

• ORBITAL CORTEX: The orbital cortex is the underside of the front of the brain, the "hot spot" in OCD. The brain's "error-detection circuit," it is located directly over the eye sockets. Here, thought and emotion combine. The orbital cortex can inform you that something is right or wrong, whether it is something to approach or avoid.

• CORTEX: The cortex is the outer surface of the brain. The frontal cortex is where the most advanced thinking and planning take place.

• BASAL GANGLIA: The basal ganglia is essentially the same as the striatum; the terms are almost interchangeable. The caudate

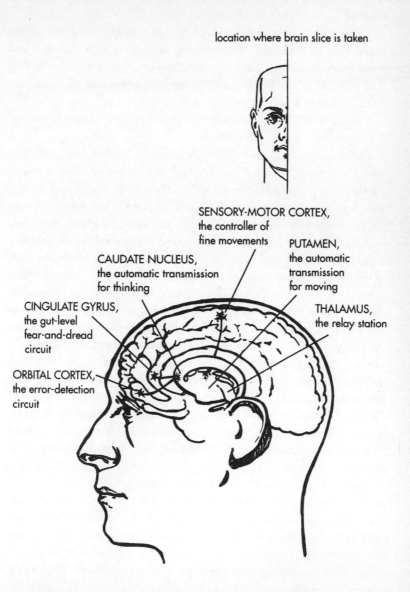

Figure 2. Illustration showing the location of the key structures of the brain that play a part in OCD.

nucleus, which enables us to shift gears from one behavior to another, is part of the basal ganglia.

• CINGULATE GYRUS: The cingulate gyrus is at the center of the brain, the deepest part of the cortex. It's wired into your gut and heart-control centers and is responsible for giving you the feeling that something terrible is going to happen if you don't act on your compulsions to wash, check, whatever.

• THALAMUS: The thalamus is the central relay station for processing the body's sensory information.

The book cover shows color photographs of the brain of Benjamin, a patient at UCLA, before and after cognitive-biobehavioral therapy for the treatment of OCD. (This PET scan image is also shown in Figure 3, on page 59.) Benjamin and other subjects in our UCLA study were injected with a tiny amount of a glucoselike solution that was then trapped in their brains for several hours, enabling us to take pictures and to measure metabolic activity in various parts of the brain. Many people feel relaxed during the scan, perhaps because of the humming of the scanner. Before we inject them, we say, "In the next half hour or so, we're going to be taking pictures of whatever your brain is doing. If you have obsessions now, that's what we're here to record, but whatever happens, happens." It's basically at rest, no challenge. Later, when we do the follow-up scan after therapy, we tell them that if obsessions or compulsions arise during the scan, they're to do the Four Steps, just as they've been taught. We have found it extremely helpful to show patients these pictures as a graphic way of helping them understand "It's not me—it's my brain." The knowledge of what's causing their urges motivates them to work to change from pathological to healthful behavior and, in so doing, to actually change their brain chemistry.

These positron emission tomography (PET) scans clearly demonstrate that the orbital cortex, the underside of the front of the brain, is hypermetabolic, or overheated, in people with OCD (see Figure 1 on page xxxiii). The colors represent different rates of brain glucose metabolism, or energy use, with red as the hottest and blue as the coolest. One thing these PET scan pictures can tell us is that the more automatic a behavior, the less energy the cortex may require to perform it. For now, keep in mind one key finding: The caudate nucleus, deep in the core of the brain, which appears to be the source of the primary problem in those with OCD, "cools down" in response to drug therapy, to drug therapy in combination with behavior therapy, and to behavior therapy alone. This is particularly true on the right side of the brain. We can now say we have scientifically demonstrated that by changing your behavior, you can change your brain. If you change your behavioral responses to OCD's false messages, you will change the brain circuits that cause OCD, which will lead to an improvement in your symptoms.

During the ten years of research that led to this truly groundbreaking finding, my colleagues and I at UCLA undertook a number of experiments that greatly enhanced our understanding of mind-brain interaction.

Dr. John Mazziotta, who heads the Brain Mapping Division of the UCLA Neuropsychiatric Institute, designed an experiment in which the subjects were required to learn to make simple finger-to-thumb rotational movements of the hand, movements that mimicked those used in handwriting. But, because they'd been instructed to make these movements precisely and in a given order, the subjects actually had to think about doing so. What happened—as expected—was that the part of the cortex that controls hand and finger movements became very metabolically activated. In other words, its energy use increased, and it heated up. Next, the subjects were asked to sign their names repeatedly. Now, you know if you've ever signed forty traveler's checks that you don't think about it a lot after the fourth or fifth check. What we learned was that when the motor task is extremely familiar, the striatum seems to take over. The cortex expends only marginal energy, but the energy use in the striatum increases noticeably. It's that smooth, automatic transmission in the striatum at work again.

Think of concert pianists: When they first learn to play, they have to think about moving their fingers, which takes considerable energy in the finger-moving part of the cortex. But once they've achieved concert-hall status, they move their fingers automatically. Then, they think about the shades and tones of the music. The cortex doesn't have to expend much energy thinking about moving fingers; the striatum does that. Thus, the advanced parts of the cortex are freed up to think about the fine points of the music. The experiment with our handwriting subjects gave us insights into this entire process.

When Dr. Mazziotta repeated the signature-signing experiment with a group of subjects with Huntington's disease, a genetically inherited disease that manifests itself at midlife with the loss of motor control, the results were different. The area of the brain that normally is stimulated by doing an unfamiliar task that requires thinking was stimulated by doing the familiar signature-signing task. Through the degenerative effects of their disease, these subjects' caudate nucleus and putamen had become malfunctional, and parts of them were dead or dying. The subjects had to use a lot of energy in the cortex to devise strategies to sign their names, since the automatic transmission and filter were broken. They told us it took thought and effort and was hard work. Before the onset of their disease, they could sign their names without giving it a thought. Now, they actually had to control their hands—physically and mentally. They had to use the cortex to take over a function the striatum would normally have been performing. In people with Huntington's disease, the striatum ultimately disappears, for all intents and purposes, and the abnormal, foreign movements characteristic of their disease, such as writhing and twisting, increase.

Whereas in persons with Huntington's disease the fact that the automatic transmission and filter are broken causes unwanted movements, in persons with OCD it causes unwanted thoughts and urges, called obsessive thoughts and compulsive urges. Just as the subjects with Huntington's disease had to apply thought and effort to sign their names because the striatum's automatic transmission and filtering system were broken, people with OCD have to apply thought and effort when doing behavior therapy to work around the intrusive OCD symptoms. With the automatic screening system of the striatum not working properly, effort must be made to change behaviors while the disturbing thoughts and urges are still there. (You'll learn more about this process in the next chapter.) But there is one big difference: OCD is largely a fixable problem; at the present time, Huntington's disease unfortunately is not, although active research is going on, and there is much hope for progress.

This experiment with people with Huntington's disease taught us much about the brains of people with OCD. We know that when the striatum is working properly, it acts as a filter, "gating" the sensory information sent to it, which is its proper role in the behavioral loop in the brain. In all likelihood, what happens in OCD is that evolutionary old circuits of the cortex, like those for washing and checking, break through the gate, probably because of a problem in the caudate nucleus. When there is no efficient gating, the person can become overwhelmed by these intrusive urges and act on them in inappropriate ways. These actions are called *behavioral perseverations,* a fancy name for compulsions. Specifically, compulsions are behavioral perseverations that a person knows to be inappropriate and genuinely does not want to be doing: The thought comes in the gate, the gate gets stuck open, and the thought keeps coming in over and over again. People then persevere in washing their hands or checking the stove, even though it makes no sense to do so. These actions may bring them momentary relief, but then—boom— because the gate is stuck open, the urge to wash or check breaks through again and again. To make matters worse, in all probability the more compulsions they do, the more rigidly the gate gets stuck.

In the absence of a fully functioning striatum, the cortex must function in a way that requires conscious effort because unwanted thoughts and urges have a tendency to interfere. It is just this sort of conscious effort that is made in behavior therapy, when a person works to manage responses to intrusive urges.

We have good reason to think that the person with OCD can't get rid of those intrusive thoughts and urges because the circuit from the orbital cortex, the brain's "early-warning detection system," is firing inappropriately. The culprit may well be the lack of proper filtering by the caudate nucleus. Evolution may play a large role in the origins of classic OCD symptoms. Think of the kinds of automatic behaviors that were hardwired into the brain circuitry of our ancestors. In all likelihood, these behaviors had to do with avoiding contamination and checking to make sure that they were safe—that the cave was neither dirty nor dangerous, for example.

STUCK IN GEAR

In behavior therapy, we try to get patients to understand what's going on in their brains so they can use the cortex to help them stop inappropriate behaviors. Because their automatic transmission is broken, they must use the cortex to shift to another, more appropriate, task. I tell my patients, "You are cursed with a lousy manual transmission. In fact, even your manual doesn't work great. It's sticky. It's hard to shift, but, with effort, you *can* shift those gears yourself." It's not easy. It's hard work because the gearshift is stuck. But when they shift gears repeatedly, by consciously changing behaviors, they actually start to fix their transmission by changing the metabolism of the striatum. Using the cortex, they work around the glitch in the striatum. And the beauty of it is that this technique gets the transmission to slowly start working automatically once again. It becomes easier to shift gears and to change behaviors as you keep working at it. Recent research in the laboratory of my colleague Dr. Lew Baxter may indicate why this is so. He has recently investigated a pathway that sends messages to the basal ganglia from the part of the frontal cortex used for advanced thinking, like the thinking used in applying the Four Steps. This pathway seems to have the ability to help the transmission to shift gears more effectively.

With behavior therapy, there is also a change in the function of the cingulate gyrus, that part of the cortex that is responsible for the feeling that something catastrophic is going to happen if you don't act on your compulsions. Before treatment, the cingulate gyrus is tightly locked to the orbital cortex, which is probably the reason why obsessive thoughts and urges are accompanied by such terrible feelings of dread. This is one of the major problems in Brain Lock. After the person follows the Four Steps, the orbital cortex and cingulate gyrus uncouple and start to work freely again, and the fear and dread markedly decrease.

Numerous neurological studies have found that when the basal ganglia or striatum is not working properly, automatic motor control is interrupted and the cortex must help out. Conscious thought is required to control shifts from one behavior to another. In a person with Parkinson's disease, the broken automatic transmission in the striatum leads to motor rigidity and on-off problems. The gearshift is stuck, and the person must think about each little movement and step.

In Tourette's syndrome, a disease that is genetically related to OCD, the person develops chronic multiple tics, or sudden movements and vocalizations that occur almost without warning. The problem—as we believe it to be with OCD—is that the striatum is not properly modulating the cortex. Furthermore, scientists know that people who have damage to their basal ganglia or to the front part of their brain will perform a behavior over and over, even when that behavior is no longer useful or, indeed, is detrimental to them. The person with OCD performs a ritual in response to an obsession, all the while knowing it makes no sense. As with these other conditions, we believe this is due to a malfunction in the modulation of the cortex by the automatic transmission and filtering systems of the basal ganglia or striatum.

Whereas one person in forty in the general population has OCD, OCD occurs in one out of five family members and relatives of those with Tourette's syndrome and in one-half to three-fourths of those with Tourette's syndrome themselves, lending credence to the theory of genetic association. Frequently, Tourette's victims develop painful arthritis or tendonitis in their joints because of the intense jerking movements that motor tics cause. In essence, they get a strong intrusive urge to move and then perform tics to relieve themselves of the discomfort. Or they may get vocal tics, starting with an urge to do repetitive throat clearing, an urge that may later develop into yips, yelps, barks, or other animal sounds. Or they may start screaming obscenities or racial slurs involuntarily, causing them great stress. Stress makes the urges much worse, as it does in OCD. Preliminary data from our PET scans at UCLA indicate that the putamen, the part of the striatum that sits next to the caudate nucleus and modulates body movements, alters metabolic function in persons with Tourette's syndrome. Many people with OCD also have motor tics, and a lot of people with Tourette's syndrome get compulsive symptoms. What is common to both, we now believe, is that parts of the cortex—probably the motor cortex in tics and the orbital cortex in obsessions and compulsions—are not being properly modulated by the appropriate parts of the striatum (problems in the putamen are related to tics, and problems in the caudate nucleus are related to OCD symptoms). Thus, problems in two closely related brain structures that modulate and filter movement or thought seem to underlie two genetically related conditions that cause difficulty with intrusive movements (tics) in Tourette's syndrome or thoughts (obsessions) in OCD.

THOSE PRAGMATIC PRIMATES

The front part of the brain is where sophisticated information processing and problem solving take place. Because of the nature of the brain structures that send signals to the underside of the front of the brain—the orbital cortex—it seems likely that problem solving that involves emotional issues may take place there. A study by E. T. Rolls, a behavioral physiologist at Oxford University in England, yielded some interesting data that may be relevant for understanding the brain's role in symptoms common to persons with OCD.

Rolls wanted to find out what is really going on in the brain when repeated inappropriate behaviors, or behavioral perseverations, are occurring, so he had rhesus monkeys trained to do a simple visual task. For example, the monkeys learned that every time they saw a blue signal on a screen, they would be rewarded with black currant juice if they licked a little tube. Now, monkeys really like juice and will work hard to learn behaviors that promise this reward. So the monkeys learned fast: When the blue color appeared—bingo!—juice was in the tube. Thus, the monkeys worked along happily and efficiently, licking the tube at the proper time. Through electrodes that had been placed in the monkeys' brains, Rolls was able to observe that once the monkeys understood that a certain color signaled that juice was coming, cells in their orbital cortex would fire as soon as that color appeared. So the orbital cortex clearly was able to "key in" on signals that meant "juice is coming."

Rolls knew that just as monkeys love juice, they hate the taste of salt water. When he offered the monkeys a syringe filled with salt water, they made the connection—syringe/salt water—and soon the mere sight of the syringe caused other nearby cells in the orbital cortex to fire to help the monkeys back off and avoid the salt water. So, there are cells in the orbital cortex that fire when there's something you want—and when there's something you want to avoid. It's pretty clear that the orbital cortex was involved in the monkeys' learning quickly to recognize environmental stimuli and to signal the monkeys, "Hey, this is something you want. This is something you don't want."

Next, Rolls wanted to see what would happen when he tripped up the monkeys. Now the monkeys had to learn that it was the green signal, not the blue signal, that would get them the juice. On the first trial, when the monkeys licked the little tube for the blue signal and came up with salt water instead of juice, other cells in their orbital cortex fired much more intensely and with much longer bursts than the cells that had fired when things were going as they had come to expect.

It's important to note that these cells in the monkeys' brains that fired in long bursts did not respond to the taste of salt water outside the test situation. What they were responding to was the fact that the monkeys had made an error. In fact, the orbital cortex fired even when the monkeys received nothing at all at times when they expected juice. After another trial or two, the monkeys stopped licking the tube for the blue signal. They learned quickly that this signal was no longer getting the job done and that it was the green signal they wanted. And, as the monkeys consistently licked the little tube for the green signal, those orbital cortex cells that fired for the winning color started firing for the green signal instead of the blue signal. So what was happening, it seems, was that as the monkeys learned that they had been double-crossed and now had to change their behavior to get the juice they craved, the orbital cortex made a change to help them quickly recognize that green was now the winning signal. The orbital cortex is able to recognize both right answers and wrong answers. It is a genuine "error-detection system"—and it's the wrong answers that make it fire in long, intense bursts.

Rolls speculated recently that these "error-detection" responses in the orbital cortex could be involved in emotional responses to situations that cause frustration. It seems reasonable that activity in the orbital cortex may be related to an internal sense that "something is wrong" and needs to be corrected by a certain behavior. The monkeys responded by changing their behavior. In OCD patients, this error-detection circuit may become chronically inappropriately activated—or inadequately inactivated—perhaps because of a malfunction in the filtering effects of the basal ganglia. The result could be persistent intrusive thoughts and sensations that something is amiss. The cingulate gyrus, interacting closely with both the orbital cortex and the caudate nucleus, could greatly amplify this internal, gut-level feeling of dread.

The monkey experiment helped us understand why people whose orbital cortex is damaged have problems with perseveration. If the error-detection system is broken, people have trouble recognizing mistakes and tend to repeat the same old habits over and over again. But Rolls's experiment with the monkeys also helped us understand what's going on with OCD. Remember, when the monkeys saw something they didn't want, the orbital cortex fired, sending out a signal: "That's no good—something's wrong." But what made the orbital frontal cortex fire *really* intensely was when the monkeys made an error because the blue signal was no longer associated with the juice. The orbital cortex firing intensely can give a strong feeling that "something is wrong." If the error-detection system keeps firing over and over, it can cause a chronic intense feeling that "something is wrong" and lead a person to do desperately repetitive behaviors to try to make the feeling "get right." What may cause this? We know that the error-detection system in the orbital cortex is strongly connected to the caudate nucleus, which modulates it and can turn it off by causing a shift of gears to another behavior. There is now excellent evidence from a variety of scientific studies that damage to the basal ganglia (of which the caudate nucleus is a part) can cause OCD, with its terrible feelings that "something is wrong," feelings that don't go away.

The end result of a caudate nucleus problem can be that the error-detection system gets stuck in the ON position, leading to a something-is-wrong feeling that will not go away. Our theory is that since the orbital cortex is modulated by the caudate nucleus, when the caudate nucleus modulation isn't working right, the error-detection system in the orbital cortex becomes overactive, and the person has terrible thoughts and feelings that "something is wrong," which lead to compulsive behaviors done in a desperate attempt to make the feelings go away. Unfortunately, these repetitive behaviors make the something-is-wrong feelings even more intense. The only way to break the vicious cycle is to change the behavior. As you'll see, this may also be where medication can be helpful.

The important role of the orbital cortex in OCD's terrible urges and compulsions is being documented more and more. In a recent study at Massachusetts General Hospital, PET scanning was used to measure blood-flow changes in persons with OCD. Researchers put each person in a scanner with a dirty glove or some other object that was sure to be very upsetting, and the person had to lie there with the dirty glove, fretting and worrying about contamination. What these researchers saw was a clear increase in orbital cortex activity, especially on the left side, when the patient's OCD got worse.

This finding is of particular interest because we now have data indicating a relationship between a change in left orbital cortex metabolism and treatment response in OCD patients. In our experiment at UCLA, drug-free patients were given PET scans, undertook ten weeks of cognitive-behavioral therapy, and were then scanned again. Post-therapy, there was a highly significant correlation between decreased metabolic activity in the left orbital cortex and a lessening of OCD symptoms. The patients who showed the most improvement had the most clear-cut decrease in left orbital cortex metabolism. It was behavior therapy alone, without drugs—the same method I'm teaching you in this book—that caused the change.

UNLOCKING YOUR BRAIN

What we have also learned at UCLA is that people with OCD have what amounts to "Brain Lock" on the right side of the brain. When a person with OCD is symptomatic, the metabolic activity rate not only increases in the orbital cortex, but locks together with the activity in the caudate nucleus, the thalamus, and the cingulate gyrus. The activity in all these parts is locked together, so that changes in the orbital cortex are tightly linked to changes in activity in the other three. Behavior therapy is the key that unlocks them and allows them to work freely again. Do your therapy, unlock your brain. Add the "water-wings" (the medication), and the response rate soars to 80 percent.

We have shown that we can literally make a new brain groove. As people with OCD apply themselves to behavior therapy, abandoning the inappropriate perseverational behaviors and responding to OCD urges and thoughts with positive, nonpathological behaviors, we see changes in the orbital cortex and in the striatum. We see Brain Lock alleviated; the circuitry has shifted. The next step is to get that new circuitry to become more functional, more automatic. As the circuitry becomes automatic, the striatum shifts gears and runs the circuitry properly because that is what the striatum normally does. *Change the behavior; create a new groove; get behavioral improvement; and, in time, you will change your brain and get relief from OCD symptoms.*

We studied eighteen subjects and found that within ten weeks, twelve demonstrated significant clinical improvement. All were treated as outpatients. None took medication. There were three main findings.

▪ Those who did respond showed significant decreases in caudate nucleus metabolism that were present on both sides of the brain, but were more robust on the right side (as in Figure 3, opposite).

▪ Whereas before treatment there were significant correlations of brain activity among the orbital cortex, the caudate nucleus, the cingulate gyrus, and the thalamus on the right side—Brain Lock—these correlations decreased significantly, which means that the Brain Lock was alleviated.

▪ There was a strong correlation between the amount of metabolic change on the left side of the orbital cortex and percentage changes in patients' scores on severity ratings of OCD symptoms. That is, the more the OCD improved, the more the orbital cortex tended to "cool down."

These findings demonstrate conclusively that it is possible to make systematic changes in brain function with self-directed cognitive behavior therapy alone.

We have scientifically demonstrated that successful therapy, without drugs, can uncouple the "fixed-worry circuit" in the OCD brain so that the person can more easily stop doing those OCD behaviors. This knowledge has been a great motivator for people who are doing

Figure 3. PET scan showing decreased energy use in the right caudate nucleus (which appears on the left side in a PET scan) in a person with OCD after successful treatment with the Four-Step Method. PRE shows the brain before and POST ten weeks after behavioral therapy with no medication. Note the decrease in "size," which signifies decrease in energy use, in the right caudate (rCd) after doing the Four-Step Method. The drawings show where the caudate nucleus is located inside the head.

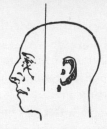

location where brain slice is taken

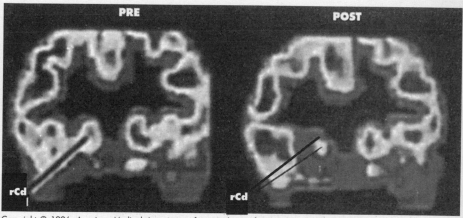

PRE

POST

rCd

rCd

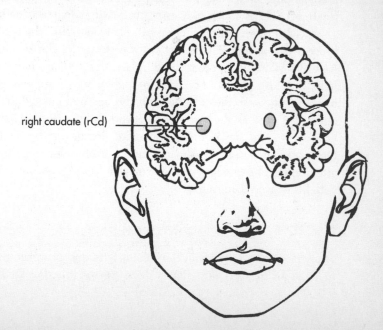

right caudate (rCd)

the hard work of behavior therapy to change their responses to OCD's false messages.

OCD is the first psychiatric condition in which a successful psychotherapeutic intervention that actually changes brain function has been documented.

When people with OCD do compulsive behaviors in a vain effort to buy a little peace, they are really only exacerbating their Brain Lock. When they systematically change their behavioral responses to OCD thoughts and urges, there is a concurrent change in the value and meaning that they place on what they feel. Before treatment, the intrusive thought might have said, "Wash your hands or else!" and the patients would usually respond by repetitive washing. After treatment, their response to the same OCD thought may be, "Oh, yeah? Go to hell!" By changing behavior, they are making alterations in brain function that, over time, result in measurable biological changes and a decrease in the intensity of intrusive OCD symptoms. It is important for patients and therapists alike to focus on these truths to help keep them motivated when the going gets tough.

As I've said, medication certainly has a role for those who need it to help them through therapy by decreasing their urges. (OCD and medication are discussed in Chapter Nine.) Using medication in treating OCD is much like using waterwings to teach children to swim. With waterwings, children can float unafraid, which helps the process of learning to swim. Then, you slowly let the air out of the waterwings until they are ready to go it alone. We use medication to help decrease the anxiety level of patients by suppressing those intrusive urges, so they can do their therapy and change their brain chemistry. Just as the swim teacher slowly lets the air out of the waterwings, we slowly bring down the dosage of the medication. Our experience in treating many hundreds of patients has been that after doing the therapy, the vast majority can get along very well with little or no medication.

KEEPING THE FAITH

Many people wonder about the role of faith and prayer in the treatment of OCD. Certainly, almost every person who has OCD has at some time prayed for relief from the dreadful feeling their disease brings on. With deep humility, they may beg for any power, supernatural or otherwise, to grant them relief from the intense pain that obsessive thoughts and urges cause. What they need to pray for is not that the OCD symptoms will go away—they probably won't—but that they will have *the strength to fight off their OCD.* There is an understandable tendency for people with OCD to become demoralized, even to begin to hate themselves because of feelings of guilt and inadequacy. One of the profound rewards of successful behavior therapy, especially from a spiritual perspective, is that people with OCD learn to forgive themselves for having these terrible thoughts because they realize the symptoms have nothing to do with their spirit or purity of mind and everything to do with a medical disease.

Using that knowledge to strengthen your will and bolster your confidence in the battle to "work around" these thoughts and urges is the critical point of mental intervention in OCD self-treatment. You need a tremendous sense of faith in your capacity to resist these urges, both to direct your mind away from the symptoms and to remove yourself physically from the site that triggers these symptoms—to leave the sink or walk away from the door. The acceptance that the painful obsessional thought is something that is beyond your capacity to remove—and that the thought is just OCD—enables you, the sufferer, to see yourself as a spiritual being who can resist this unwanted intruder. And always remember at least two principles. First, God helps those who help themselves. Second, you reap what you sow.

It is almost impossible to fight off an enemy as vicious as OCD if you are bogged down with feelings of self-hatred. A clear mind is required. Properly directed prayer can be very effective, but anything that helps you to develop the inner strength, faith, and confidence needed to reach that state of mindful awareness will further your progress along the road to recovery. The power of the Impartial Spectator can then guide your inner struggle to fight off the urge to do a compulsion or to sit, paralyzed, listening to some ridiculous obsessive thought.

Doing cognitive-biobehavioral self-treatment can truly be viewed as a form of spiritual self-purification. Remember, "It's not how you feel but what you do that counts." In self-directed therapy, you concentrate your effort and use your will to do the right thing, perform the wholesome action, and let go of your excessive concern with feelings and comfort level. In so doing, you perform God's work in a very real and true sense while you perform a medical self-treatment technique that changes your brain chemistry, enhances your function, and greatly alleviates the symptoms of OCD.

Strengthening your capacity to exert your spirit and will in a wholesome and positive way has far-ranging benefits that are, in many ways, even more important than merely treating or even curing a medical disease.

FINDING ANSWERS—WITHOUT FREUD

Here are a few of our patients' descriptions of their battles against OCD:

KYLE

Kyle, a mortgage company employee, had struggled for years with violent thoughts of shooting himself, jumping out a window, or mutilating himself. Sometimes he thought he should just kill himself and get it over with. He prayed, "If there's a weapon around and I do it, please don't send me to hell." His obsessions were "like a movie running through my mind, over and over." He described his OCD as "a monster." But through behavior therapy, he has learned, "I can bargain with it. I can stall it." Crossing a street, he no longer has to push the WALK button a certain number of times, afraid he will be struck dead. He says, "Okay, I'll push it again next year," and he walks.

DOMINGO

Domingo, whose grab bag of obsessions included the horrifying feeling that he had razor blades attached to the tips of his fingers, said, "Every day, OCD is here. Some days it comes in waves. Some days are livable, some are miserable. On the miserable ones, I tell myself, 'You're just having a bad day.'" Pasted to the mirror door of his bedroom closet is a color photo of an OCD brain, a PET scan—the same photo that's on the jacket of this book. When things get rough, Domingo focuses on it. "I tell myself, 'Okay, now that's reality. That's the reason that I feel like this.'" That gives him strength to cope and helps make his pain recede. "Once you know what you're fighting," he said, "it makes it easier." Domingo is one of those whose brains we scanned. When he looks at his scan, he laughs and says, "It was pretty busy in there."

ROBERTA

Roberta, who became fearful of driving because of unshakable thoughts that she had hit someone, first sought treatment with a Freudian therapist who suggested that there was something in her past that was causing her obsession. Looking into her past didn't help her one bit. What did help her was behavior therapy. Once she understood that the problem was biochemical, she said, "I relaxed. I wasn't as afraid. At first, it was like this thing had control of me. Now, while I can't keep it from happening, I *can* tell myself, 'This is a wrong message, and I feel I have control over it.'" Most days, she is able to drive wherever she wishes, no longer having to weigh her need or desire to go somewhere against her awful fears. "I just go on my merry way."

BRIAN

Brian, the car salesman with the morbid fear of battery acid, also had experience with a Freudian therapist who diagnosed just about every mental aberration, but not OCD. One therapist tried to treat him with basic exposure therapy. Brian laughed as he recalled, "I walked into this guy's office, and he had two cups of sulfuric acid on his desk. I said, 'Adios, guy! I'm outta here!' There was just no way I could do that." Brian's OCD fears and compulsions had become so overwhelming, he said, that "I just wanted to crawl right out of my skin, just crawl right out." He told one doctor, "I don't own a gun and it's a damned good thing I don't because I would blow my brains out."

In self-directed behavior therapy, Brian began using the Four Steps. He shook his head as he described what he went through. "It's work, I'll tell you, it's work. It's a war." The moment of truth came when, on a new job at a car dealership, he spotted six palettes of batteries right outside his office door, inches away. His first instinct was to order them moved. Then he told himself, "No, you've just gotta put your foot down, take a stand, and fight." He left the batteries there, and the batteries were still there the day he left that job. Brian knew that if he didn't hold his ground, if he didn't Relabel and Reattribute his fear of battery acid, "I would just have to keep running away." He was even able to joke that the batteries were still there, "and I haven't been eaten yet." He tries to practice the Four Steps religiously, always reminding himself, "This is OCD. This is nonsense." Sometimes he backslides. But if he lets his OCD get the upper hand, he knows, "Everything will wind up being contaminated in my mind, from the phone to the microwave oven."

ANNA

Anna, the philosophy student, had been diagnosed by a therapist who told her that her jealousy and doubts about her boyfriend were "just a Freudian obsession with your mother's breasts." Though Anna knew that this was "totally stupid," she didn't know she had OCD until she was diagnosed at UCLA. She and Guy are now happily married, but they came close to breaking up because of her relentless and senseless questioning of him: What had he eaten that day? Who had he dated as a teenager? What did she look like? Where did he take her? With absolutely no cause to do so, she interrogated Guy over and over about whether he looked at girlie magazines and whether he drank to excess. Although Anna understood that she clung to certain insecurities because of past relationships with men who had drug or drinking problems, it wasn't until she learned that she had OCD that she began to understand her absurd actions.

In high school, Anna had become obsessed with Cheryl Tiegs after Anna's first real boyfriend, who wasn't very ardent in his affections, mentioned in passing that he thought Tiegs was good-looking. "This woman drove me mad," Anna recalled. "It was making me physically ill." Some time later, Anna learned that her boyfriend was homosexual, which explained why he wasn't more amorous. But this knowledge only exacerbated Anna's insecurities, and years later she would lie in bed with Guy and suddenly think, "What if my husband is gay?" Naturally, it was another of the questions with which she bombarded the poor man.

Each day, Anna would grill Guy about his activities, down to whether he had butter or margarine on his bread for lunch. If there were minute discrepancies in his answers, since he repeated them somewhat absentmindedly, Anna's whole world would crumble "because there was one card in the house of cards that would fall down." She couldn't stop her questioning, even though she realized her behavior was "appallingly shrewish."

Through our Four-Step self-directed therapy, Anna was gradually able to conquer her obsessions. She considered it a significant sign of recovery when a Victoria's Secret catalog came in the mail and she was able to leave it lying around where Guy might see it. Now, if an obsession intrudes, she tells herself, "Okay, it's not going to help me to dwell on this now. If it's real, and there's a real component, it'll be clearer when the OCD is not intruding." Of course, it never is real. This is another example of that crucial principle: If it feels like it might be OCD, it *is* OCD.

Anna sees "sort of a Zen aspect" to coming to a mindful awareness about OCD. "If you truly accept OCD, it's a very profound acceptance and it really requires a certain mind control." Anticipation helps her. She knows, "It's not easy to remain unruffled when terror is shooting through my body." But she has learned that "the body can do crazy things. It's something that I have to live with, even though I really hate it. That's my life. I'm now well acquainted with OCD's tricks, and I don't fall for them as I once did."

When first told that she had a brain disorder, Anna reacted with mixed feelings. "Though it was hard to feel good about having such a brain defect, I felt enormously glad to find that the disease wasn't me." She could begin to rebuild her shattered self-esteem. Now happily married and a mother, she's able to look back and say, "Though lack of character was not what got me into OCD, quite a bit of character and stamina, combined with a well-considered approach (the Four Steps) would be absolutely essential to get me out of it."

JILL

Jill, a real estate agent in her mid-40s, has been battling a contamination obsession for twenty-five years. It started when, as a bride of 18, she went to the funeral of her husband's best friend, who'd been killed in a car accident. Looking at the body in its open casket, she was suddenly seized by the feeling that things she came in contact with were contaminated. She would clean her house over and over, in a way that made no sense. Dirty dishes could be piled in the sink, but Jill would ignore them while relentlessly scrubbing the walls, floors, and ceiling—which were perfectly clean—with Lysol or rubbing alcohol. Sometimes, she remembers, "My lungs would hurt from inhaling the fumes."

Jill could never explain how, or why, an object might become "contaminated." And she knew it was crazy to spend her days scrubbing. "You're sitting there thinking, 'Hey, other people are out there enjoying themselves and doing things, and you're in here cleaning this imaginary contamination!'" Still, she couldn't stop. It was easier to clean and thus force those awful feelings from her mind for a little while.

For an entire year, she left her house only to buy groceries, and even then she could go to only one store, which she had decided was still "clean." Her obsession started with one store being contaminated, or one neighborhood. "It grew to where I'd contaminated whole towns and states and I had to leave, I had to move. We moved an awful lot because of my sickness." In some way she can't explain, "I contaminated my parents, my sister, and my brothers and couldn't see them for sixteen years." If one of them chanced to call her, the telephone would then be contaminated, and she would have to "alcohol" her whole apartment (Jill uses that word as a verb). She'd even have to wash the cat and take the vacuum cleaner apart, pole by pole, and pour alcohol into it. If it was Christmastime, she'd have to take all the ornaments from the tree and submerge them in big pans of alcohol. She might feel an imaginary blob crawling up her arm from the hand in which she'd held the telephone and would have to shower five times to get rid of it. About the same time, Jill began to associate any official document with contamination, a throwback, she figures, to the stress of her divorce many years earlier. If she got a traffic ticket, for example, she would have to come home and "alcohol" the house and shower. She couldn't bear to touch the registration certificate in her car or visit a government building.

Jill and her two teenage daughters were living in North Carolina at the time, but her OCD was getting worse and the rainy weather further depressed her, so she decided to drive to Florida, to see if she could find a noncontaminated place to live. She'd left the girls with friends temporarily and, anxious to make sure they were all right, she stopped regularly along the way south to telephone them. Because she had discovered that the girls had lied to her about places they had been and things they had done—to avoid the silly rituals they'd have been required to perform if they had told the truth—they had now become "contaminated," so this was tricky. Jill always chose to make those phone calls from big hotels that she knew would have health clubs. She developed a routine for avoiding "contamination" when calling her daughters: She'd head for the health club, put her clothes in a locker, wrap herself in a clean towel, and go to a pay phone in the lobby. She laughs, "A lot of businessmen would come by and stare at me. I was hoping nobody would notice that I didn't have a bathing suit under that towel." After talking to her girls, she'd wash the phone with soap and water, take at least four showers, wash her hair, and dress. In this way, she avoided contaminating her clothing and herself and would not be forced to toss out all the possessions piled in her car.

Jill still has urges to shower excessively, but for the most part she has overcome her contamination fears and the fears about death associated with them. The first hurdle in behavior therapy was "just accepting OCD, not making myself feel bad that I have it." Occasionally, she gives in to an intense urge to wash or clean. That's when her anxiety level is so high that she reasons, "Sure, I might be OCD-free if I don't do the compulsion, but I might have a heart attack if I keep putting myself through all this stress. So now I try to be a little bit easy on myself and, if I feel really good, I'll tackle something a little harder. If I'm not feeling really good, I'll try to do a little something, anything."

If she lets her OCD have its way, she has learned, "It's kind of like you give it more credibility. It becomes a habit, and you keep on doing it and it becomes worse and worse." Her compromise might be one shower instead of five. "Just take those little baby steps," she advises—with the Four Steps as the helping hand.

"So much in my life has changed by just being able to Relabel this thing," Jill says. "If you give in to it, it snowballs. It starts out with one person contaminated, then ten people, then ten stores, then the whole state." Often, for Jill, Relabeling is enough. She takes a deep breath, relaxes, and the intrusive urge goes away. "If you face it right away, Relabel it as OCD right away, it's not going to get to the point where it's going to take hours of your day to deal with it."

Before she started self-directed therapy, Jill was on medication. But, she says, "medication was just like a cold tablet. It helped take the edge off, but it didn't really make it better," as behavior therapy has. "If I'd known the Four-Step technique years ago, I would have saved myself a lot of aggravation, a lot of time, and a lot of heartache."

KEY POINTS TO REMEMBER

•Step 2 is the Reattribute step.

•Reattribute means answering the questions "Why do these thoughts and urges keep bothering me? Why don't they go away?" The answer is, because of a medical condition called OCD.

•OCD is related to a biochemical imbalance in the brain that results in a malfunction of the brain's gearshift: The brain gets "stuck in gear."

•Because the brain is stuck in gear, its "error-detection circuit" keeps firing inappropriately. This causes very uncomfortable feelings.

•Changing your behavioral responses to the uncomfortable feelings and shifting to useful and constructive behaviors will, over time, make the broken gearshift come unstuck.

•As the brain starts to shift gears properly, the uncomfortable feelings begin to fade and become easier to control.

3

Step 3: Refocus

"Wishing *Won't* Make It So"

> **Step 1. Relabel**
>
> **Step 2. Reattribute**
>
> **Step 3. REFOCUS**
>
> **Step 4. Revalue**

Step 3: **Refocus** tells you what to do when you are trying to overcome those urges to do the compulsive behaviors. It instructs you to "work around" those nagging, troublesome thoughts by Refocusing your attention on some useful, constructive, enjoyable activity, such as gardening or playing a computer game. The key to the Refocus step is to **do another behavior.** When you do, you are repairing the broken gearshift in your brain. Your brain starts shifting more smoothly to other behaviors. The more you practice the Refocus step, the easier it becomes. That's because your brain is beginning to function more efficiently.

I like to tell the story of the chameleon and his therapist to illustrate the futility of trying to think away the nagging symptoms of obsessive-compulsive disorder. The therapist tells the hapless chameleon, "Listen, you've got to calm down. The more you worry about changing color, the less progress you'll make. Now, why don't you put yourself on the green background again?"

With the OCD patient, the problem is exactly the same. The more you worry about trying to drive some foolish and bothersome idea from your mind, the less chance you'll succeed. Eventually, you'll just give up. OCD will win. A key principle in self-directed cognitive behavioral therapy for OCD is this: *It's not how you feel, it's what you do that counts.*

And perhaps the most critical thing you must do during an OCD attack is to Refocus on another activity. What do I mean? Here's one way to look at it: Refocusing is like learning a martial art. Your opponent, OCD, is very strong, stronger than the power of your mind to make it go away. But you have one clear advantage: OCD tends to be very stupid. The closest OCD comes to being clever is the fiendish way it puts doubts in your mind. Now, if you stand right in front of this stupid but powerful opponent, it will knock you right over. Therefore, you have to take advantage of its stupidity. You have to step aside, put the OCD thought aside, and work around it by putting your mind in another place and doing another behavior, one that is more pleasant and functional.

This is Refocusing. You Refocus on another behavior. It can be a physical activity, such as taking a walk, doing needlepoint, shooting a few baskets. Early in therapy, physical activity seems to be especially helpful. But the important thing to remember is that whatever activity you choose, *it must be something you enjoy doing.* You may listen to music, cook, knit, play a computer game, or water your geraniums. The object is to pursue the activity for at least fifteen minutes— instead of acting out some silly ritual in response to an obsessive thought that has come from your brain. This is the fifteen-minute rule.

Now, fifteen minutes is only a guideline. At first, five minutes may be the limit to your staying power. The important thing is that for at least a few minutes, you will not be sitting and dwelling self-destructively on the bothersome thoughts and urges that have invaded your mind, and you will not be acting on those thoughts and urges. Instead, you will be consciously Relabeling those senseless thoughts as OCD and Reattributing them to a wiring problem in your brain. Relabeling and Reattributing help you get "centered" and ready to bring your mind away from OCD and back to reality. Now you're ready to work around those thoughts by Refocusing your attention on another, more wholesome, behavior.

The one-line summary of Refocusing is: *Do another behavior.* When you do, you'll learn that the OCD urges change and tend to diminish over time when they're not acted on. (It's also true that medication tends to make the OCD fade more quickly while you're following the fifteen-minute rule; see Chapter Nine.)

ONE STEP AT A TIME

Don't just plunge in and try, through some kind of frenetic, nonstop activity, to dismiss all the bothersome thoughts at once. (Let's not forget good old Professor Gallagher and his poor patient with the fear of snakes, heights, and the dark in Chapter One.) Rather, you take things gradually; slow and steady wins the race. You can't do everything at once. Let's say you have an obsession about contamination and that dreaded thought comes up again: "I have to wash my hands." First, you *Relabel* and call it what it is—an obsession. Then you *Reattribute* and place the blame squarely where it belongs. You remind yourself, "It's not me—it's the OCD." Then you *Refocus:* You walk away from the sink without washing your hands and do something worthwhile that makes you happy. You do not attempt to make the OCD go away through some kind of magical understanding of what it is and what it means. That's a fruitless struggle. You will only become demoralized, literally beaten down internally.

By Refocusing and changing to another behavior, you shift those sticky gears in your brain and resist the urge in an intelligent way. When you do so, the urge slowly begins to lessen because you're working to change the chemistry of your brain. When you pay the urge no attention, it starts to go away. When you shift behavioral gears, you improve how your brain works. This is what our research at UCLA has shown.

The Refocus step is at the core of self-directed cognitive-biobe-havioral therapy. The key to Refocusing is to realize that you must go on to another behavior even though the OCD thought or feeling is still there. You're not going to let those thoughts or feelings deter-mine what you do. Your battle cry is never "I have to get rid of this feeling." If it were, you'd be the guaranteed loser. You can't do much of anything to make the awful feeling quickly go away, just as you can't make the annoying false alarm in the car shut off. You must work around it. One of the great ironies of life is that when we don't really care whether we get something, it often comes our way. The same principle applies to fighting the symptoms of OCD. When you say, "Hey, who cares if they go away or not? I'm going to do some-thing constructive," you actually increase the chance that they'll go away. Meanwhile, you are doing something that gives you pleasure, rather than pain. You are using your Impartial Spectator—that observing voice of reason within you—to say, "Oh, that? That's OCD. Let me do something else." By doing another behavior, you'll also be improving how your brain functions.

As our research at UCLA has proved, the ability to work around the OCD is a powerful weapon. When you do it, you actually change the way your brain works—in essentially the same way that medica-tions change brain chemistry. You fix the broken filtering system in the brain and get the automatic transmission in the caudate nucleus to start working again. When those OCD urges come on, you try to wait at least fifteen minutes without acting on them. At the end of that time, maybe you'll be able to say, "Well, it's still bothering me, but not as much. I've noticed a change." If it doesn't happen on the first try, be patient; it will happen in time. As you learn to manage your anxiety, your powers of observation will improve. You will develop a powerful mind, a mind that is sensitive to subtle changes and able to see the implications of those changes. The applied use of your Impartial Spectator is the ultimate in mental power. So after one successful fifteen-minute wait, you may assess the situation and decide, "Hmmm . . . it's not bothering me as much. I'm going to wait another fifteen minutes." People who can do so always get better. I have yet to see anyone who reaches that level of mental resolution who fails to improve.

IF YOU'RE WORKING, YOU'RE WINNING

Now, how do I define "getting better"? Since OCD is a chronic disease, my definition of getting better is reaching a point where the OCD affects your everyday functioning far less, where it is no longer making you act in ways that you regret, no longer interfering with your performance on the job, no longer interfering with your personal relationships, no longer commanding your constant attention. And I can guarantee that you can do this for yourself. Even though your OCD may still try to sneak in and make your life miserable, you now know that it's not how you feel, it's what you do that counts. As our research at UCLA has shown, when you focus on working around your OCD, you start to feel more comfortable inside because your brain starts to work better. On the other hand, if you just sit there, repeating over and over, "I have to feel more comfortable," you're not going to change your behavior, you're not going to change your brain, and you're not going to get better. You need to be active; you cannot be passive.

Just because your orbital cortex is stuck in gear and sending you false messages doesn't mean you have to listen to it. That's the important mind-brain discovery around which our UCLA team has structured the Four-Step program. Many scientists and philosophers have been inclined to say, "If the orbital cortex says it's a go, it must be a go." But it's not a "go"—unless *you* go. *You're* the one who decides whether you're going to listen to those foolish messages and act on them, not your orbital cortex. Your orbital cortex may be telling you, "Wash!" but that doesn't mean that you must wash. As it turns out, if you refuse to give in and wash, you'll start to make positive changes in the way your orbital cortex works. Your orbital cortex will tell you, "Wash this! Check that!" If you listen to it, it will get hotter and hotter and hotter. But if you refuse to listen to it, we have learned, it will cool down. (Remember those brain photos on the book jacket?)

By learning to put off acting on an obsessive thought for fifteen minutes—or even five minutes—you are teaching yourself response prevention. You do not need to spend hours in therapy with a medical professional, as was once thought necessary. This is truly self-directed therapy in the sense that you are your own therapist. Of course, you can always get additional help and support. But you will find that as you apply the Four Steps—Relabel, Reattribute, Refocus, Revalue—you will be able to expose yourself for longer and longer periods to those terrible thoughts and urges without performing compulsive rituals in response to them. Initially, you may have to remove yourself from the sink very quickly so as not to give in and wash your hands again or move away from the door so as not to check the lock again. It's okay at first to put some physical distance between yourself and the sink or the lock. But never say to yourself, "Oh, my God. I gave in. I'm terrible. I'm a loser. I'm never going to get better." If you do a compulsion, just tell yourself that OCD won this round—and vow that next time you're going to work to ignore the sink or the door and try to Refocus on doing something worthwhile and pleasurable. Just realizing that this is a form of behavior therapy, even if you're doing a compulsion at the same time, prevents you from taking the compulsive behavior literally at face value (it's not "washing your hands," it's "doing a compulsion") and keeps your Impartial Spectator active and in play.

Typically, a person with OCD experiences the urge to perform a compulsion many times during a day. However much time you're able to put between getting the urge and acting on it is time well spent, even if it's only a minute or two. At the end of that period, it's important that you reassess the bothersome urge and make a mental note of any change in the intensity of the urge during the time you were able to hold it at bay. Even if there is an almost imperceptible change in its intensity—which often happens—you will have learned that you can control your behavioral response to the OCD thought.

RECORDING YOUR SPIRITUAL SUCCESS

It's important to keep a journal or diary in which you record your successes at Refocusing. It can be just a little spiral notebook to tuck into your pocket or purse. Why is this important? Well, for two reasons. In the heat of battle against a compulsive urge, it's not always easy to remember which of your Refocusing behaviors was the most effective. What's more, having a written record will help you place these helpful behaviors more firmly in your mind. Your diary can also help you build confidence as you see your list of successes grow.

There is a spiritual aspect to overcoming OCD, as well as a biological one. In the Bible, the Book of Galatians says: "Be not deceived; God is not mocked: For whatever you may sow, that you will also reap." It seems that the way God wired the human system, when people focus too much on how they *feel*, they don't *do* what they must to overcome OCD. You can change your brain. But you have to do the sowing to reap the rewards. No one can do the work for you.

From studying OCD, we have learned a great deal about the relationship between how the brain works and what's going on in the human mind. I continue to enjoy doing research on the causes and treatment of OCD largely because people with OCD are very rewarding to work with. They're not only hard workers, in general, and very appreciative of help, but tend to be creative, sincere, and very intense. One woman in my OCD therapy group said, "Whatever I do is serious, even if it's choosing a breakfast cereal." In learning the Four Steps, this intensity is an asset. However, people with OCD also tend to become de-energized, worn out from what they have come to view as a hopeless struggle against a fiendish disease. Refocusing helps to re-energize them.

The best Refocusing activities require concentration and strategy and involve other people. Jogging alone, for example, is less apt to take your mind off your obsessive and compulsive thoughts than a good game of bridge or even solving some work problem—as long as what you do gives you pleasure. (This is not to deny that jogging alone can be helpful for many people.) Here again, my patients are very creative. One man used to be afraid to shave because he was terrified of hurting himself as punishment for having obscene obsessive thoughts. Now he can use shaving as a Refocusing activity when these thoughts arise. The result is that both his face and his mind have become very clean!

THE MIND-BRAIN CONNECTION

The study of OCD is intellectually stimulating. Unlike those who suffer from many other psychiatric diseases, people with OCD can tell you in pretty clear language how they feel and what's bothering them. They can describe in minute detail ominous feelings and intrusive urges and the misery and suffering that these feelings and urges cause. As a result, we have a pretty good idea of what's going on in the mind of a person who has these urges to wash or check or whatever. Since we now know a fair amount about what goes on in the brain of a person with OCD, we can gain a better understanding of the relationship between what goes on in the brain and how the person feels inside. Understanding the relationship between what the brain does and a person's internal life is very important, both for medical reasons and because it is such a fascinating subject in its own right. Three factors are at work here: the capacity of people with OCD to tell how they feel inside, the emerging understanding of the underlying brain problems that cause OCD, and the intriguing fact that among all psychiatric conditions, OCD is one of the few that does not respond very well to so-called placebo treatment— blank pills. Even with schizophrenia and depression, when people are given blank pills—pills that they think may be helping them—a fair number of them actually improve in the short term. But with persons with OCD, generally less than 10 percent get better when they are given placebos, so if something active isn't being done to combat their symptoms, nothing really happens—or they get worse. Put all these findings together, and you can begin to see why studying OCD can be so revealing about the relationship between the mind and the brain. Both the strong evidence that the brain changes when people with OCD improve (and they tend to improve only with truly effective treatment), and the fact that people with OCD can accurately relate how they think and feel before and after treatment add up to powerful sources of information on the relationship between the brain, behavior, and a person's mental life.

STAY ACTIVE!

I firmly believe that allowing or encouraging patients to be passive is a problem with much of modern medicine. A person goes to a doctor, the doctor does what the doctor does, and the person waits to get better. Our UCLA treatment method teaches people what they can do to help themselves. Medications are fine, if used to help people help themselves (the "waterwings" theory). In treating OCD, medications make it easier for many people to learn to do the Four Steps. They certainly make the unpleasant OCD symptoms fade more quickly when you do the fifteen-minute rule. But eventually, as you keep working at your self-directed cognitive-biobehavioral therapy, you find that you can do it successfully with less and less medication. And that's a good thing.

The bottom line is that as you do fewer and fewer compulsive behaviors and pay less and less attention to your obsessive thoughts—work around the thoughts—those thoughts and urges will fade more and more quickly.

So the familiar brain trio—the orbital cortex, the cingulate gyrus, and the caudate nucleus—have ganged up on you. The orbital cortex is sending you false messages that "something is wrong"; the cingulate gyrus, which is wired right into your heart and guts, is making you feel, "Oh, something terrible is going to happen if . . ."; and the caudate nucleus is not shifting gears to enable you to abandon repetitive, nonsensical behaviors and move on to other, appropriate behaviors. But once you start using the Four Steps, you will no longer act unthinkingly and automatically on those false messages. You will know what's going on up there and you will stop reacting like a puppet. Your Impartial Spectator will keep you in touch with reality and tell you, "That's good, that's bad," just as your tongue tells you, "That's sweet, that's sour" and your eyes tell you, "That's red, that's green." You will look at yourself and be able to ask, "What is this feeling?" The answer? It's Brain Lock. Once you realize that the feeling has no deep meaning, that it's just a false alarm, you will be able to largely ignore it and go about your business. You shift gears and *do another behavior.* (And preferably, since you've Anticipated and planned ahead, you'll know in advance what behavior you will do.)

WHAT IT MEANS: NOTHING

But if you take OCD's false messages at face value, you will spend your time fretting and worrying. "Did that guy touch me? Maybe he scraped against me when I wasn't looking. Oh, my God. What does it mean?" Deep down, to be honest, you know it doesn't mean any-

STEP 3: REFOCUS ▪ 79

thing. You know that you are not contaminated because of your "encounter" with that mystery man. But without the Four Steps as tools to reassure you, the feeling is so strong that you're apt to buy into it.

What you *don't* want to do right off the bat is say, "You know, those two hundred compulsive behaviors I have, well, tomorrow I've got to stop doing them." Do what's easiest first: Tackle one and try to wait fifteen minutes before responding to its silly commands. It may be wise to start with the one that causes you the least stress. Keep a list, a kind of stress meter, if you think it will be helpful (see Chapter Eight: The Four Steps and Traditional Approaches to Behavior Therapy).

As a member of the human species, you have a little edge at the starting line. Dogs can get a disorder that causes them to lick their paws, fur, and skin, compulsively and destructively—a condition that, Dr. Judith Rapoport of the National Institutes of Health found, can be treated with the same medications that are used to treat OCD. But you cannot say to a dog, "It's not you—it's just your canine dermatitis. It's caused by urges from your brain. Refocus. Go dig in the back yard." However, as human beings we have the capacity to observe our own behavior, to use our Impartial Spectator, to increase our mindful awareness, and to make thoughtful decisions about how we're going to value and respond to the signals our brain is sending us. Our patients at UCLA have developed their own techniques for distracting themselves from doing their compulsions. One young man snaps the fingers of both hands. One woman gently slaps her face a few times. You do whatever works.

In Refocusing, at first even a minute is progress. But several weeks down the line, you'll have to push the edge of the envelope. This is fighter-pilot territory. You will no longer be able to cling to your mental timer that's set for five minutes or ten minutes. You will have to make yourself increase your tolerance of your discomfort. It's a perfectly good idea to promise yourself some treat—a theater ticket or a yogurt or an ice cream bar—if you manage to wait at least fifteen minutes before you act on some obsessive thought. Then you should record your success in your behavior-therapy journal. Many people come to see recording their successes as the biggest treat of all. A woman in our therapy group who has battled body dysmorphic disorder, an OCD-related condition, for many years, finally made up her mind that she was no longer willing to live with the lights dimmed and the mirrors covered with newspapers to prevent herself from scratching and picking relentlessly to rid herself of imaginary skin flaws. For every fifteen minutes that passed that she resisted the urge to pick, she would give herself twenty-five cents for new clothes. It definitely helped.

When the going gets tough and the job of Refocusing taxes your willpower, keep in mind that there will be a payoff down the line. As time goes on, you will begin to get a lot more mileage out of diligently practicing the Four Steps. You will change the inner workings of your brain. By Refocusing, by working around your OCD—by accepting it for what it is, not for what it isn't—you will come to understand that your whole life doesn't depend on controlling those awful, intrusive feelings and that your world isn't going to crumble because your OCD won't go away.

DERAILING THOSE ANXIETIES

Performing an activity that requires your full attention is an excellent way to divert yourself from your OCD symptoms. This is what Howard Hughes was probably doing when he was piloting his airplane. Hughes thought nothing of flying a plane, but was gripped with fear at the thought of touching a doorknob that he imagined was contaminated. In his day, his friends were totally perplexed by his behavior, but if we analyze it in terms of what is now known about OCD, it's really not difficult to understand. The doorknob gave him a morbid fear of death, but he did not associate his airplane with contamination, so he had no feelings of fear associated with flying. Flying was a form of behavior therapy for Hughes. At the controls of his airplane he Refocused away from his OCD onto an activity that required total concentration. In an airplane, the pilot is in control. For a person with OCD, the mundane action of touching a "dirty" doorknob may cause the dreaded thought that a disaster is imminent. In the short run, the feeling of fear is uncontrollable, probably because it is caused by misfiring in the cingulate gyrus. But it can be worked around and, in that way, can be controlled.

After a time, the Four Steps become almost automatic. Michael, who obsesses about his pants being too tight, says that the Four Steps gave him "the discipline that I needed. I learned to tell myself, 'You do this today, and you'll feel better tomorrow. Do this tomorrow, and you'll feel better the next day.' The Four Steps were a beginner's guide. Now, it's like I'm still doing the Four Steps, but without really thinking of the Four Steps. I think most people sort of improvise what works for them, but they're still doing the basic method. You know, you don't have to think, 'Now I've gotta do the First Step. . . .' And you don't have to think, 'Okay, this is a biochemical problem.' You just have it in your own mind exactly what it is you have. You don't have to have a name for it. Basically, you just know that you have to do something else. You improvise, but you always try to improve. You're always figuring out exercises that will help you help yourself." This is good advice on intermediate-level behavior therapy.

Sometimes, Michael says, Refocusing is "sort of like pushing the thought out of my brain. I almost feel like something is hitting my brain and then leaving it. And that's not like OCD feels at all. It sort of feels good." He finds physical exercise very helpful in working around his OCD thoughts. "If I could play basketball twenty-four hours a day, I'd be great. I'd never feel bad." When Michael's anxiety level is low, his powers of concentration become very intense, and he is able to perform his stenographic job extremely well. "People say, 'Oh, that's good. You have a decent job and you're able to do it, even with your OCD.' But my comeback is—and I think this is good for me—that I don't want to be doing this job; I want to be doing something I enjoy." As his OCD continues to improve, he becomes more optimistic about getting a better job. For a long time, he could read very little because his OCD symptoms would intrude, causing him to read and reread every page, but now he is reading voraciously and learning new things—"I can read more books now in a month than I used to read in a year. With my behavior therapy, and getting more insight every day into what this OCD is all about, coming to grips with it, I hope I can have more job success."

In his battle against OCD, Michael figures he's about 70 percent of the way there. "You have to keep working. That's the only way to get above 70 percent. I realize now that something in me, be it biochemical, genetic, whatever, will never allow me to be 100 percent. But I always want to work to get close to that. At the same time, I want to be realistic. It's important to me not to have unreachable goals, but just to work and reach whatever it is that I can attain and to realize that my anxiety is not going to kill me."

For Michael, coming faithfully to the weekly OCD therapy group at UCLA is like doing a homework assignment, part of his ongoing behavior therapy. In short, it is vigilance. He has, however, abandoned the idea he once had that his primary mission was to try to help others in the group who have not yet achieved his level of success. With the best intentions, he once brought to the group the exterminator's business card that he'd carried around, reasoning it would be effective exposure therapy for others with a fear of pesticides. After all, it had worked for him. Instead, he recalls, "It made some people go nuts. I realize now that I can't be Mother Teresa."

There's an important lesson to be learned from Michael's experience as a "therapist." Each person must fight the OCD battle on his or her own terms and at his or her own pace.

Jack, who conquered his hand-washing compulsion, remembers that I gave him a finger puzzle whereby the more you tug, the tighter it grips. You have to calm down, use your brain, and extricate your fingers. It's the same when OCD grips you. You tend to panic and start to push and pull the wrong way. What you need to do is stay calm and use the Four Steps to unlock your brain. For Jack, staying calm took real perseverance. He admitted, "I had that kind of personality where I would prefer to have some big force come in and do everything for me. I used to have a drinking problem. Alcohol would make me a different person, and I wouldn't have to face myself or make any effort to change. So it fit right in with my personality." Before seeking treatment at UCLA, Jack was on drug therapy, suffering terrible side effects and making little progress in fighting his OCD. Looking back, he says his doctor acted "kind of like he was trying to knock a virus out of me." When Jack would call the doctor to say that the drugs were giving him explosive headaches, the doctor advised him, "Just hang in there. You don't abandon ship if it develops a little leak." Eventually, Jack realized that medicine just wasn't going to do the job for him. He told himself, "This is it. It's up to you now. You've got to change your behavior. You just can't rely on chemicals to change your life." Years earlier, Jack had developed an intolerance for alcohol.

Jack faced facts: "I was running out of options. I had to start relying on myself," not on medication. "Winter was coming, and I couldn't stand the thought of having dry, cracked hands again. Something had to be done. Until then, I had thought that even having my hands like this was better than having to endure the anxiety that would follow if I didn't give in and wash them. But I began to wonder if it was worth it.

"I began trying not to give in to the thoughts that my hands were dirty and would spread contamination everywhere. Of course, I was anxious, at first, when I didn't wash, but then I discovered that the longer you don't give in and find out that nothing happens, the easier it gets the next time. You begin to have a history of incidents in which nothing really happens when you ignore the obsession. Being in the therapy group was helpful because it was hard to keep going to group and not show any progress. And once you made progress, you were encouraged to continue, so you wouldn't let others in the group down.

"I found that when I ignored the unpleasant, intrusive thoughts, their intensity would decrease. It was when I started to pay attention to them that they would begin to bother me. I also tried to work at reducing the excessive checking that I would go through when I left my house or car. This was difficult because there are so many fears associated with what might happen to an unprotected dwelling or automobile. Of course, being clean and protecting your property are real concerns that everyone has. It's just that, with OCD, you don't know when to stop. Eventually, you have to walk away from your house or car after telling yourself that you did everything you reasonably could to make sure they were secured. When OCD gets really bad, you can stare at a locked door or see that a window is closed, but not get that reassuring feeling that they're all right.

There comes a point when you have to assure yourself that everything is okay."

As Jack began to make himself spend less time checking, he realized, "You don't have absolute control over things. All you can do is your best—and then you have to decide when you've done enough. The amount of checking may go up or down, depending on the amount of stress that you're going through, but you must not let it get out of control. You have to give yourself credit for every little improvement you make. As I learned in the group, the more you change your behavior, the more your thoughts will change."

Sometimes Jack found it difficult to tell if what he was experiencing was really OCD. For example, one symptom common to people with OCD is hoarding useless objects. But at times, Jack had the reverse problem: He became obsessed with getting rid of things he felt he no longer needed. At first, getting rid of things gave him pleasure, but later the situation got out of hand and it became a major preoccupation. He didn't know when to stop rearranging things and sorting through things. That's when he decided it was probably an OCD symptom. He was right: If you think it's OCD—it's OCD! Reality doesn't feel like OCD.

Jack was in the group for three years and continues to practice self-directed therapy. Today, he estimates, his symptoms have decreased 90 percent. He washes his hands only a "socially acceptable" number of times each day.

MEETING THE ENEMY HEAD-ON

Christopher, who had contamination obsessions, as well as terrible blasphemous thoughts, worked out a no-nonsense self-directed therapy technique. When his neighbors went on vacation, they would ask him to walk their dog. Now, for someone who is terrified of contamination, walking a "dirty" dog on a "dirty" street is a challenge. Christopher met it head-on: He would stop, pick up some dirt, and rub it on his hands and arms. That done, he would focus on walking the dog. When he returned home, he didn't allow himself to wash the dirt off until he had to go to work or to bed. And he never developed a washing compulsion! Since he was following the guidance of his Impartial Spectator, he had a clear view of reality.

Since Christopher works in a kitchen, he must wash his hands frequently. For a while, he said, "I developed this kind of quirky obsession that if I washed my hands several times, that would be developing a compulsion. And *that* was the obsession." But this obsession didn't prevent him from washing—again, self-directed behavior therapy. And since reality doesn't mimic OCD feelings, he could always be confident that when he felt the need to wash, it wasn't OCD. In this particular case, OCD would have made him *stop* washing. One of his tasks at the restaurant was to put tomato sauce on the pizzas. It was agonizingly hard for him to do because he had developed an obsession that the tomato sauce was actually blood. But he had no choice. This was something he had to do repeatedly every day. It was, in effect, constant exposure therapy. In time, Christopher overcame his thoughts about the sauce being blood and had no difficulty tending to the pizzas.

Amy, who had a morbid fear that if she picked up a pen or pencil she might write something obscene, recalls her moment of triumph over this obsession. On her birthday, the family went to an Italian restaurant for dinner. Amy panicked when the maitre d' seated her party right next to the waiters' station, where pens and pencils and pads were clearly visible. She wanted to flee, but she did not. She remembers, "I just consciously said, 'I'm going to stick it out.' I told myself, 'This is not real. You're not going to get up there and do anything. You're going to sit here like a normal person. You're not going to act on your fears.'" Having done so, she was able to Refocus on the birthday celebration and socialize with the rest of her family. She realized that by fighting back against the OCD, she was giving herself the best possible birthday present. Through self-directed cognitive biobehavioral therapy, Amy has become pretty comfortable with pens and pencils. It is interesting to note that when her typewriter broke down, she made a conscious decision not to have it repaired. She knew that by forcing herself to use pens and pencils, she would hasten her recovery.

Brian, who had the awful fear of battery acid, knew he needed professional help when his obsession reached the point where he asked a physicist friend to figure out how long battery acid would cling to the tires of his car after he had driven through a spill. (For the record, his friend estimated that all traces of the acid would be gone in about four revolutions of those tires.) Now Brian is able to see his obsession as "totally bizarre." But he still remembers the agony of those nights when he would follow the police and fire vehicles, cleaning up real or imaginary acid spills on the pavement. He shakes his head. "I would actually go out and clean public streets. That's pretty damned bizarre. Somebody must have seen this idiot out there with buckets and baking soda."

Like many others who suffer from OCD, Brian sought help when he'd "had a bellyful" of that nonsense. "I got so damned tired of that stuff, so tired of the depression it caused. I couldn't do normal things. Every minute of the day, my mind was concentrating on battery acid."

Brian is quick to say that the Four-Step Method "is the only good tool out there right now for people like me. . . . You've got to get to the point where it's mind over matter. You've got to say to yourself, 'Man, there's just no way.' And you know what the hard part is for me? Well, with somebody who's afraid of cotton or dustballs or whatever, theoretically there's no real danger, but theoretically sulfuric acid is dangerous. So it was real hard for me to make that split. You've got to have a healthy respect for it, but at the same time you can't let it go over that edge. I was living over that edge all the time, I mean, acid was everywhere. It was in my bedroom, on the walls of the house." For the record, OCD can make a person just as frightened of a dustball as Brian was of acid. It's hard to overstate how bizarre and ridiculous OCD symptoms can be.

With the help of the Four Steps and some medication to help get him through his therapy, Brian has been able to work around most of his obsessions. His garden is where he tends to do his best Refocusing. "I have a lot more success on weekends when I'm working in the yard, and working hard. I'm an avid gardener and I can get out there and mow and plow and pull and sweat. That's a great escape for me." The general principle is simple: If you have a hobby you love, use it as much as you can to Refocus. Then you'll be getting two benefits for the price of one.

THE POWER OF SELF-DISTRACTION

Anna, the philosophy student who interrogated her boyfriend relentlessly because of her unfounded fear that he was being unfaithful, recalls, "The third step—Refocus—was essential to my recovery, but it was a very difficult step to learn. Waiting is about the last thing you want to do when life itself seems to be hinging on whether a compulsion is performed. Distracting myself by doing something else helped. However, even if I couldn't really concentrate on another activity, letting time pass still had a salutary effect. Usually, when I managed to make it through fifteen minutes and would try another fifteen minutes, I was in much better control of myself when the time had passed."

Anna then made an important observation: "Those who have compulsions can sometimes remove themselves from the place where they perform their rituals—the sink or the door. But removing oneself physically from one's own thoughts is impossible." Still, she has found that the fifteen-minute rule, though difficult to implement, gives her space "to stand back and assess an obsession as OCD, not as a matter of significant content."

Using shorter periods, even one minute or thirty seconds, is perfectly acceptable, especially in the beginning. The key is to keep making mental notes and Relabeling: "This is just OCD—nothing is really wrong." By conscientiously turning her thoughts to other matters, Anna learned over time that she was able to resist her urges to ask her poor, beleaguered boyfriend all those crazy questions and to Refocus away from her OCD thoughts and urges, rather than to pour more energy into them, as she had done before treatment. Consequently, the intensity of her OCD attacks diminished. "Over a period of months, these small gains added up to a significant improvement in my mental health."

Although she still has the obsessions and compulsive urges to a greater or lesser extent, depending on the stresses in her life at a given time, Anna is now "more likely to let OCD thoughts wash over my brain, rather than allow them to seep in and infect my whole thought process. For example, almost every time I see a sharp knife, a strong, intrusive thought or picture comes into my mind." (Her obsession with knives was totally unrelated to her jealousy obsession.) "Completely involuntarily, I envision the knife slicing through my own flesh, and this vision is vivid enough to cause me to wince. Or, if someone is in the room with me, I have the thought that I am stabbing that person. But because I now know that these are simply unwanted, and basically senseless, thoughts, I just let them go by without trying to figure them out, as I once would have done. I don't let them ruin my peace of mind. My success in implementing the Four Steps increased quite a bit as I gained confidence that I could prevail, rather than give in, when OCD attacks strike. I am not free from OCD, but most of the time I manage it, rather than allow it to manage me." This is a great description of applying the principle, "It's not me—it's the OCD."

Karen, the compulsive hoarder, also found that Refocus is one of the most helpful of the Four Steps. She advised, "Do something you like to do and get involved in it. Plant an herb garden. Read a short story. Arrange some flowers. Go Rollerblading. The compulsive urge will pass if you can redirect your attention and behavior. If it does return, it may not be as strongly compelling. Again, do another behavior. It works! I use this technique when I encounter a garage sale or an attractive trash can. If I can stall the compulsion long enough, the sale will be over, and someone else will have taken the trash-can item. More likely, however, I'll be tired, and the urge will have passed."

As your behavior changes, Karen promises, so will your attitude. "The taste of each success has a unique sweetness, and it urges you onward to further success. You know you can do it this time because you have done it before. Your whole outlook changes from negative to positive, from darkness to light."

After two years of cleaning out and tossing out, Karen and her husband are about three-fourths of the way to a junk-free home. And she now knows the huge satisfaction that comes from having a tidy house and a pretty yard—and feeling free to invite friends over to share them. But, she says, "I got an even greater reward. Somehow I went over an invisible line in my mind and told myself, 'I am going to beat this thing.' And that's the real jackpot. The promise of behavior therapy has come true. The old, disturbing thoughts and feelings that make me want to hoard may reappear—I'm sure they will—but they will never again have the same power over me. The fruits of success and self-confidence are much sweeter than the false promise of future security that the stockpiling of material things gave me. I have the tools of behavior therapy, and I have the power of the belief in a God who cares what happens to me. That thought comforts me and gives me strength." Karen—the new Karen—has started a small business. She is successful and forward looking. This is the power of faith based on personal knowledge and experience!

DON'T WORRY, YOU WON'T DO IT

One thing our patients at UCLA learn early is that no matter how real their obsessive thoughts with dangerous content may seem, they will never act on them. *No one ever does anything morally objectionable because of OCD.* Lara, whose obsession about doing some violent act was so strong that she was terrified to pick up even a butter knife, now understands, "I have never acted out an obsessional thought that would harm anyone. I will not, nor do I want to. It is repulsive to me. I know I have control over the thoughts and urges, no matter how strong or disruptive they become." It's important to remember: OCD cannot take over your will, certainly not in a way that would make you do something you believe is wrong.

Lara has also learned the cardinal principle of behavior therapy: "The harder I fight to make the obsessions go away, the stronger they get. So I shift and reframe my thoughts. I try to focus on something else—a project, a book, a television show. I shift my thoughts, alleviating the symptoms. If I can redirect my behavior and energy onto another path, I can usually get on with another task." When her obsessions worsen, Lara tends to feel sorry for herself, thinking she no longer has any control over them. "But then I shift. I call someone, I start cooking, I go to the gym. I am not always successful in being able to shift my obsessional thoughts. Sometimes I just have to ride out the storm. The obsessions are difficult to walk away from. They stay with me wherever I go as 'added baggage.' So I must work harder not to pay attention to the obsessions." Again, Refocusing your attention on something else, even for brief periods, can be very helpful with bad obsessions, if only to prove to yourself that the bad thought doesn't have to totally leave your mind before you can Refocus. This is what I mean by "working around" it.

In Lara's case, there is an interesting dichotomy: Although compulsive shopping is one of the compulsions with which she struggles, she will sometimes use shopping as a way to divert herself from her disturbing thoughts or urges. "I will go out to get out of the house, to be busy. I'll go shopping basically because I don't want to come home and be alone with my obsessions, because I know they'll get worse at home. If I'm out, looking around, I can quell them a bit." In essence, she is Refocusing away from her obsessions.

For Carla, whose awful obsession was that she was going to murder her infant daughter, the Four Steps are now so automatic that "it's like writing my name or drinking water. When you keep doing them on a constant basis, all day, it automatically clicks, like a lightbulb going off. It's the greatest defense." This is when the transmission in the brain starts to become automatic again.

Keeping busy is part of that defense. Carla is on the advisory board of her daughter's school and collects clothing for distribution to the needy. "When you do these positive things for people," she has learned, "it gets you off yourself. It doesn't make the OCD go away. I will not tell anyone that I do not have OCD. I still have OCD. I take medication every day. But there are so many things other than OCD, and I want people to understand you have a life beyond OCD, and you deserve that life. Don't think you've done something bad or horrible or maybe God wasn't with you when this thing, OCD, happened to you." This is a beautiful example of the kind of spiritual acceptance that makes all aspects of the Four Steps work better.

Jill, who had terrible fears about contamination and would "alcohol" her entire house, also learned this vital lesson: "When I'm not working, my OCD gets worse because I have more time to let it get worse. The busier I am, the healthier I get." Now that her OCD is under control, she is "ready to get back into the mainstream." Before she took time off from working to get treatment for OCD, Jill had been a real estate agent. At that time, it suited her needs; the flexible hours gave her time to take care of her disease and to cope with rearing her two daughters, who are now young adults. Today, she thinks she is ready to "do something more creative." It's a big leap forward for someone who was once so overwhelmed by her OCD that she couldn't leave her house and literally had to clean the air that she breathed with alcohol swabs.

Gary had been plagued since his teens by intrusive thoughts that told him to "strike out" at people with whom he might be talking or to make rude and inappropriate remarks to them. Of course, he never acted on these weird thoughts. As we've learned, people with OCD never do. Nevertheless, the thoughts were ruining his life. As he worked diligently at doing the Four Steps, with low dosages of medication as his waterwings, Gary was able to Refocus on other behaviors for gradually increasing periods. Assiduously working around his OCD thoughts, he found that he was spending less and less time repeating senseless phrases in his head and doing other compulsive rituals that he had once thought were the answer to making his violent thoughts go away. Gary's social life began to improve as he became more confident that he could cope with the bothersome thoughts when they intruded while he was talking to others. In fact, he used social interaction itself as a Refocusing tool. He made new acquaintances and became friendlier with casual acquaintances at work. After fifteen months of behavior therapy and medication, Gary was able to get off medication. No longer fearful of letting anyone get close to him, he is dating for the first time in years. And as part of his Refocusing, he is doing volunteer work for AIDS Project L.A.

Joanne, who at one stage was "coming unglued" as a result of the dark, brooding thoughts that smothered her, remembers clearly the day when she experienced for the first time the sensation of having her mind "move on," get unstuck. This is the awareness of the brain unlocking. Until then, she says, "I had no concept of how that felt; my brain had no idea how that felt. Everyone is always saying, 'Live in the moment,' but that's hard to do when you get stuck in that moment. I've learned that, for me, time cannot stand still, even for a moment. Now, I always try to keep moving forward." Today, she says, "My life is so different. From the outside, I probably haven't changed much. No one knew the torment going on in my brain. But now I have joy, I can focus on the things I want to do, I can be who I was meant to be. I can live a life! When the dark voice inside starts to bother me, I know what it is. I Refocus on something else and tell myself to move on. I have been given the tools to help myself, to have control over a voice in my head that was destructive and affected everything in my life."

What Joanne has learned is that she has mastery and control over her OCD. If, early in treatment, people can be taught to Refocus, to ignore their intrusive thoughts by working around them—for even a couple of minutes to start—it gives them some sense of control. This sense of mastery and control is very helpful and important, and it is to be reinforced and encouraged. In the beginning, even extremely small steps are meaningful. This is how people learn that it is not necessary that they fully control the intrusive thoughts or totally remove them from their awareness to make significant functional progress by doing behavioral therapy. The big effort it takes to make a very small Refocusing step in the beginning will be enough effort to make a large step later on. The same effort yields greater results as time goes by, because your brain is changing as you work at the Four Steps.

Jenny, who for years has battled numerous obsessions, including one that nuclear radiation was going to jump off her and onto others, is now able to put all this in proper perspective and even make light of the avoidance techniques she once used to deal with her OCD. At one time, she developed a not uncommon obsession that she had struck and killed someone while driving. Her attempt at a solution? She simply decided not to own a car. "I would make up stories—'I can't drive at night because my eyes are bad' or 'I'm too broke to own a car.'" And her checking compulsion? Well, because she couldn't bear to look at other people's stoves—the knobs might be a tiny bit askew—she found a way to avoid that neatly, as well. "When I went to parties at other people's houses, I would avoid the kitchen by bringing a dish that you didn't have to heat up." Of course, none of her symptoms abated until she faced up to her problem; called it OCD; and then Refocused on other, positive behaviors. She learned behavior therapy as an outpatient at UCLA and later, in my weekly therapy group, was introduced to the Four Steps.

Although Jenny still has "a little mixture of all the classic OCD fears," she is now able to "just kind of move on" when the feelings strike. She has a good job and a lot of friends. She drives a car. And she can bring a dish that needs to be heated. And, she says, "I feel I can move anywhere in the world and go on to different careers."

Dottie, who performed ridiculous rituals out of fear that something terrible was going to happen to her son's eyes, was hospitalized for a year in the 1970s—but that did little to help her OCD. She now understands that she was largely to blame, even though the techniques we now have for treating OCD had not been developed at that time. She remembers that in the psychiatric hospital, "We had group therapy every day, but no one ever knew what was wrong with me. People would say, 'Now, Dottie, it's your turn. What do you want to tell us about yourself?' Well, I liked to help everybody else, but I would never talk about me and, of course, that's the worst thing." One day she just ran screaming from the group session—"It was the only emotion I ever showed in that hospital." Why hadn't she been able to tell the others about her horrible, obsessive thoughts? "Because I thought if I talked about them, they might come true." After four years of attending our program at UCLA, Dottie is off medication, is able to hold down a part-time job, and talks about how she hopes to use what she has learned to help others who have OCD. The ultimate in Refocusing—doing cognitive-biobehavioral therapy with others.

OCD AS AN APHRODISIAC?

Domingo, whose obsessions include his fear that he has razor blades on the tips of his fingers and is going to hurt his wife when he touches her, has a most interesting—one might say unique—take on how OCD has affected his sex life. Tall, dark, and wiry with a big smile, he is attractive to many women and had his fair share of girlfriends before he recently married. (The following interview took place before his marriage.)

During sex, Domingo explained, "It's hard to concentrate because of my OCD. Half of me is with the woman. But the OCD thoughts keep coming, and I can't concentrate and the time keeps going by.

I'm still with her, but my mind is somewhere else. So I keep from having an orgasm. Women find that's a very good idea because it lasts forever. I just go on and on and on. They tell me I'm a rare species of man." Just what kind of OCD thoughts does Domingo have during lovemaking? "It could be, 'Did I close the front door?' 'Did I bring the stereo in from the car?' 'Did I feed the dog?'" Do his partners notice that his mind is not entirely on them? He grinned. "They say, 'Are you with me?' I say, 'I'll be with you in a second. Enjoy it.' They understand."

Although new obsessions tend to sneak into Domingo's mind even as he conquers others, he figures that, as a payoff for his diligence in doing the Four Steps, he is halfway home in his fight against OCD. When one of the terrible thoughts intrudes, he notes, "I just take a deep breath and say, 'I can do this. I have things to do. I can't wait fifteen minutes every time I'm upset because I will see fifteen minutes lead to two hours. It's one obsession after another. If I wait fifteen minutes, I will sit here and do nothing all day." So he simply mentally eliminates the possibility that he will perform the compulsion at all and goes on with his business. At UCLA, we call this Active Revaluing.

Not everyone has willpower as strong as Domingo's. But he is not the only person who has been able to use the Four Steps as a sort of launching pad for behavior therapy and then to learn over time that he no longer needs to perform them as though he were reciting a litany. With practice, people like Domingo can bypass the Relabeling and Reattributing steps, which they find kick in automatically, and move directly to Refocusing behaviors, as a result of having very rapidly Actively Revalued the intruding thought or urge as worthless, miserable OCD.

This, of course, is the ultimate goal.

KEY POINTS TO REMEMBER

•Step 3 is the Refocus step.

•Refocus means to change your behavioral responses to unwanted thoughts and urges and focus your attention on something useful and constructive. DO ANOTHER BEHAVIOR.

•This is the no pain, no gain step. You must be ACTIVE. You cannot be passive.

•Use the fifteen-minute rule: Work around your symptoms by doing something wholesome and enjoyable for at least fifteen minutes. After fifteen minutes, make mental notes of how your symptoms have changed and try to Refocus for another fifteen minutes.

•Use your Impartial Spectator. It will strengthen your mind.

•When you change your behavior, you change your brain.

4

Step 4: Revalue

"Lessons Learned from OCD"

> **Step 1. Relabel**
>
> **Step 2. Reattribute**
>
> **Step 3. Refocus**
>
> **Step 4. REVALUE**

Step 4: **Revalue** is a natural outcome of diligent practice of the first three steps—Relabel, Reattribute, and Refocus. With consistent practice, you will quickly come to realize that your obsessive thoughts and compulsive behaviors are **worthless distractions to be ignored.** With this insight, you will be able to Revalue and *devalue* the pathological urges and fend them off until they begin to fade. As your brain begins to work better, it will become easier to see the obsessions and compulsions for what they really are. Your brain will function in a much more normal, automatic way. As a result, the intensity of your symptoms will decrease.

People who suffer from obsessive-compulsive disorder (OCD) feel a pain so great that they reach deep into their souls to seek an answer to the question "Why me?" Too often, they wind up thinking, "What a terrible person I must be for having such 'bad' thoughts."

If you do not actively Revalue these thoughts as nothing more than false messages coming from the brain—messages with no spiritual significance whatsoever—you will certainly become demoralized and filled with self-loathing. The key is to realize that the thought is happening *in spite of* your will, not *because* of it.

A religious person, for example, can examine a blasphemous obsessive thought and understand that it has nothing to do with having objectionable feelings about the Virgin Mary or Jesus Christ—and everything to do with a medical condition, OCD. With this knowledge, you should see this as an opportunity to reaffirm your faith through spiritual self-examination. The knowledge that the blasphemous thoughts are nothing more than the reflection of a disease—not a reflection of your spiritual purity or integrity—is key to developing the capacity to "work around" the obsessive, blasphemous thoughts.

The general principle that is embodied in the Revalue step is, *The more clearly you see what OCD symptoms really are, the more rapidly you can dismiss them as worthless garbage that is not worth paying attention to.* The practice of the first three steps gradually removes the fear and anxiety that OCD causes when its false messages are taken literally at "face value." As you learn that OCD need not control your behaviors or thoughts, you come to devalue it and can begin simply to ignore it as nothing but a bothersome pest. In fact, the more consciously and *actively* you can come to Revalue it as mere foolish nonsense, the more quickly and smoothly you can perform the Relabel, Reattribute, and Refocus steps and the more steadily your brain's "automatic transmission" function returns. Revaluing helps you shift the behavioral gears! Furthermore, as people come to understand their disease more clearly and use the Four Steps as their weapon to defeat this enemy, they commonly gain a new ability to Revalue their lives and their feelings about themselves and others.

Lara put it this way: "Having OCD has made me a more intense, sensitive, and compassionate human being. I have been humbled by my disorder. It has built character even while tearing at my soul, my heart, and my self-esteem. It has enabled me to fight harder, to strive for the good and the truth inside me. It has made me less critical and judgmental of others who suffer in their lives."

"GOD LOVES ME"

Having been given the tools to fight back against OCD—knowing that it need never again take over their lives—people begin both to think of the time and opportunity they lost and to look to the future with a renewed zest for living. Often, they experience a spiritual awakening.

Joel, having largely overcome his hoarding and contamination compulsions, finds that for the first time in years "there is an intrinsic value in life itself. I never had the type of depression where I would want to kill myself, but life was just really drudgery." Carla tells of her gratitude that her daughter—the daughter she obsessed that she might kill—is now a happy, healthy 6-year-old. Although Carla is devoutly religious, in her darkest moments she had questioned whether there was an Almighty power capable of forgiving her for having these awful thoughts. Now, she understands, "God loves me." She has Revalued her life. No longer wallowing in her guilt and anger, she is "fired up," determined to do something more meaningful than just working to pay her bills. She says, "I want my life to make a difference. I want to help others. Having OCD has pushed me to work a little harder. There are so many people out there with needs. I feel like my life has been spared, like I have this illness for a reason, that now I must make a difference."

God can certainly tell the difference between what is in your heart and is real and what is just a false message coming from your brain. It is important never to forget that point. Cognitive-biobehavioral self-treatment presents a real opportunity to actively reaffirm your faith in God's ability to know who you really are. It is only when you allow yourself to take the blasphemous OCD thoughts at face value—and to mistrust your deepest inner feelings about God's capacity to tell what's real and what's not—that you develop a sense of self-loathing. Like all battles worth winning, in the end it's a test of faith.

You must continually remind yourself, "This is not a blasphemous thought. This is an OCD symptom. I don't believe it, and it is not a reflection of what I feel in my heart."

Perusing a conservative religious magazine, Christopher—who suffered from recurring blasphemous thoughts—read an article stating that it was wrong to receive Communion in the hand, even though it is common practice today in the Roman Catholic church and one that he had followed since childhood. Because he is very conservative by nature, Christopher became frightened that he would offend God and, for a long time afterward, would take communion only directly in the mouth. He also obsessed that nearly everyone around him was unknowingly committing this terrible offense of receiving Communion in the hand. This obsession made him feel so miserable that he came to dread Sunday Mass and would start getting nervous on Friday or Saturday. Finally, he forced himself to take the risk of offending God by confronting the obsession and taking the Communion wafer in the hand. The first time he did so, he broke out in a sweat and his heart was pounding so hard he could hear it. But, of course, God did not punish him.

The symptoms of OCD frequently have a religious content or overtone in people of faith, and this fact is not always appreciated adequately. For instance, the fact that when Christopher first sought professional help for his disease, he was rudely questioned when he tentatively explained that he had considered that his symptoms might be a form of demonic possession should serve as a wake-up call to the psychiatric community. Too many psychiatrists today seem to have a blatant inability to empathize with the perfectly reasonable content of religious thoughts in the minds of some religiously observant people. Being an intelligent and insightful person, Christopher basically understood that he had a medical disease and that demonic influence had nothing to do with his terrible thoughts. He knew, through spiritual self-examination, that he was not under the influence of demonic powers and was confident that he was suffering from a neuropsychiatric condition. He had already considered and discarded the possibility of demonic influence before he consulted a psychiatrist. The stressful nature of the initial interaction between Christopher and the psychiatrist who misunderstood him was probably more a reflection of the all-too-common ignorance and arrogance of psychiatrists than of anything that was going on inside Christopher as he tried to describe and explain his terrible pain.

ELUDING OCD'S TRAP

In the context of the Four Steps, Revaluing can be understood as an accentuation of the Relabel and Reattribute steps. By refusing to take their symptoms at face value, people with OCD come to think of their bothersome feelings and urges as, in one person's words, "toxic waste from my brain." Doing so enables them to work around the thought or urge so quickly that the Relabel/Reattribute steps become virtually automatic. They no longer have to shift gears manually, gear by gear, to change to another behavior. They now recognize the OCD thought or feeling for what it is almost the moment it occurs. Ongoing self-treatment results in a decrease in the intensity of symptoms, which, in turn, enhances Revaluation by lessening the effort required to dismiss the OCD symptoms as the worthless rubbish they are and to Refocus on a positive behavior.

Here's a reasonable way to conceptualize this:

■ Self-treatment with the Four Steps leads to changes in the brain, which result in diminished fear and a lessening of the intensity of symptoms.

■ This tends to enhance Revaluation of the symptoms because it makes it easier to see them for what they really are, which, in turn, intensifies the Relabel, Reattribute, and Refocus steps and leads to further changes in the brain. Thus, a therapeutic, self-enabling feed-forward pattern is established.

■ During the Refocus step, it is likely that the actual chemistry of the brain is changed, which causes the urge to diminish, making it easier to Revalue.

▪ Revaluation results in easier Relabeling and Reattributing and leads to more Refocusing, which causes further changes in the brain and an even greater decrease in symptoms, which leads to more Revaluing, and so on.

The end result is usually a clear decrease in the intensity of symptoms and a marked improvement in controlling behavioral responses to the thoughts and urges that may remain.

We know that the traditional behavior therapy technique of having the anxiety-besieged patient just passively "ride it out" for an hour or so, waiting for the anxiety to subside, after exposure to a stimulus that causes intense OCD urges, is not a readily achievable self-treatment method for those who suffer from OCD. What people with OCD can more readily do is modify the traditional behavior therapy technique by practicing self-directed response prevention, using the Four Steps for gradually increasing periods. This means telling yourself, "It's all right—it's just OCD" (Relabeling); then Reattributing it to a brain glitch; Refocusing on a constructive, enjoyable behavior, rather than washing your hands or checking the lock—and finally, Revaluing the meaning of those thoughts or urges.

In Revaluing, you realize that your obsessive thoughts and compulsive urges are not important, that you can deal with them. You are, in essence, *devaluing* those silly thoughts. By trying to wait for at least fifteen minutes and then working to gradually increase the length of the time delay even more, you are giving yourself space to work around the OCD thoughts. And fifteen minutes of doing focused self-directed behavioral therapy with the Four Steps gets you a lot further toward genuinely getting past the OCD urge than fifteen minutes of unfocused waiting it out. A powerful mind—which you will develop by practicing the Four Steps—will be increasingly able to make note of even subtle positive changes in the OCD symptoms and to understand the profound implications of those changes. And what are those profound implications? Namely, that you're changing how your brain works by changing your behavior, and you're getting back control of your life. A powerful mind is a mind that can take note of subtle changes and understand the implications of them.

Anna, the philosophy student with the irrational fears that her boyfriend was unfaithful, says that her recovery depended, in part, on being able to look at OCD thoughts and urges in a new light. "Once I learned to identify my OCD symptoms as OCD, rather than as 'important' content-laden thoughts that had to be deciphered for their deep meaning, I was partially freed from OCD. As the process of Relabeling became automatic and I learned how counterproductive it was to act on urges and dwell on obsessions, it became easier to ignore the tricks that OCD was always playing on me." She finds it helpful to personify OCD "as someone clever and devious who tries to ensnare me." Since Anna's disturbing, intrusive thoughts are by nature unsolvable—"How does one ever know for sure that one's lover is faithful in action and in thought?"—her OCD obsessions are impossible for her to think her way out of and are extremely painful. But, she says, "Now that I've seen OCD's tricks many times and learned how to think and work around OCD, I no longer get suckered into obsessing or acting compulsively, as I did before." Practicing the Four Steps has brought her not only relief from OCD suffering but "a greater sense of self-mastery and confidence to tackle almost any problem."

A BATTLE OF WILLS

Because obsessions follow you around and you cannot walk away from them as you can from a stove or a door, it is harder to work around them. As one person put it, "You can't leave your brain." Obsessions cannot always be refuted by logic. A plane may crash after a person ignores the inner voice that's warning, "Do this compulsion or else. . . ." The fact that there is no connection between the plane crash and the person's failure to do the compulsion may not be metaphysically provable. However, we know for certain that the person who continually does compulsive behaviors based on an obsessive fear of a plane crash (or an earthquake or another calamity) will live a life of hell.

I suggest that you Actively Revalue the obsessions with the help of two substeps of the Relabel and Reattribute steps: the two A's— *Anticipate* and *Accept*. The first A reminds you to anticipate that obsessive thoughts will occur hundreds of times a day and not to be surprised by them, even if they are violent and extremely upsetting. It is an amazing fact of OCD that people can have the same obsessive thought a thousand times a day and still be startled and upset by it every time—if they don't make the effort to consciously anticipate it. By Anticipating your particular obsessive thoughts, you will recognize them as soon as they arise and Relabel them right off. In this way, you will be simultaneously Revaluing them. You will learn to go onto the next thought or behavior even though the obsessive thought is still there. As you do so, the second A, Accept, will come into play. When you Accept that your problem is a treatable medical condition, you do not allow yourself to get down on yourself, to criticize your inner motives. You don't want that OCD thought to be there, but you Accept that *it exists despite yourself—not because of yourself.* Patients with obsessions tend to ruminate, to ponder, "What's going to happen if I actually do that inappropriate behavior? If I punch someone or sexually attack someone?" They visualize themselves being carted off to prison in handcuffs as everyone shouts, "See, he did it! He did it!" So it is very important to Actively Revalue obsessions, rather than let the Revalue step take its course, as it tends to do when you deal with compulsions. And, of course, the answer to the invariable question, "How do I know I won't do it?" is always, "Because I don't really want to! Its only an obsession, a false message from my brain. It can't take over my will."

Lara, who is overwhelmed by violent thoughts about knives, was confronted by a psychologist friend: "How do you know you're not going to act on them? Certainly, Charles Manson was obsessional. Jeffrey Dahmer was obsessional." But Lara now understands, "They were also psychopaths; they had no guilt. For me, there's guilt, there's depression, there's a feeling of 'I don't want the consequences.'" What's more, it's extremely doubtful that these two evil men were really obsessional in any true OCD sense. They weren't getting false messages from their brains; they were ruminating about evil things they *wanted* to do. Lara and I have talked about this difference. She has told me, "I won't do it because I don't want to do it. I don't want to hurt anybody. I could never do that." She is right.

EASY TO SAY—HARD TO DO

As a medical professional, it is very humbling for me to watch people struggle to overcome their obsessions and compulsions. Many times, people with OCD have told me, "It's easy to say. It's hard to do." Believe me, I do understand how hard it is, and I never say "Just do it" in some glib, offhand way. It's a hard job, a tough assignment, but the rewards are great. Furthermore, it's a battle that can't be avoided because OCD gives no peace; any peace from it must be earned!

The ultimate goal, of course, is for the anxieties to disappear forever. At UCLA, we have found that using *progressive* time delays that gradually increase to fifteen minutes or longer, breaking the task into manageable bits, reassessing the situation while you are still anxious, and noting changes in your response make this goal more attainable. Of course, you can always try to put a series of time delays together to lengthen the time span. Always practice the Four Steps during the time-delay periods. Recording in a journal the activities you do during the Refocusing and Revaluing steps, as achievements you want to keep track of, strongly reinforces this process. As you note each decrease in your anxieties and urges and record which activities cause the anxiety to decrease, these signs of progress will strengthen your resolve to persevere at the hard work of doing the Four Steps. As a result, you will view each little improvement as a victory, rather than see your inability to totally overcome your anxieties the first or second or third time as a demoralizing sign of failure. You will see that you are actively helping yourself, being your own therapist.

One of the ironies of OCD is that it enables some people to function at a very high level because their attention to detail is so great. Years of practicing OCD rituals appear to create skills that increase their powers of observation and memory in ways that can be highly adaptive. Unfortunately, however, people with OCD also tell us that they can't help but wonder how much they might have accomplished had they not spent so much time dealing with their obsessions and compulsions.

Michael, who obsesses that his pants are shrinking, stated flat out,

"My OCD has killed my success. I'm intelligent and I used to have so much potential in so many different ways, but it really killed me. I wake up in the morning and drive a 1983 Dodge Colt to this steno- graphic job that I don't want to be doing. The OCD is what did that. I hate my OCD because it hasn't allowed me to do what I want to do."

In an effort to understand better how it has affected his life, Michael reads a great deal about mental illness and its causes. He seeks answers to why he developed OCD. He wonders, "Was it more than biochemical that I was this sad eight-year-old kid in school? Or was OCD the result of emotional factors, as well as other corrupting elements, such as genetics? I want to know how I got to the point where I am today and how I can maybe someday reach the point where I want to be. It's an incredible mystery, and one that I want to keep studying on my own. I think that's a part of the recov- ery process." Some days, he says, he would like to "take a knife and stick it in my head and cut out the sick part of my brain." He wakes up tired and asks himself, "Why aren't I doing more?" (Many people with OCD report that they have interrupted sleep patterns that cause them to be constantly fatigued. If these interrupted sleep pat- terns are chronic, the possibility that the OCD is being complicated by depression must be seriously considered.) There was a time, Michael says, when he would wake up feeling "like I'd run a marathon in my sleep." Medication—as an adjunct to behavior ther- apy—helped him to sleep more soundly and to function more effec- tively on the job, probably by treating a depression at the same time it was treating the OCD.

LOSING AN "OLD FRIEND"

When people successfully Revalue their OCD symptoms and take back control of their lives, it is not uncommon for them to go through a period of grieving the "loss" of OCD. As his obsessive urges became less and less frequent, Jeremy (whose anxieties included his fear that alcohol had somehow contaminated his food) recalls, "I felt an emptiness in my life that I had never felt before. For years, OCD had run, and been, my life. I thought about it more than anything else. Now it was, for the most part, gone. So the emptiness was real. I actually mourned my OCD. This feeling lasted until I started filling the emptiness with positive actions. Positive thoughts and feelings followed. Dining is no longer torture. When I realized that OCD was bullshit noise, I realized I could enjoy my meals. I haven't ruminated about my food obsession for more than two years." Jeremy has also overcome his fear of using a public toilet and most of his other anxieties. He says, "It feels great."

Other people with OCD may use their medical condition as a convenient way to excuse their shortcomings or to rationalize behaviors that are essentially self-destructive. Psychiatrists generally refer to these excuses as the "secondary gains" of having OCD. Barbara (who obsessed about Mr. Coffee) was a temporary worker with an Ivy League honors degree. She reflected, "Although it's hard to admit, I can take jobs beneath my capabilities and blame it on my OCD. It also enables me not to take risks. Of course, these are self-esteem issues, not OCD issues. I have to watch that because I can't use OCD as an excuse my entire life." Barbara readily acknowledges that she always takes these lesser jobs "not necessarily because of the OCD, but because I lack some belief that I can do the job. So I do stuff that I could do with my hands tied behind my back. Certainly, I don't need a college education for it." But Barbara has always had a self-esteem problem that she believes has nothing to do with her OCD. Alcoholism is rife in her family, and, at one time, she drank to excess and indulged in sprees of compulsive overeating to cope with the stresses of living with an alcoholic father.

She says, "I know I'm smart, I'm competent—and at the same time I don't think I'm good enough. It's the same as with OCD. I know the doors are locked, I know the stove is turned off. At the same time, I don't believe it. On paper, I look great, but I undermine myself completely. Not long ago, I was offered a great job. I signed the contract and then I got out of it. I used anxiety as an excuse. I told them I was too anxious and, of course, they just flipped out. It was very unprofessional of me. And I know I'll probably never get another job in that field." It's worth noting, however, that as her work with the Four Steps has improved her OCD, her level of comfort with responsibility has also increased.

Self-esteem has also been an issue for Carla. When you have OCD, Carla says, your self-esteem is so low that you tend to direct your anger inward, even when it is not justified. "Maybe if someone said something to you that was negative, or something negative happened to you that day, instead of dealing with the issue—and only the issue—you internalize it. Anxiety is a part of it. You have a tendency to take the anger and say, 'Okay, why didn't I do such-and-such differently, why did I say that to someone, why didn't I say this?' It's like with OCD, you second-guess yourself all the time instead of considering that the problem might have nothing to do with you." It may well be that OCD can contribute to bad habits in your thinking pattern. Practicing the Four Steps can help solve both problems.

Although Jill is largely free of her washing and cleaning compulsions (she no longer "alcohols" her house), she is vigilant about coming to our OCD therapy group at UCLA. For one thing, she says, the group is helping her to Revalue her life, to realize that she is "a lot better off than a lot of people." It also reinforces her determination, since she sees how frequently people can "use OCD as a crutch, an excuse not to do anything with their lives, not to try to better themselves. There are a lot of productive, really talented people who are just wasting their lives because of this disease." She wants to encourage others with OCD to use the tools, the Four Steps, "baby step by baby step," just as she did, on the road to recovery.

In treatment, Jill learned to Revalue her OCD-driven fears about death and contamination. In her mid-40s she realized, "I couldn't keep falling apart every time someone close to me died." Her first little step was self-enforced exposure therapy. She set a mousetrap, but when she found a little mouse glued to that trap, she felt so terrible that she began bringing him water. "I knew he was going to die. In a way, I did it so I could face death." Her beloved cat, which had been part of the family for eleven years, was sick, and Jill was using the mouse to prepare herself for the cat's death. She was consumed with a terrible fear that "the cat would stop breathing in my face, and then what would I do? Would the whole town then be contaminated?" By the time the cat died, Jill was in therapy and was able to deal with it. She kissed the cat good-bye, showered, and that was that. She remembers, "We even stopped on the way to the vet to drop off a video, so I wouldn't be charged for another day's rental. To maintain my composure like that was just unbelievable to me."

Jill's biggest test was to come later, with the death of her mother. She knew the end was near, and on the day her mother died, she had a big debate with herself over what to wear to work. Surely, if she got the dreaded call from the hospital that day, whatever she was wearing would become instantly "contaminated." Ultimately, though, she forced herself to wear her best white linen suit. When she got the phone call, she did not feel compelled to throw away the suit.

Another hurdle for Jill was her mother's funeral. Because Jill traced the onset of her OCD, with its terrible contamination fears, to the funeral of a friend when she was only a teenager, she had never been able to attend another funeral. Feeling great guilt about not wanting to be at her mother's funeral services, she consulted a priest, who wisely assured her that her mother would not have wanted her to make herself sick over this. Jill engineered a compromise: She and her daughter took flowers to the beach and had a private, meaningful ceremony in honor of her mother.

OPPORTUNITIES LOST

In therapy, Josh, who obsessed that he might flip paper clips into colleagues' coffee cups (causing them to choke) and loosen hood ornaments on cars (causing them to fly through the windshield on the freeway), came to understand clearly how his guilt, his decreased ability to function, and his deteriorating relationships with family and friends—all fallout from his OCD—were harming both him and others. "To put it into really sophisticated economic terms, there are profound opportunity costs for doing the compulsions." In economic terms, this means that time spent on OCD results in lost opportunities in business and elsewhere in life. Part of Josh's guilt was over what he perceived as his inadequate commitment to financial support of a shelter for the homeless. So he'd tell himself, "If I can avoid this obsession, I can get out there and make more money and give more of it away." Sometimes that reasoning helped. Josh was truly Revaluing.

Josh's concept of opportunity cost is valid. It really is the answer to why there's no value in doing a compulsion. Even if you're not able to realize that your time is valuable in an economic sense, doing a compulsion to avert some imagined and illogical catastrophe is still not a good trade-off. Why? Because the effort that you expend doing the compulsion is robbing you of time and distancing you from other people and from doing some wholesome and productive behavior. I'm not necessarily talking about saving mankind. It could be something as basic and simple as having time to sit and talk with your family.

A common and serious error that people with OCD make is to say, "Well, I'll just do the compulsion because otherwise I'm going to worry about it and it'll distract me from my work." First, doing the compulsion is only going to make the compulsive feeling get worse, as you have learned. But there's another issue: One compulsion leads to another. The amount of time you spend doing all those compulsions can be spent doing something that is genuinely useful. Therefore, you've not only wasted time doing the silly compulsions, but you've also lost the opportunity to do something useful with that time. So keep in mind: If you do something useful instead of OCD, that's also Refocusing, which is the primary way of making your brain change and getting better. And that's creating new opportunities and better value by anyone's definition.

Brian, who struggles to control an urge to scrub down public streets at night to rid them of battery acid, says, "Time that people with OCD spend doing just totally irrational things is the biggest waste. It's time you'll never get back. It's time I should have spent with my kids instead of out on the streets, scrubbing. All that time— just a waste. OCD consumes every ounce of energy, takes over so much of your life. I'd be out there at 1:30 in the morning, washing down the street, then go home with my butt dragging and wake up just deadbeat tired." He was physically exhausted from lack of sleep and mentally exhausted from constantly dwelling on his obsession. Had he not been a part-owner of the car dealership where he worked, Brian says, "They'd have said, 'Go to hell.'"

At his lowest point—before Brian began behavior therapy in our UCLA group—he was so desperate that he swore that if he died and was somehow offered a second chance to live, he would turn it down if it meant coming back to earth as a person with OCD. Each day was sheer agony. "I can honestly say I hated the damned sunrise. Another damned day of OCD, another damned day of being afraid. I prayed that I'd get a terminal illness. I just prayed, 'Lord, take me. I just can't take this anymore.'"

Brian went through a rocky period in his marriage and troubling times with his children, as do many people with OCD. But today, he's able to look at his progress and speak with pride about the "gallant gains" he has made in fighting his disease. His battle with OCD, however, remains an ongoing struggle.

"A LITTLE LIGHT IN MY SOUL"

Those who have Revalued their OCD symptoms and gone on to Revalue their lives offer us some deep philosophical insights, as the following examples illustrate.

Joanne, who for years had been plagued by dark, brooding thoughts, found that after she began practicing the Four Steps dutifully, "My fear started to go away and my life started to make sense. I could finally see a little bit of light in my soul. For the first time, I was able to experience the feeling of having my mind 'move on,' not stuck in the moment, but moving forward. It was incredible! I know what is happening to me, and I can help myself. Some say about life that all bad things that happen to us have a reason or a lesson. I'm not sure that I go along with this. All I can say is that, in the end, I have learned about compassion and I feel so lucky because it has helped me to become a better human being." Her account is also an elegant description of someone with improved brain function: moving forward, Brain Lock relieved, no longer "stuck in gear."

Lara, who has built a productive professional life despite having OCD and Tourette's syndrome, says, "'Never give up' is my motto. No one with OCD should ever give up. I managed to get both bachelor's and master's degrees and to become a counselor. Now I help others work through the everyday struggle against OCD. Having

OCD and Tourette's has helped me to be more in tune with my clients. I probably will always struggle with my disorder, and that is okay. Maybe I can help others with OCD or Tourette's. I often think how wonderful life would be without Tourette's or OCD and what I would be like. Unfortunately, I'll probably never find out. But that's okay, too."

Karen, the compulsive hoarder who had allowed junk to take over her house and her life, set both pragmatic and spiritual goals for herself once she recognized that she was dealing with a medical disease called OCD. She wanted a home filled with fresh air and sunlight—for too long she'd kept the windows barricaded to hide her terrible secret. She also wanted to savor every hour of the new leisure time she would have, once she had freed herself from her time-consuming compulsion. She says, "You have no idea how much time I spent each day rearranging things so I could fit in more. I spent hours of frustration looking for things that were hopelessly lost in the clutter and chaos. The hours it took to acquire all that stuff—and the hours, years actually, it took to clear it out—added up to at least a decade out of my life. Years of hassle and stress and frustration, feelings of helplessness, hopelessness, and grief."

What she truly wanted most, Karen said, was serenity. "I guess that would be the number one goal of anyone with obsessive-compulsive disorder. OCD is hard work. It leads to internal (and seemingly eternal) unrest; frenzied activity; and physical, mental, and emotional exhaustion."

While doing behavioral therapy at UCLA, Karen came to see, "I am not a bad person because I feel a need to scavenge things out of trash cans." She learned that although she could not keep her compulsive urges from coming on, she *could* control what she did about those urges. She says, "You're never going to hear me say, 'Oh, I'm so glad I have OCD because it is such a challenge and it changed the whole direction of my life.' It is, and it did, and I know I'm a stronger person today because of it. However, I lost a decade of my life to OCD, and that can never be replaced. Why couldn't I see earlier that material things can be replaced, but time lost is gone forever and can never be retrieved?"

Karen is now in her 50s, a time when people typically reassess their lives. And she has done just that. She is philosophical: "I'm not going to beat myself up over those lost years. I did the best I could at the time." Her biggest mistake, she now knows, was to let her false pride keep her from seeking help before useless rubbish took over her life. She knows, "You really must have human help to get yourself on the road to health. Trusting another to lead you will be the most difficult thing you ever do, but you must do it. Get a loving buddy, a friend, or a family member to help you and encourage you. Don't be a victim to this disease. Be a victor over it. Take the risk. Do it now. Get your life back. Your future is in your own hands."

Time—the extra hours in the day that OCD patients find they have when they're no longer spending them doing compulsions— also became a big factor for Jack, the compulsive hand washer. But he found it a mixed blessing. "You can fill up vast amounts of time with OCD, and then you've got a problem. After behavior therapy, you can get stuff done faster, especially around the house—watering, feeding the cats, doing laundry." At home, he now felt in control, and he liked doing things in a time-efficient manner. Unfortunately, this feeling only led to greater frustration at work. Because he was in a temporary job that basically bored him, he became more frustrated. Jack had a patchy work record, with problems of concentration and an inability to deal with people. "I'd just get mad and think, 'Here I am, wasting my time. I could at least be out looking for a worthwhile job or at home doing those chores.' My wife would say, 'Nobody's going to care if you do the laundry. Why don't you look for better work?' But it's funny. With OCD, there's a lot of resistance to change."

Jack developed good habits in Revaluing OCD urges as he worked on his hand-washing compulsions with the Four Steps. As he described it, "Of course, I was anxious at first when I [resisted the compulsive urges to] wash, but then I discovered that the more time that you don't give in and find out that nothing happens, the easier it gets the next time. You begin to have a history of incidents in which nothing really happens when you ignore the obsession." Now he's learning to apply the Revalue principle in a more general way to improve his self-confidence and begin to overcome the resistance to change. "I try to work on my OCD every day—to work on some of the more subtle symptoms and thought patterns. I try not to pay attention to intrusive thoughts. I try not to be too hard on myself. It's hard to get rid of this problem completely, but you have to give yourself credit for any improvements you make." By learning to take note of his achievements and to make mental notes of a self-supporting nature, Jack has improved his confidence level. He is now more comfortable at job interviews, and his overall function continues to steadily improve.

SELF-SUPPORTIVE STATEMENTS

It's impossible to overstress the importance of learning to make self-supportive statements as a regular part of doing the Four Steps. In brief, you are working to learn how to Revalue your OCD *down* and Revalue your behavior therapy achievements *up*. For instance, never demean or underestimate the importance of even a small time delay before doing a compulsion. You may say, "I want to do even better," but never demean the achievements that you actually make. Of course, keeping a journal record of your achievements in behavior therapy will help you accomplish this goal.

Benjamin, whose PET brain scan is on the book jacket, is now in his early 40s and has been battling OCD compulsions, including checking and cleaning, off and on since he was about 6. Washing his car could take six hours; it had to be done just right. The garage, the closets, and his files had to be in precise order. Disarray and disorder were not to be tolerated. Having a repairman come into his house was a trauma because this stranger would be intruding on Benjamin's tidy environment and might make something dirty or get it out of order. Benjamin's compulsions and anxieties began to take up so much time that he could not take a full course load in graduate school. Finally, he "hit rock bottom" in productivity.

Because Benjamin, who is now a school district administrator, came from a family of highly successful, efficient people, he felt guilty and ashamed; he was basically in denial. He knew his behavior was abnormal and reasoned that he must be a bad person, the rotten apple on the family tree. Until he learned he had OCD, a medical disease, Benjamin "had always operated under this kind of illusion that one day my life would be a dream life, with everything perfect. I would be successful and happy. So it was very difficult for me to accept the fact that my life was going to be more of a struggle than other lives, that things weren't perfect."

While learning the Four Steps of behavior therapy, he also learned to take what, for him, were "major, major risks." He forced himself to live with a certain amount of physical disorder, to touch things that he once would have felt were contaminated. Something as insignificant as leaving a drawer open, some papers askew, was a huge victory. While gaining the upper hand over his OCD, Benjamin also began to Revalue his life, to rethink his priorities. He says his struggle against his disease "made me much more sensitive and aware and empathetic to people who have disorders and physical disabilities. It also made me a much more spontaneous person, more realistic. Life is a risk, it's a chance, and it's also a great opportunity. That's what makes it exciting and enjoyable. OCD was really difficult for me to accept initially, the idea that it will always be there to varying degrees. At the same time, I now know that when you heighten your self-awareness, it makes you more human. The degree to which you accept what and who you are measures your success as a person. You no longer operate in some fantasy world of perfection."

Today, by Benjamin's own assessment, his OCD is 80 percent under control, but, on a scale of one to ten, he rates himself only a five in terms of personal relationships. "I want to be more useful to other people, more helpful. At one time, I thought having an ordered environment—an orderly life, an orderly office—was the greatest good, but now I have transferred to things that are more genuine and lasting and worthwhile, less material. I want to be a better family member, a better person on a personal, intimate level. In the past five or six years, I've gone though a major value shift that started with seeing Dr. Schwartz. I guess the reassuring message here is that if you get the basic elements of your life under control, the natural tendency is to move toward things that are more emotionally gratifying."

Like so many of our OCD patients, Benjamin has Revalued his life. He understands that "a person's value is the degree to which they can accept and move forward with what they were given."

KEY POINTS TO REMEMBER

•Step 4 is the Revalue step.

•Revalue means don't take your symptoms at "face value"—they don't mean what they say. See them for what they are.

•Work to Revalue in an active way, by seeing the reality of the situation as quickly and clearly as possible. Strengthen the clarity of your observation with assertive mental notes, such as "It's not me—it's just OCD."

•When you Revalue and devalue unwanted thoughts and urges, you are strengthening your Impartial Spectator and building a powerful mind.

•A mind that can take note of subtle changes and understand the implications of those changes is a powerful mind.

•A powerful mind can change the brain by altering responses to the messages the brain sends.

•This is true self-command. It results in real self-esteem.

The Four R's

Step 1. Relabel

Step 2. Reattribute

The Two A's
Anticipate
Accept

Step 3. Refocus

Step 4. Revalue

PART II

Applying the Four Steps to Your Life

One who is slow to anger is better than a warrior; and one who rules his spirit is better than one who takes a city.

—King Solomon, *Proverbs 16:32*

Though a thousand times a thousand men are conquered by one in battle, the one who conquers himself is truly the master of battle.

—Gotama Buddha, *Dhammapada 103*

5

The Four Steps and Personal Freedom

The struggle to overcome the scourge of obsessive-compulsive disorder (OCD) almost always begins for the most pragmatic reasons. Your life is being taken over by a strange power that seems to be stronger than you are. In this book, my goal has been to teach you the most effective strategies for neutralizing this opponent called OCD, whose tricks can be so devastating to those who don't know how to fight back effectively. Like most other bullies and aggressors, much of its power comes from its ability to intimidate the naive and uninitiated. When seen from the clear-minded perspective of the Impartial Spectator, the true nature of this deceptive opponent comes into focus. With this insight, fear and dread begin to fade, and the path to victory comes into view. This is what training yourself to do the Four Steps is all about.

The power of the Relabel step is something that should never be underestimated. It's the difference between knowing what's real and living in fear of shadows. When you Relabel and make mental notes and remind yourself, "That's just OCD—I don't have to listen to that"—a very powerful process is initiated. A change in the value and meaning that you give to the unpleasant obsessive thought or urge begins. The power of the Impartial Spectator is called into play, which profoundly changes the nature of the interaction between you and your internal opponent. Now the battle is being fought on your home turf—reality—not on the playing field of your opponent, who relies solely on deception and illusion. Always remember that a firm grasp of reality is your greatest ally in the fight against OCD because in the end, fear and false messages are OCD's only weapons. If you Reattribute those fears to their true causes, as you've trained your-self to do, and Refocus on a wholesome behavior for at least fifteen minutes, you may not win every battle, but in the end, you'll win the war. With the power of your mind, you will change your brain. Where once there was Brain Lock, a freer and more smoothly running thought process is now in place.

People frequently ask, especially early in treatment, "Will I ever be cured?" As I've tried to explain through the stories of courageous patients, a cure cannot be guaranteed, especially if you take it to mean that you will never have an OCD symptom again. But if cure means the freedom of never again running scared from the plague of OCD symptoms and not having the direction of your life dictated by the tyrant OCD, then that goal is within the grasp of essentially every person who suffers the misery of OCD. (I know this to be true. I've seen it too many times to doubt it.)

The larger meaning of the effort that people put into following the Four Steps is a message about what we all can accomplish when we let go of fear, practice mindful awareness, and decide to take control of our lives. The increased mental power that people with OCD develop, the power to notice small changes and understand their significance and to go forward in the face of pain and fear, have wide-reaching effects not only on the lives of people with OCD but on the lives of those around them. This greater mental power can go beyond the realm of OCD. It can lead you to a much deeper insight into what it means to Revalue your internal experience in light of new and more productive ends and goals. In doing so, you can expand your mental and spiritual horizons in ways you may not have considered before.

Consider the power of the simple question "Why am I doing this?" In many ways the entire Four-Step method boils down to bringing the perspective of the Impartial Spectator more clearly into mind when answering that question. No doubt, new information about how the brain works helps people with OCD answer this key question more realistically and more courageously. Yet it seems crucial to realize that what these new brain discoveries have in essence done is enabled people to see their own minds with greater clarity. And doing so enhances their ability to find their true goals and objectives.

We live in an age when many people who fancy themselves sophisticated thinkers—whether they are doctors, scientists, or philosophers—can state with the greatest authority that the mind is just something that "somehow emerges" from and is fully determined by the physical properties of the brain. Anything that may be called a spirit, they're too embarrassed even to talk about. Somehow it doesn't seem sophisticated to them. For them, science must relegate the spirit and the will to the realm of mere superstition. To my mind, this is all very unfortunate. Far worse, I believe it reflects a profoundly false way of thinking. And one of the great accomplishments of our research on OCD, I believe, is that it helps us perceive more clearly just how the conscious and comprehending mind differs from the brain and cannot be solely dependent on it.

Consider what goes on inside a man who is fighting off an OCD symptom using the Four Steps. The intrusive obsessions keep bothering and imposing on him—"Go wash your hands. Go check the stove." Before training in the Four Steps, he listened right away, which tended to make the Brain Lock worse and worse, tighter and tighter. After Four-Step training, his mental response is very different. He now says, "I know what you are. You're just OCD, just an alarm system in my brain gone bad. I'd rather be dead than listen to you, you miserable brain circuit from hell." Then he goes and listens to Mozart or practices his golf swing or whatever. He considers his goals, reflects on his options, exercises his will, makes a new choice, and does another behavior. In this way, he changes how his brain functions. Over time, his brain changes enough so that, with new advances in technology, we can measure the change, even take a color picture of it (as is shown on the book jacket). Now, although some academics may say that this is just an example of the brain changing itself, any sensible person can see that the person in our example is clearly *using his mental power* to make the effort and do the work that it takes to change his brain and conquer the symptoms of OCD. A genuine spiritual (willful) process has taken place, resulting in a scientifically demonstrable biological change in the body's main organ of communication—the brain.

THE FOUR STEPS AND THE REST OF YOUR LIFE

The really big message for people who use the Four Steps is that by strengthening the Impartial Spectator and practicing mindful awareness, you will increase your mental power in every other aspect of your life. Mindful awareness will help you in your relationships with other people, it will help you at work, it will help you with problems of mind wandering and excessive daydreaming. You'll begin to see improvements in all the problem areas of life in which the cravings to which the mind is so vulnerable cause pain and distress.

For example, consider how much time and energy people spend ruminating and stewing about personal relationships. The Relabel and Refocus steps and use of the Impartial Spectator and mindful awareness are particularly helpful for modulating the intense ruminating that almost everyone does under stress—about boyfriends and girlfriends: Should I ask her out, shouldn't I, should I call, should I wait? That's one category. Then there's the did-the-boss-look-at-me-funny? group and all those What-do-people-think-of-me? Am-I-good-enough? Do-I-look-okay? types of thoughts. And let's not forget the life-would-be-great-if-only category. At the point that thoughts like these get out of control and start taking on a life of their own, they become extremely unpleasant ruminations. Anyone can become controlled by these types of thoughts. But people with OCD may be particularly vulnerable to them. However, I have seen many patients with OCD teach themselves how to break these streams of ruminative thinking when they learn the power of Relabeling and develop the technical ability to make mental notes. They can then use the Refocus step to get on a better track.

It may sound funny to say that you need to remind yourself of what you're thinking about, but all people need to develop that ability, and a lot more so than they may realize. As mindful awareness increases and making mental notes (in which you consciously notice your thought stream) becomes more natural, you will quickly realize just how much of the time you spend thinking about things that you didn't even know you were thinking about. These principles apply to everyone. People with OCD who do the Four Steps develop abilities that are very helpful in life—abilities that people without OCD may never develop. That may be one of the genuine silver linings of having OCD and using the Four Steps to overcome it.

OCD can function like an exercise machine in your head. Just as working out on an exercise machine increases your physical power, working on OCD increases your use of the Impartial Spectator, which will increase your mental powers and insight into both your own and other people's behaviors. What's more, your control over your internal mental life, even in things that have nothing to do with OCD, will be greatly enhanced. You will genuinely increase your personal freedom through the exercise of the Four Steps because the essence of having a mind that is free is the capacity to tame and direct the restless wanderings into which the unattended mind inevitably falls. With the making of mental notes, you will come to realize quite rapidly that much of the content of your mental life, of your ongoing thought process, concerns subjects that are not conducive to living a wholesome and happy life.

One of the most amazing things that you learn when exercising mindful awareness and using the Impartial Spectator is how much the mere observation of the content of your thoughts tends to direct them in a much healthier manner. In other words, knowing what you're thinking at any given moment tends to direct the mind away from destructive ruminations, onto more constructive and wholesome subjects.

Mindfulness itself is an extremely helpful and wholesome mental state. Any moment in which the mind is exercising mindful awareness or using the Impartial Spectator is a moment in which an unwholesome thought cannot arise. Thus, the longer the period that mindful awareness is applied, the stronger the mind becomes and the less you actually experience the unwholesome and destructive types of thoughts that tend to lead to pain and suffering. Unfortunately, however, with unimaginably rapid speed, the mind can make the transition from a wholesome and mindful condition to an unwholesome and negative one. The bright side is that by reapplying mindful awareness, you can reestablish a wholesome mental state just as rapidly. For instance, if a string of unwholesome ruminations on craving or anger, greed or ill will, is broken by making a mental note that "I am now thinking a thought related to greed" or "I am now thinking a thought related to ill will or anger," the very breaking off of that stream of unwholesome thought processes by wholesome mindful awareness will itself lead to further wholesome thoughts concerning something functional and healthful to both you and others.

This makes the Refocus step much easier to apply. As time goes by and this process becomes more and more a natural pattern of living, your mind will become sharper and more at ease and your life will be smoother and happier.

To sum up: Having OCD is a curse, but your natural ability to use the Impartial Spectator and practice mindful awareness is a blessing. If having OCD leads to your developing wholesome mental abilities that you otherwise might not have acquired, there truly is a silver lining inside of the cloud. That's what practicing the Four Steps is about.

KEY POINTS TO REMEMBER

•Keep in mind the power of the Relabel step: It's the difference between knowing what's real and living in fear of shadows.

•Always ask yourself, "Why am I doing this?" and keep the perspective of your Impartial Spectator in mind when answering.

•Make mental notes to remind yourself what you're thinking about. Just the act of observing tends to direct thoughts in a wholesome direction.

•Any moment the mind is using the Impartial Spectator, an unwholesome thought cannot arise.

6

OCD as a Family Disorder

Obsessive-compulsive disorder (OCD) is, in the truest sense, a family affair.

Typically, people with untreated OCD find themselves increasingly isolated from others, preoccupied with their terrible thoughts and urges, and choosing out of fear or shame, or both, to share their awful secret with no one.

Within families, this can be devastating. Again and again, our patients at UCLA tell us, "I'm driving my wife crazy, pushing my friends away from me. My family can't stand it anymore. I have to stop doing this."

JUST SAY NO

Commonly, people with OCD fall into a pattern of using OCD as a "weapon" in interpersonal conflicts. In one frequently observed personality disturbance, dependent personality disorder, the person with OCD becomes dependent to a pathological degree on the people he or she lives with to get things done. Family members become part of the OCD—enablers—actually doing the compulsive behaviors for the person to keep peace in the household. The person will demand, "Check that lock for me" or "Scrub the walls for me." By giving in, of course, the family only ensures that the person will continue to get worse; nevertheless, out of sheer desperation, they usually give in.

Spouses have told us that if they refuse to be drawn into the bizarre behaviors, they are met with tantrums and tears. Eventually, all their energy may be poured into trying to cope with the person's illness. They may cajole or plead with the person to stop—or they may lie and say that they did such-and-such a thing or avoided doing so-and-so. Lying, of course, is not helpful to the person with OCD in the long term. The wife of one man with severe OCD acknowledged that she does not tell her husband the truth about where she has been if the truth will cause him to react violently because of his OCD fears. Once, she went someplace that was "off-limits" and thought for a moment that she had seen him. "I actually began having palpitations. You'd have thought that I'd robbed a bank and the police were right behind me." If he asks her outright if she went where she wasn't supposed to go, she will tell little white lies. She reasons, "If I say no, this man gets to have a nice dinner and a lovely evening and so do I, instead of an episode of swearing and slamming doors." Lying makes her life bearable. She knows she shouldn't be buying into his illness, but after years of coping with OCD, she's weary. "So I'm an enabler. One little word and my evening's nice." Doubtless, there are thousands of women who can relate to her predicament. What she does is perfectly understandable, perfectly human. But, in truth, she is sabotaging his progress. When she learns the Four Steps herself and works to help him apply them, they'll both be much better off. She'll stop being an enabler of his OCD and start being a behavior therapist. The one-line message for family members is: "Don't enable the OCD—enable the behavior therapy."

A child with OCD can totally disrupt a family, waking them many times during the night with demands and dictating their lives down to where they must sit in a given room and at precisely what time they must do X, Y, and Z. Too often, parents allow themselves to be sucked into this behavior because they have heaped guilt on themselves, convinced that they are responsible for the child having this awful illness. As you shall see, both environment and genetics play a role in most cases, but the biological factors are the *primary* reason the person has OCD. However, emotional and environmental factors are often the critical ones in determining whether the person does behavior therapy and gets better.

OCD AS A WEAPON

Although the family cannot force the person with OCD to get well, they *can* take charge of their own lives, refusing to participate in enabling symptoms, to be prisoners in their own homes, or to be what in popular psychiatric jargon is called codependent. The confrontation may not always be pleasant, but the end result is that the person is apt to improve. The bottom line is always this: Is the family member helping or hindering the person's efforts to do the Four Steps?

Consider the case of a family in which one member has a contamination obsession. Parts of the house may become off-limits to the entire family. The person keeps everyone out because of an overwhelming fear that they will make the area dirty and he or she will then have to start on an out-of-control cleaning binge. (Ironically, when cleaning compulsions get really bad, whole rooms may become profoundly filthy because the person with OCD is afraid to start cleaning, and no one else can enter the room.) In some cases—and they aren't that rare—people have actually ended up living in tents in their backyards. Even when the obsession doesn't get to that stage, the usable inside space tends to keep shrinking and shrinking. In addition, objects become off-bounds; perhaps none of the dishes or eating utensils can be used, or certain items of clothing cannot be worn.

The partner or spouse must take a stand. After the 1994 earthquake in Los Angeles, Olivia began obsessing that water from the toilet was somehow flowing into her washing machine. She would check and check and then ask her husband to stick his hand inside, just to make sure. When I talked to them together, I advised him to start telling her that he would look, but he wouldn't put his hand inside. He would also remind her to Relabel and Reattribute. He was to reassure her, "There's no water. It's just an obsessive thought, a false message from your brain. We'll check it quickly to get the compulsion out of the way and just move on." After a few days, he was to go one step further and ask, "Are you sure you really want me to do this? Let's Refocus on another behavior." The strategy paid off. In time, her urge to check decreased markedly.

When those with OCD ask others to help them do their dreadful tasks, they may simply be so overwhelmed by intrusive thoughts and urges that they feel they need more hands to help them perform their bizarre rituals. On the other hand, they may well have a hidden agenda that they may not be aware of themselves: people with OCD frequently use it as a weapon in interpersonal conflicts. For example, if they want to annoy another person or get even for some real or imagined hurt, or if they perceive that they are powerless in the relationship and that their OCD can give them power, they will be less motivated to fight off their urges and the uncomfortable feelings the urges cause. Moreover, when they feel that their suffering is being demeaned or underestimated by other family members, they may be especially apt to try to get even by making other people's lives miserable, either quite willfully or only half-consciously. A psychological tug-of-war ensues.

In behavior therapy, we draw a line in the sand right off, explaining very clearly to both the person and his or her family that this is not acceptable behavior. Involving family members in treatment is essential, both for support and to educate them about OCD.

WHO IS THIS STRANGER?

In time, through faithful practice of self-directed behavior therapy, people can and do change their brain and conquer their OCD symptoms. But as the person with OCD gets well, family dynamics are apt to change, often with devastating psychological consequences. Roles become reversed, and the once-powerless partner may make a power play. Others in the family may resent that the person has improved because now the family has to start facing its own realities and shortcomings, which may not be related to the OCD. The person is no longer an excuse for the family's failings or a doormat. He or she is someone with newfound self-esteem, demanding to be dealt with as a fully functioning member of the family. Suddenly, there is a stranger in their midst.

Thus, when the person starts to improve, the family may unconsciously begin to undermine the treatment. For example, for years one woman with OCD had made her husband jump into the shower as soon as he came home from work because she thought he was contaminated. When she began to get better in therapy, he preferred to keep doing so than to have a well wife who might start asserting herself in more worrisome ways.

Dr. Iver Hand, the distinguished University of Hamburg psychiatrist who has been studying OCD for 20 years, believes that intimacy issues are a primary fueling factor in maintaining the disease, that people get a "secondary gain" from the OCD—that is, they use it to keep others at an emotional distance. At UCLA we have demonstrated that people can be taught to let go of their OCD without addressing intimacy issues, but these secondary gains are the primary reason why some people do not respond to treatment. In other words, if a person with OCD has a well-entrenched pattern of fending off people, he or she will also find reasons to fend off doing the hard work of behavioral therapy. Although I am convinced that OCD is more a biological than an emotional disorder, there is almost certainly an interface between the two. In therapy, the person must be honest about these underlying issues if he or she is to get the maximum beneficial effects.

EMOTIONAL BURNOUT

At UCLA, our patients have taught us a great deal about the nonbiological manifestations of OCD—how it affects personal relationships, professional goals, and life paths.

Christopher, who had terrible blasphemous thoughts, is young and single and would like to have a girlfriend but is unsure of whether a "normal" woman could be attracted to him. And, he says, "I have this rule that I really can't have a relationship with girls who themselves have OCD or some other kind of mental disorder. I can't have that because I don't really want OCD or, more generally, mental disorders to have any more of a part of my life than they already have had."

Michael, who has the obsession about his pants being too tight, until recently felt extremely uncomfortable in most social situations, unable to "fit in"—and relationships with women were no exception. He believes that his OCD, which he has had since childhood, is at the root of these feelings of social inadequacy. In grade school, he tended to be distracted by OCD compulsions, such as repetitive counting, and although he knew there was something strange going on, he never felt able to talk to his parents about it. As a consequence, they put his poor performance down to his being "lazy and kind of disturbed," a bad person. (Kyle, who had violent OCD thoughts about himself and others, had an even worse childhood experience: His parents heaped guilt on him, telling him that his odd behaviors were just the "Satan in him.")

In retrospect, Michael wishes he had felt free to tell his parents about his crazy thoughts. "But," he says, "I'm sure my parents would have sent me to an institution, where it wouldn't have been understood what was going on. . . . To this day, my father doesn't really understand. I don't think mental illness is included in his vocabulary." (Michael is probably right; little was known about OCD thirty-five years ago, and many people still don't understand it.)

Michael yearned to communicate to his parents what he was experiencing, yet he never could. "All my life," he says, "I was just wanting someone to say, 'I'm sorry. I wish things were better. I realize you try.'" But because he never heard these words, he never felt fully loved or fully accepted—and he learned to bottle up his own feelings. As he has grown older, that trait has worsened. "One thing I see in common with people with OCD is that their feelings get numb. When I get into a relationship, I immediately close down my feelings and really sabotage myself. And that's when the OCD will be the strongest. At the moment you want to really feel something, all you feel is the OCD."

OCD-fueled fears can be much stronger than any other emotions, including love and grief. For instance, an elderly woman in the UCLA OCD therapy group has a death-related obsession that is so strong that she cannot with comfort go anyplace where people have died, even centuries before. A family vacation to Tombstone, Arizona was traumatic for her. Everything she had worn there or taken with her became contaminated. She has alienated herself from dear friends because they can't understand her silence when they lose loved ones. But she cannot bear to pay condolence calls or even to pick up the telephone and say how sorry she is. She rationalized that by this avoidance she was keeping her anxiety level low, even at the risk of losing friends. That's not very clear thinking, though it's understandable that someone would be willing to make that tradeoff. In reality, it's not a true tradeoff. By not making condolence calls, she is just setting herself up for her intense obsessional fear to worsen and worsen. If her fear is to go away, she must confront it. Another woman was unable to say good-bye to her father as he lay dying because compulsions prevented her from leaving her house to get to the hospital on time.

Recently, things have turned around for Michael, who has faithfully practiced the Four Steps, reinforced by regular attendance at the OCD therapy group at UCLA. For years, he had used medication to bolster therapy, but he came to believe that "medication was really leveling out my personality. I was just very numb. My feelings were very much kept in check. In order to fight their OCD, people have to really let their feelings go."

Although his OCD was largely under control, Michael felt that he had reached a plateau, and he wanted to do better. Therefore, he decided to go off the medication and felt better almost as soon as he did. Although he has experienced some escalation of his OCD thoughts and urges since then, he uses the Four Steps to effectively control them. "I'm going downhill now, rather than fighting my way uphill, caught on the treadmill of OCD." And, for the first time in years, he is experiencing deep emotions. He remembers, "When my mother died a few years ago, I didn't cry at all." Again, that numbness. "But when my favorite baseball player, Mickey Mantle, died"—this was after Michael went off the medication—"I was hurt very badly and I cried and was able to let out my feelings." When he is able to do so, he finds that his OCD level is very low, whereas when he suppresses his feelings his OCD is at its worst.

The isolation felt by people with OCD is largely the result of their decision to keep their terrible secret from others as long as they can. Michael, on the other hand, likes to tell people that he has OCD— "It's a very liberating feeling, a real catharsis. You know, 'Hey! I'm crazy. How are you?'" But he has also learned that most people either don't care to know about his problem or react by bombarding him with a list of physical or mental symptoms of their own.

TO TELL OR NOT TO TELL

Barbara, who obsessed about whether she had unplugged Mr. Coffee, told everyone when she was first diagnosed, figuring that "if people knew the very worst about me and still thought I was okay, then I was okay." But she quickly learned to keep quiet about her OCD. At work, people would respond either by making jokes at her expense or looking perplexed and responding, "Why don't you just stop it?" Barbara realized that being forthright about OCD was a bad career move. Unfortunately, that is all too frequently the case.

Benjamin, who once had to live in a totally organized environment, says, "I don't see anything productive about telling people I don't have to tell because of people's general lack of understanding about mental disorders." He doesn't tell work associates or new friends, for example. But he has been open with his girlfriend and with his family, and both have responded positively. The decision to be honest with his family was a tough one: "Because I come from a highly successful family, high-powered people who were successful socially and professionally, I had sort of built this brick wall around myself" in an effort to hide this defect from them. Telling them about his OCD was "a great relief. After I opened up, they opened up much more. It had a positive snowballing effect. Their response was much more empathic and understanding than I had anticipated. I no longer have to carry around this big defense. I'm a much more open person, more able to admit other weaknesses and to laugh at myself."

He learned that "people respect other people for accepting themselves for what and who they are. And people do have a high level of tolerance for a physical disorder—if they see that the person is trying to function and interact as well as he can."

Benjamin has observed that others can sense in people with OCD a preoccupation and lack of spontaneity that inhibits intimacy. As he gets his OCD more under control and is less preoccupied with himself, he hopes to expand his social contacts. "I know I've got to step around the OCD. I've got to function like other people do. I have a responsibility toward other people. I am constantly evaluating myself: Is it my OCD that's keeping me from being a loving person, a person who can have an impact on other people's lives? A person who can be helpful, caring, more empathic?"

Not everyone, of course, has had as positive an experience. Christopher found that his parents never really understood his OCD and just counseled him to try to "think good thoughts all the time." This lack of understanding led to tense encounters with his father whenever the subject came up. "I was actually forced at one point to quit seeing a doctor because I supposedly didn't really have a problem and the 'psychiatric stuff' had gone on long enough." Several months later, Christopher persuaded his parents to allow him to go into the OCD program at UCLA, where I introduced him to our Four-Step program. He continues to make progress and is a regular in our OCD therapy group.

OCD patients frequently talk about having OCD personalities, of being extremely introverted, afraid of aggression, and unable to deal with aggressive people. Jack, the compulsive hand washer, has bounced from job to job and has learned, "I really don't like dealing with people that much. Those seem to be the jobs I do the absolute worst in. I had a summer job as a bank teller, and it was terrible. Customers demanded speed and friendliness, while I was just concentrating on what I was supposed to do. I was definitely not the friendly bank teller." He also taught school for a while. "Can you imagine? At the high school level, it's all assertiveness and discipline." Not Jack's strong suits.

USING COMPULSIONS TO CONTROL

In an interview for this book, Dr. Iver Hand confirmed that those with clinical cases of OCD may tend to settle into menial, undemanding jobs. "People with OCD can be pretty successful" at the right job, he said, "like being a mechanic or a computer programmer. Their OCD can actually help them do a good job. But if they get a promotion, they have no skills to lead. They don't know how to handle competition problems. Within a very few months, people who, from their point of view, were pretty happy with their professional lives completely overcompensate and develop compulsions that make them absolutely unable to go to work."

Undoubtedly, environmental and genetic factors both play some role in the development of OCD. Several people with OCD have told me that they grew up in households headed by either a very rigid father or a dominating mother (which, of course, could be the result of the parent having undiagnosed OCD) and that they believe this background contributed to their having very low self-esteem. To compensate, Dr. Hand found, these people may develop controlling compulsions. "They have to be perfect" as a way of controlling their social environment. Still, he said, "Nobody knows why some people who have grown up under these conditions later develop OCD and others don't, or develop other disorders." Nevertheless, the scientific evidence for a biological pattern of genetic inheritance has grown quite strong.

Low self-esteem can set people up for failure. A man with OCD, for example, who tells himself, "I'll never get married because no one will deal with this stuff," creates a self-fulfilling prophecy, cuts himself off from social outlets, and ends up alone.

It is clear that many people with low self-esteem grow up to have latent aggressive personalities. They are insecure, even if they manage to function passably well both socially and professionally, but they lack real social skills and distrust those around them. In a marriage, if they have the biological predisposition, they may develop obsessive-compulsive behaviors to control their spouses. Or in self-defense, a child who grows up in an emotionally tumultuous environment may develop OCD as a counter-weapon. "They build up their own safe little world," Hand noted.

Sometimes, but not always, Hand said, children will respond with hatred. They may seek affection elsewhere, perhaps from their peers. In interviews with OCD families, he sees a lot of anger and aggression among the members. "It's horrible, frightening—the whole family, one after another, will say they had thoughts of killing the other one." The OCD plays a role, certainly, but it may not be the major one, and the real, underlying problems come out during treatment.

LOOKING FOR LOVE

When a parent has OCD, a child may grow up harboring fierce anger and resentment for having been denied a "normal" life, having had to participate in the parent's bizarre and time-consuming rituals. Dottie, who washed excessively to try to rid herself of the fear that something would happen to her son's eyes, explained to him when he was old enough that she had an illness called OCD and that she did crazy things because she could not help herself. But when he went off to college, he upset her greatly by saying, "I've had enough of you, Mom." A single parent, she had done everything she could for him to try to make up for the turmoil she created. "I thought I was a good mother, but a couple of years ago he told me, 'I thought you were the most terrible mother there was.' If someone had taken a knife and stabbed me . . . I mean, that was the worst thing anyone's ever said to me, ever. Whether he really understands or not, of course, it doesn't matter now. I did the best I could."

The story of Karen, the compulsive hoarder in our UCLA group, is a strong argument for the role of both environment and genetics in the development of OCD. Karen's father demanded perfection of everyone else in the household, though he was far from perfect himself. Without doubt, he had classic OCD—checking and contamination obsessions and an over-the-edge compulsiveness about not wasting anything. Karen actually "learned" OCD at his knee. He showed her how to check the knobs on the stove just so and lectured her about the dangers of bacteria and viruses. She recalls, "Taking care of a splinter was practically like performing surgery. There was this whole routine to make sure no infection developed." If Karen failed to carry out one of his orders, his face would contort with rage, and she knew a beating was coming. Desperately seeking his love and approval, she found ways to get them. He insisted that the family buy everything secondhand, usually at church rummage sales, and he would take Karen to the city dump to pick up junk that he would fix up or make something out of. Karen took to salvaging items from trash cans in alleys and bringing them home. Her finds always resulted in a pat on the head. Karen says, "In my middle age, these ideas and values of my early years came back to haunt me— and very nearly ruined my life."

Most of the time, Karen compensated for the lack of affection at home by being a "good girl," getting all A's at school and obeying her father's ridiculous demands. Still, he never let up on her. One day she exploded to her mother, "I hate his guts!" Certain that he had heard her, she dreaded coming home from school that day to face the consequences. When she walked in, she found him lying dead on the kitchen floor. He had had a heart attack. Karen says, "I was 15 years old. I felt I had killed my father as surely as if I had held a gun to his chest and pulled the trigger." From then on, she strove even harder to be perfect, reasoning that somehow her father would know and that would make things right between them. Her quest for perfection proved costly. She developed anorexia nervosa and a binge-and-starve eating compulsion and wound up in a psychiatric hospital the day of her high school graduation, where she was to have been honored as the girl with the highest grade-point average.

Children often respond quickly to therapy. An 11-year-old girl with no history of psychiatric illness developed obsessions and compulsions after experiencing her first earthquake soon after the family moved to southern California. She obsessed that her parents would be injured or that she would be separated from them. (There was some logical basis for her fears because the family's home was near the epicenter and sustained some damage.) The child developed sleep disorders and compulsive behaviors. Whereas she had once been a typically messy 11-year-old, she began arranging her desk and belongings just so. She devised a ritual whereby for thirty minutes at bedtime she would have to write on an inkboard, "Nothing is going to happen to Mommy and Daddy." She also brought a glass of water to her bedside each night, convinced that it would keep her mother, her father, and her rabbit safe. Since the child's father is a psychiatrist, he immediately recognized that she had a problem, and the family sought professional help five weeks after the behaviors began. In therapy, the therapist told the girl that she was developing a disorder called OCD and explained what it is and what it does. The girl was also told that she must resist her compulsions or they would only get worse. After three months of treatment, her symptoms had virtually disappeared. Less aware parents might have continued to cater to the child's OCD, thinking it was a passing phase, and OCD could have dug in and eventually thrown the family into emotional chaos.

A SHARED SICKNESS

Frequently, family members will accommodate the person with OCD to an absurd degree—Karen's husband, for example, allowed the junk to pile up in their house until they had only a narrow path that was navigable. It had been years since they had allowed people in. Still, he tolerated her bizarre behavior. Was he himself sick? Dr. Hand thinks so. "Only people with their own severe psychological problems," he believes, would let such a situation get absurdly out of hand. He mentioned a case of a couple who moved six or seven times, thinking that things would be different in a new home, but it never took long for the new place to become filled with junk.

Hand insists that the family be involved in the diagnosis but allows them to decide on the degree of their involvement in therapy. The person with OCD may be very artful in covering up whatever other problems he or she has—such as difficulty in one-on-one relationships—and may resist too much delving by the therapist. "They are afraid," Hand stated. "They develop an attitude of learned helplessness. They have their problems, but those problems cannot be solved. If they're in a stable relationship, the relationship is usually sick as long as they have their OCD. Both sides have no hope that any real improvement is possible but, at the same time, they are very, very scared to disrupt everything. So they prefer to live in bad relationships."

What Hand calls "interactional dynamite" often develops in families. This term means that the person with OCD harbors long-term aggressions and at crucial, and inappropriate, times uses the OCD to attack his or her spouse for some real or perceived violation of their relationship. Thus, a "sudden outburst" of very intense compulsive behaviors can occur, causing chaos that disrupts the lives of other family members, with the resulting distress and aggravation.

Hand related some case histories from his practice in Hamburg, Germany: One woman who lives with her daughter and son-in-law constantly nagged her daughter about her house not being clean enough. Ultimately, the daughter developed a defensive compulsion. When making the beds, she spent hours and hours smoothing the sheets just so and increasingly neglected the rest of the house. When the mother tried to break her daughter of this habit, the two fought and the mother threatened to have a heart attack. In reality, Hand found, this was just the culminating battle in a long-standing war for dominance. The power struggle, in which the mother insisted that the daughter be a better housewife, developed into a paradox in which the daughter used her compulsions to get the upper hand.

Another woman became obsessed with her belief that twenty years earlier, her husband had an affair. When she confronted him, calling him a "dirty pig," he denied it. Ultimately, she was hospitalized with pathological symptoms of jealousy. When she returned home, she developed a massive cleaning compulsion that resulted in 80 percent of the house becoming virtually uninhabitable because in sixteen hours a day of furious cleaning, she could get only 20 percent of the house "clean enough." When her husband came home from work, she demanded that he undress, and she would bathe and disinfect him from head to toe. Her rationale was that the long-ago affair had made him dirty, and though she could not rid him of that inner dirt, she *could* rid him of his outer dirt. This gave her a feeling of control. In therapy, it came out that what consumed her even more than the suspected affair was the fact that her 6-year-old daughter, her favorite child, had continued to show open affection toward her "errant" father. The woman improved and stopped her cleaning rituals, but she said that she was forced to stop only because she had developed arthritis in her knees, a diagnosis that was never confirmed. She even persuaded her husband to join a dance group with her: The exercise, she explained, would be good for her arthritis.

Still another case was a husband who had a compelling need to repeat simple sentences over and over for hours at a time. He had to do so in front of his wife, so she could assure him that he had correctly pronounced all the words in each sentence and that his voice had the proper intonation. When his wife tried to wiggle out of this chore, he would lock the doors. Finally, he took to locking her inside the bathroom while he stood outside the door, repeating his sentences. Hoping for release, she would occasionally shout through the door, "Good!" or "Correct!" This only aggravated him further because he figured she was not being honest with him. One day, the wife managed to escape from the house, get into her car, and pull out of the driveway. Just then, her husband rushed into the street, flung himself in front of the car, and forced her to stop. He won.

In treatment, Hand tells patients that they must work out the advantages and disadvantages of clinging to their OCD. If they are in therapy not because *they* want to be—but because someone forced them into it—he believes treatment is futile. And, he added, the therapist and person should work together to develop behavior therapy strategies. For example, the housewife who gets even with her husband by developing cleaning compulsions might be told how their relationship could be reorganized so she could get the same power benefits without the OCD behavior. This technique can be thought of as a broadening of the application of the Reattribute step—it is not *only* the brain that is causing a person to be plagued by OCD symptoms, but the fact that OCD is being used as a mechanism to manipulate others in his or her interpersonal life. This is the "secondary gain" element of OCD symptoms, and the Reattribute step can be used to actively address it and begin to deal with it. By recognizing the role OCD can play in your emotional life, you can make the healthy changes that decrease your tendency to use OCD symptoms in this ultimately self-defeating way. This is another example of how the Four Steps can be used to help enhance the process of better managing the OCD.

UNDERSTANDING, NOT PAMPERING

Let me assure you that it is not true that OCD and healthy marriages and relationships always go together like oil and water. There are cases of couples working together using the Four-Step program to build stable, loving, and supportive relationships.

But the obstacles that OCD can throw in their path should not be negated. People with the disorder may develop sexual anxieties linked to the fear of losing control. One person may have violent thoughts that he or she will never act out, while another may obsess that some wild and uncontrollable sexuality will be unleashed. The person with OCD may take out latent aggressions by initiating conflicts, often involving OCD symptoms, that result in the avoidance of intimacy. Deep down, the motivation may be to avoid the risk of being hurt by opening up emotionally—the old self-esteem issue.

Another case related by Dr. Hand was a teenage boy who developed bizarre food behaviors. He could eat only one thing—a rare and costly fish—and had to be fed by his mother in a ritualistic fashion. His parents were allowed to talk to one another only in his presence and only on topics he chose. He regressed in some areas to age 2 and began dirtying his bed at night. Significantly, all these symptoms came on after the father threatened to have an affair and break up the marriage. The boy achieved what he wanted: When he got sick, his father broke off the affair. The boy, however, became sicker and sicker, withdrawing from his teenage friends and from the outside world. A vicious circle developed: The father came back home, but the marriage was a marriage in name only, with no mutual affection. The mother now took care of her emotional needs by devoting herself to her son, enabling his OCD to escalate. The boy used his illness to dominate his parents. He kept the family together, but at his own expense. They were all together—and all sick. This story did not having a happy ending. The boy improved greatly in family treatment but later relapsed. The social deficits he had developed proved to be disastrous when he tried to reconnect with his peers. His mother lapsed back into her old enabler role. It was family business as usual.

Finally, a woman came to Dr. Hand seeking help after her neighbors complained that she made too much noise when she unlocked the door to her apartment; she explained that she just wanted to know how to calm the neighbors. In therapy, she began to talk about her compulsive Bible translating. As a young woman, she had joined a monastery, eager to withdraw from normal social contacts. She gave the monks a chunk of inherited money, but when she left, disillusioned, a year later, they refused to give back the money. Soon afterward, she began translating the Bible, intent on showing the pope that all existing translations were in error, since they had provided the ethical guidelines for the monks who had treated her badly. Bible translation became her sole mission in life. A part-time secretary, she lived like a nun in her apartment, translating and translating, sending her work to the pope, but her compulsions betrayed her. Instead of getting even with the monks, she developed bizarre behaviors that became her only purpose in a lonely life.

FORGIVING OCD TOGETHER

When families work together, however, wonderful things can result. One patient told me that she got better with her husband's help: "Together we forgave my OCD."

Lara, who has violent thoughts about knives, says that she tends to withdraw when she is obsessing, to become quiet, sullen, sad. Her husband will say, "Lara, stop obsessing. I can see the wheels turning in your head. Stop it." This Relabeling helps snap her back to reality. He gets upset, she says, only because the OCD causes her so much pain. And he is protective. "If there's a horrible accident on TV, like a plane crash, well, he knows I'm kind of drawn to catastrophic things, so he'll say, 'You don't have to watch that. You're already afraid of flying'"—another reality check. She has found him to be caring and understanding, and he does not let her OCD frighten him. Sometimes, though, it frightens her in hard-to-explain ways. She and her husband have talked of adopting a baby, but Lara obsesses that the adopted child—who, of course, as yet has neither a name nor a face—will come to harm. "I have a gnawing, pulling, tearing sensation that the child will always be in danger—have an accident, become ill, get kidnapped, or die." Therefore, the adoption decision has been put on hold.

Carla, who obsessed that she might kill her infant daughter, struggled with intimacy problems in her marriage. "That was the last thing I could think about. OCD takes twenty-four hours a day. I was just trying to survive and function. It was very difficult for him to understand our relationship, and how I had changed." Before OCD, she had been the superefficient wonder woman, easily coping with her job, volunteer work, and caring for frail parents. With OCD, she could no longer juggle everything and became very frustrated, taking her frustration out partly on her husband. He was puzzled because in fourteen years of marriage, she had always been a take-charge person. Now, she was demanding time off to take care of her own needs, and he wasn't used to it. "Unfortunately, I didn't have time to deal with what was going on with me and with him, too. And I didn't really share what was going on in my head. The details were too scary."

Family members can be most helpful by offering support, understanding, kindness, patience, and encouragement in doing the Four Steps—but not by pampering or indulging the person's OCD. Reinforcement is essential; every improvement should be recognized. People with OCD need to feel good about themselves, since it's been a long time since they've done so. What they don't need is angry criticism; they are already critical enough of themselves. Nor should they be pushed too fast to get well; their goal will be reached by taking a lot of small steps, not giant leaps. Sure, there will be times when the partner is tired and out of patience with OCD and needs his or her own time out. That's okay, too. There should be no guilt feelings about that—in fact, the person with OCD should encourage it.

Jack, the hand washer, and his wife had some rough spots in their marriage before he sought help. Both she and their daughter were fed up with his continually asking, "Did you wash your hands?" He understands now, "It was like telling someone they're dirty." His OCD-warped mind kept thinking that she was somehow going to contaminate the meals she fixed for them, and the thought almost drove him crazy. But he forced himself to stop asking her if she had washed her hands. "It still bothered me, but I figured that if I kept on, it would create a worse catastrophe—like my wife leaving me." Insights like this can be great motivators for doing the Four Steps.

In treatment, Jack mentioned his frustration that his family didn't seem to notice how he was improving, that they wanted the OCD to be gone right away. His wife would say, "I know what you're doing and why you're doing it, but it's still driving me crazy." Before he was diagnosed, she would get angry with him, telling him his hands were going to fall off if he didn't stop washing, but she just thought he was a little weird. He laughs and says, "Once there's a diagnosis, once this thing has a name, people know they can bug you about what you're doing. Before, they don't know what the heck is going on and they don't want to ask questions." He asks, "Can you imagine living with someone who wants to change you all the time, every waking moment? 'You know why you're doing that.' 'What are you doing in the bathroom?' 'Why are you washing again?' It would drive me crazy, so after a while she took the attitude that I was getting professional help and she sort of laid off. Once she started crying and said, 'I wish I could help you.' I told her she was, by being intolerant of my OCD, by not indulging me and just making the OCD worse." Of course, there are better and worse ways for family members to be "intolerant" of OCD.

Jack's wife drew the line at going with him to group therapy. She'd say, "Why do I want to go see people doing what you're doing?" He didn't push her. "I think a little fear had crept in, too. Before, she'd thought these were just my quirks. But suddenly I had a mental disorder. She didn't want to think about that."

Karen recalls that she was frequently so depressed, tense, and frustrated during bad bouts of OCD that she became extremely irritable. "My husband called me a bitch, which infuriated me, since I felt too much of a burden already. So my response was, 'Well, you certainly ought to be an expert on that. There are enough of them in your family.'" Their fights escalated, and their sex life diminished. In therapy, she learned that her husband also had OCD, which explained why he had tolerated her hoarding all these years.

Because they were kind of coconspirators in this ridiculous ritual of collecting worthless junk, there were no reality checks, and things got to a tragically absurd crisis state. Old friends from out of town came to visit, but could not be invited in, so they all stood around the yard talking. When friends from Canada called to say they were coming to town, Karen and her husband arranged to meet them at her mother's house. Nevertheless, Karen was terrified that they might show up unexpectedly at her door. "I felt compelled to park our cars several blocks from our house, so they would think we were not at home. We went to bed as soon as it got dark, so they would not be attracted by lights and drop in on us."

Barbara's husband was loving and understanding about her checking compulsions, even though he found them difficult to understand. But when she came home and announced that she had the awful feeling that she had hit someone that morning while driving to work, he lost patience. "That was the final straw for him," she says. "It was too ridiculous, too bizarre, too completely detached from reality. It shook him up, really sent him over the edge." Whereas she understood that it was just another of OCD's dirty little tricks, he did not. He snapped, "You would have heard a 'thunk' if you'd hit someone with your car. You would have seen a body in the road." She was stunned by his overreaction: "I knew it was the same thing, whatever this thing was that was happening to me." Soon afterward, she read a newspaper article describing a person with severe OCD who had the same symptoms as hers. At last, Barbara knew what she had.

As Barbara progressed in self-directed therapy, her husband handled his role well. He refused to check things for her unless she was completely exhausted. Then he might make a joke out of it, announcing, "Check!" This is actually a form of Relabeling. She says, "He knows he can't fix me, that I have to fix myself. So he never got overinvolved. He is an amazingly tolerant, well-adjusted, normal person. If I'd married someone like myself who had all sorts of dysfunctional family issues, it would have been a disaster. He's had to deal with other problems, not just my OCD. I was an alcoholic and had to recover from that. I had a crippling self-esteem issue. I had a lot of baggage before OCD." That baggage included a mother with mild OCD who used to send her daughter back into the house to double-check the stove before they could leave. Barbara admits, "I didn't even go into the kitchen. I'd come back and say, 'Oh, yeah, Mom, it's off.'" What irony—years later Barbara would ask her husband to check the stove for her.

Today, Barbara's OCD is very mild and under control. But when it was at its worst, her husband was there for her. "I could unload on him and decompress, and he'd just sit there patiently and talk to me until I felt better." He did complain occasionally, "You know, you're not connecting with the world. You're in a cocoon. You have no involvement with the world or other people. It doesn't matter to you that you live in a vacuum." True, sometimes she would just lie in bed on weekends. Sometimes he would come in and hang out with her; other times he wouldn't. Barbara has since had a baby and quit her job. Now that she's started to feel less stressed out, she is initiating social contacts and is becoming much more interested in the outside world.

The fifteen-minute rule is very helpful in enhancing communication between family members and the person with OCD. If family members can say in a supportive way, and it must be done in a therapeutic manner—"Let's just wait fifteen minutes. I'm not going to do this for you now, but I'll do it in fifteen minutes. I know your OCD is really bothering you right now, but let's just wait fifteen minutes and see how it goes"—the person with OCD is apt to reevaluate the situation at the end of that period. Again, this intervention must be approached with goodwill, or it will only make things worse.

DON'T PUSH, DON'T RUSH

Because they have had years of practice, people with OCD are clever at hiding their illness when it is to their benefit. A number of people have told us that for many months into an intimate relationship, they had no reason to suspect that their partner had a mental disorder. There may be quirky little behaviors that can be shrugged off and rationalized. Domingo's ex-girlfriend, Kathy, told of how, very early in their relationship, Domingo had a bad OCD day. She knew almost nothing about OCD and had no idea what to do. "It was like, 'Oh, my God, oh, my God,' I didn't know the magic words to tell him to get him out of it, and I'd be saying all the wrong things, everything that would make him angry." Sometimes Domingo would make light of it, telling her, "Why don't you just get naked and stand in front of me, so my mind's thinking of something else?" When his OCD was that bad, she said, she was willing to try anything to snap him out of it, but "nothing short of a bomb going off next to him would help."

She laughed as she told us, "The funny thing is, our dog has the same anxious behaviors. You know how they say animals pick up your personality? Well, it's weird. This dog is a real clingalong. He has to be next to us all the time. We created a monster. If we leave and he has to stay home, his breathing gets funny, and he starts licking and gets this really goofy look on his face. It reminds me of Domingo's anxious feelings. I tell him, 'You two guys are just the same.'" There is, however, no clinical evidence to show that dogs of people with OCD develop OCD.

Moving can be traumatic for people with OCD, as can any disruption of their routine. Frequently, they resist the idea of travel, especially when they have contamination obsessions. Travel means using public bathrooms and sleeping in beds where strangers have slept. Domingo bought himself a $500 mountain bike and fixed it just the way he wanted it, but when Kathy suggested a day's outing to the mountains, she practically had to drag him and his bike out the door. He remembered, "I was afraid the bike would get scratches on it.

But, the funny part is, when I went to the mountains, suddenly it was not *my* bicycle, so I was able to enjoy riding it. I didn't care if I broke it or scratched it. OCD is weird."

Although Domingo and Kathy lived together as a couple, they each had a bedroom. She used to tease him and call his room "the mausoleum," a space where he had his precious collection of art objects arranged just so. She knew better than to rearrange anything. "If I ever clean his things," she said, "it just freaks him out. He has to go and check for damage. I don't even do his laundry. I'm a terrible washer. I tend to get bleach spots on things, and he freaks out about that, too."

Kathy came to see that Domingo's resistance to change and disruption in his life had an unexpected side benefit. She told us, "If he didn't have OCD, he'd probably have ten girlfriends because he is, by nature, very promiscuous. But because of the OCD—and this is the part I love—he's faithful. He's Latin, right? But if he wanted to cheat on me, he'd have to tell me. For one thing, there's the contamination thing. He'd have to tell me if he'd touched somebody else." Domingo confirmed what she said. "Once I'm used to something— somebody—my anxiety gets less and less. With somebody new, I have to start from the beginning. Those of us with OCD are different. We get used to things." There is security in familiarity.

Kathy used to come to our family support group, where she met parents and family members of other people with OCD. Many of them had been through hell with OCD and, Kathy remembers, "a lot of them were wondering what I was doing with Domingo. They couldn't understand why I would be involved with this guy if I had a choice not to be. I wasn't born to it. I wasn't a parent." The answer was that, OCD or no OCD, she appreciated him for his good qualities.

It's not that they didn't go through some tough times. Kathy's natural instinct was to pull away, to withdraw, when she saw the OCD coming on. "I would be like, 'Oh, God, I've got to get out of here. I can't deal with this. How can I deal with this for the rest of my life?'" But when she asked me what her role should be, I told her that if she chose to be with Domingo, she had to take an interest and be involved in his treatment.

After five years, Domingo and Kathy split up for reasons other than his OCD. It was a terrible time for him, and he suffered a relapse in treatment. He explained, "I get used to people and things very fast. If that pattern is broken, my peace has been broken. Then I have to struggle a little so I can get my peace back." He recently married a woman he met after the breakup. Ironically, they met when he went to a health-food store to buy the weight-gain supplement that Kathy insisted he continue to take. The first time his wife met him, she told him later, she sensed there was something "different" and "interest-ing" about him. He took her out to dinner and laid it all out for her about his OCD. She had never heard of OCD and really didn't under-stand, but she is learning. Domingo told her right off, "Never push me, never rush me, or you can expect me to get aggressive. Don't ever tell me, 'Hurry up!' because that brings out my bad side. I get really mad when people rush me because they don't understand what I'm going through": why it takes so long for him to do simple things like put on a pair of socks or take a shower. Domingo gets lost in his rumi-nations. If he sees a catsup spot on his pants, he may obsess that it is blood and stare at it until his mind understands that it is only catsup.

"Don't rush me" is good advice for anyone living with a person who is struggling with OCD symptoms.

JILL AND HER DAUGHTERS

When Jill's older daughter, Erica, was 11 years old, Jill's best friend died in a car crash. Jill was devastated—the two women had worked together in a real estate office and often shared confidences over din-ner afterward—but Jill could not go to the morgue to identify Mari-lyn's body, nor would she attend the memorial service. She couldn't. If she had, her whole world would have become "contaminated."

The day Marilyn died, Jill remembers coming home to find both her daughters—Erica and 8-year-old Tracy—at the door waiting for her. "They were crying and I was crying and they reached out to hug me and I said, 'Stay away from me. I'm dirty.'" Jill then took her clothes off, right there, and went in to shower.

She stayed in the house for weeks. "I couldn't go anywhere where Marilyn and I had been together. It was the contamination thing." For more than twenty-five years—since she was a teenager and had to go to the open-casket funeral of her boyfriend's best friend—Jill had suffered from contamination fears tied to death and dying. Though it would be years before she would be diagnosed, she was suffering from severe OCD.

The day of Marilyn's memorial service, the unthinkable happened: Knowing that Jill was devastated by the loss, friends dropped by to bring her a fruit basket. When Jill peeked out the window and saw them standing there, she told Erica and Tracy not to open the door. These were the people who had identified Marilyn's body for the coroner. They were contaminated. The fruit basket was contaminated. Jill, her daughters, and her house would be contaminated if they came inside.

"It was horrible," Jill says. "All I could do was stand there and say, 'I can't take it, I can't take it, I can't take it!' But I wanted to take it, so finally I told Erica to open the door, take the basket, take it into the bathroom, and stand in the tub. My friends left, and here was Erica, just standing there in the tub, holding this basket of fruit. I didn't know what to do with it. She was contaminated and the basket was contaminated."

It was Erica who jolted her back to reality, screaming, "Mom, you can't just wash Marilyn down the drain!"

Jill told Erica to put the basket on top of the refrigerator, where she could see it but couldn't touch it, and then to take a long shower. The basket stayed on the refrigerator for a long time and then Jill threw the fruit away. But the memory of that day has stayed with Erica and Tracy.

Tracy listened recently as Jill told that story. She is now 22, and only in the past few years has she been able to let go of the anger she felt toward her mother for what her mother did to her and her sister when they were growing up—the bizarre cleaning rituals; the moves from city to city and state to state, in search of a place that wasn't "dirty"; and the embarrassment of trying to explain to their friends why they could never come into the house.

Jill married when she was only 18; by the time she was 20, she had two babies. Several years later, she and her husband divorced. Stress piled on stress. She was a single mother now, trying to hold down a job, and she was sick. She didn't know what this sickness was, but she knew it wasn't normal. She knew it wasn't normal to talk to relatives through a closed door or to forbid her girls to kiss their grandfather because he was a meatcutter and had touched blood. Sad and depressed, she wouldn't leave the house for months on end except to buy groceries or drive the girls somewhere.

For sixteen years, she cut off all contact with her mother, father, brother, and sisters. They were contaminated, and she couldn't even talk to them by telephone. Jill, Erica, and Tracy moved repeatedly because whole neighborhoods and whole towns would be contaminated.

Tracy is able to laugh now as she remembers, "We always had to find a two-closet apartment." Setting aside one closet as the "dirty closet" was Jill's way of dealing with the fact that her girls had to go to school—where they could become contaminated. She devised a routine to keep them and the house "clean": When the girls came home from school, Jill would open the door to let them in. They weren't allowed to touch the doorknob. They would then tiptoe through the house to the "dirty closet," where they would strip off their clothes and dump their book bags. They would then tiptoe to the bathroom to shower. If they had homework, the routine was a bit more complicated. They would have to sit in the closet with the door open doing their homework. Then they could shower. Jill, of course, never went near the "dirty closet." Tracy remembers that if she or her sister had to use the bathroom while doing homework, they would have to shower first (to keep the bathroom clean), go back to the closet to finish their work, and then shower again.

Erica and Tracy went to a private school and missed a whole year of school when the family's finances got tight. Jill was always in a bit of a Catch-22. "If I got very sick, I couldn't work because I was spending all my time cleaning. We'd have to move a lot because we couldn't pay the rent."

When they were very young, the girls just thought, "Oh, well, this is what everybody does." Later, though, they had a hard time explaining their mother's peculiar behavior to their friends. Certainly, their friends found it puzzling that they were never invited in. "Mom would tell us stories to tell people," Tracy remembers, "how to make excuses for this or that. It bothered me a lot, the peer thing. 'How come your mom can't take us all to the skating rink tonight?'" Tracy would mumble something about, "Well, she just can't."

When Tracy was in third grade, her whole school became "contaminated." If she or her sister had to go the principal's office, that was a kind of double-dip contamination. Tracy says, "I remember one time when I knew I was going to have to go in and see the principal. It was a Catholic school, and I was really religious at that time. And I was really praying to God that I wouldn't get called into the office because I knew that then I would have to go through all this extra nonsense." A trip to the principal's office meant two or four showers when they got home—always an even number.

Tracy began telling little lies. When interrogated by Jill, she would say she hadn't been to the principal's office when she had. Sometimes she'd sneak a schoolbook out of the "dirty closet" and take it into her bedroom to study.

When Jill found out her daughters were lying, "This rage would come over me. Now, everything was dirty because I had no idea where they'd really been or what they had touched after they'd been there. I'd get itchy all over and start hyperventilating." When Tracy was in ninth grade, she broke her silence and told her best friend about these strange things her mom did. "It was a breakthrough for me, finally talking to somebody." Her friend told the other girls, of course. Pretty soon the girls at school were joking, "Hey, I think it's so cool. Can I come over and stand in your closet with you?" To Tracy, it was not funny.

The girls hated their mother's OCD—but they learned to use it to their advantage. Tracy says, "Erica and I would tell her, 'If you're not going to let our friends come over, then you need to give us money to go out.'" They weren't allowed to earn money by baby-sitting because the child or the child's family might be contaminated. Though Jill was struggling to keep afloat financially, she would give them what they wanted.

There was no logic, of course, to Jill's obsession about contamination, and this fact was thoroughly confusing to the girls. Tracy recalls, "Erica and I used to spend a lot of time asking her, 'Well, how come this is dirty now and it wasn't dirty before?'" If a "contaminated" person should telephone, Jill would spend hours scrubbing the wall by the phone while dirty dishes piled up in the sink. "That's what would make my children really upset. Sometimes I would even take all my clothes off first, so I wouldn't have to clean them. They'd come home and find me standing there, naked, with a paper towel and a bottle of rubbing alcohol. It was bizarre. They'd say, 'Mom, you're an alcoholic.' And, of course, seeing them get upset would make me upset. It's terrible when your kids are ashamed of you."

"I hated her," Tracy says. "I would tell her all the time, 'I hate you. I hate you for making me do this.' OCD affected every little thing in my life—the lying to people, the conflict I felt. When she'd make me shower four times, I'd tell myself, 'I'm doing this because I love her.' And then I hated her. I'm still like that now. I've hit her, I got so angry. And I love her. I don't want to hit my mom."

Once, for a lark, Tracy and a girlfriend decided to hang out one night in a graveyard. When Jill asked where they'd been—as she always did—Tracy told her the truth. For weeks, Jill dwelled on it: graveyard-death-contamination. When Tracy's girlfriend later came by to visit while Jill was out, she knew she had to lie about it. There wouldn't have been enough alcohol in the world to make the house clean again. As it was, Tracy says, "We'd go up to the city and buy literally cases and cases of alcohol—three, four, five cases. By that stage, all she was doing was cleaning."

Things had gotten out of hand, and the girls were fed up. Tracy was 16 and the family was living in North Carolina when "the big blowup" came. Erica confronted Jill and told her that she and Tracy had been lying to her for years, doing things she'd told them not to do and not doing things she'd told them to do. "We told her, 'We're not going to live with this. We're not going to have a life like this,'" and they left, going to stay with families of school friends. Jill was devastated. She knew she couldn't have them with her if they were going to betray her, but she was too sick to really understand what she had done to them.

Erica, who was 19, did not come back. She and Tracy took an apartment, but after a while Tracy came home. "I missed her. I loved her. I felt bad for her. I knew she was hurting."

The homecoming, of course, triggered a massive "alcoholing" of the house, since Tracy was now badly contaminated. Jill remembers, "I ended up cleaning the cat, too." Tracy says, "We're talking even books, page by page, and photo albums. My award certificates from school got smeared with alcohol and had to be thrown out. It killed me. I was very mad at my sister for having us tell mom all that because she had destroyed everything and now I had to come back and pick up the pieces." Jill, unhappy and depressed, had been thinking that life might be better in Florida. She decided to drive south and take a look. But first, all their possessions had to be drenched in alcohol before she put them into storage.

It was spring break, and while her mother went to Florida, Tracy planned to go to Montgomery, Alabama, to visit former school friends, but she knew that to Jill, Montgomery was "really dirty." So she lied. She told her mother she was going to visit other friends in Savannah, Georgia. They made plans to rendezvous in Florida. But Jill became suspicious and, en route to Florida, called Tracy's friends. Her worst fears were confirmed: Tracy had gone to Montgomery, after all. Jill "felt betrayed a second time. It was breaking my heart that they could just lie to me like that. And I was still so confused about my disease." Tracy was now contaminated; they could no longer live together. Tracy says, "She couldn't even talk to Erica or me on the phone."

Eventually, Jill and Tracy sort of worked things out and, for a while, were sharing an apartment near the UCLA campus, where Tracy is a student. For years, Erica and Jill were estranged. Erica had trouble forgiving her. She lives in a different section of the country, and they have seen each other only once in the past five years, but they have spoken by telephone. Jill understands, "She still has a lot of the old hostilities. But things have mended. She no longer blames me for taking her family away. Understanding that I have this disease has taken a lot of the pressure off. She's forgiven me. She knows that it's a sickness, not me."

Although Jill and Tracy haven't totally resolved their conflict, they're working at it. When Jill's compulsions affect her, it makes Tracy angry—"I don't want to be a weirdo." Deep inside, she's a little scared that she may have some OCD tendencies. Tracy herself has a little problem dealing with death and dying and is extremely squeamish about what she will eat.

Jill has shared with Tracy what she has learned about OCD and its treatment from me and from other members of the OCD therapy group, which she attends faithfully. Recently, Jill got a traffic ticket and was taking a driving-school-at-home program. There was one problem: She couldn't touch the manual because of an old contamination obsession about official papers that started at the time of her divorce. (When Erica was 16 and wanted to get her driver's license, she had to wait three years because Jill couldn't go into the department of motor vehicles, an official building.) So Tracy flipped the pages for her. But at the end, Tracy told her, "OK, you've got to sign it." And she did. Tracy said, "Well, since you signed it, do you want to go ahead and try to touch it?" Tracy, seeing that Jill was nervous and jittery, thought a minute and then told her mother, "I think it would be really cool if you touched it. And you'll get a big gold star." It wasn't easy, but Jill reached down and touched the manual. "Suddenly" Jill said, "my hands and arms got all these red splotches, and I was itching between my fingers, but I knew I wanted to touch it. I had to—for my behavioral therapy."

Today, Jill's obsessions and compulsions are largely under control. She no longer "alcohols" her house. Her mother's death two years ago caused a setback—her family members, who had become uncontaminated, suddenly became contaminated again.

But she's working on that problem, practicing her therapy every day. "You know," she says, "I've always had a real strong survival instinct."

BRIAN AND HIS WIFE

For most of the fourteen years of their marriage, Sara has shared Brian with his OCD, his morbid fear of battery acid, and his compulsive need to scrub public streets to avoid being contaminated by it.

She minces no words as she talks about her husband, his illness, and how it has essentially destroyed their marriage: "OCD has ruined my life. It steals your husband. It steals your lover, your companion, your friend. It steals your time, money, and energy. It takes all there is to take and gives nothing back. And it never says 'thanks.'"

Sara and Brian met at the office where they both worked and had known each other six years before they married. In all that time, she had seen no signs of his illness. But they had been married only a few months when she began to notice strange little behaviors— "He'd ask me not to walk in certain places, drive certain places, wear certain shoes"—but she was able to convince herself that these were simply his little eccentricities.

Of course, there were those long, long showers he'd take, but, again, she just "put it down to his being very neat."

Then, when they'd been married about a year, there was a battery spill at work, and, she remembers, "He just went ballistic" and had to be hospitalized. The gates of hell had just opened for both of them.

Night after night, Brian would lie in bed, listening for the sirens that would tell him that there was an accident nearby. He was always on the alert, ready to grab a bucket and baking soda and drive to the scene and start scrubbing.

Sometimes, Sara said, he would be in the middle of a sentence when he would hear those sirens and would just jump up and disappear for five hours, forgetting even to close the front door in his panic.

The family—which included his son and her son by previous marriages—was being torn apart by OCD. "My kids didn't know what was going on," Brian says, "All they knew was that dad was deathly afraid of batteries and battery acid and that I wasn't fit to go out in public. I mean, it was terrible. Terrible. If my wife could have left me and not felt guilty, she'd have done it. I couldn't do anything. I wanted to crawl under a rock."

Of course, the boys couldn't have friends over because Brian couldn't control where those friends might have driven or where they might drive next. Once, they came home from school and confided in Sara, "Man, we did chemical experiments today and we had sulfuric acid everywhere." That was a secret they kept from Brian, knowing he would grab the boys on the spot and start scrubbing them down. Looking back, Brian says, "My son was real anxious to join the Marine Corps. I think he just wanted to get away from me, get away from the problem."

As his OCD progressed, Brian could no longer work. "I was an absolute basket case. I felt like acid was all over me and I couldn't get clean. It was in my bedroom, it was on the walls. One day a friend of my wife came to the house and I learned that he'd driven down a street where there'd just been a traffic accident. Now it was on his tires. I spent all night on my hands and knees, washing the carpets with baking soda and water. Then I rented one of those vacuum things at the market and cleaned and cleaned."

Brian says, "It got to the point where this thing was just completely out of the stratosphere." He was scrubbing streets all night long, waking up exhausted, and then starting the cycle all over again.

Was he crazy? Was she crazy? Sara was so confused by this time that she wasn't sure.

Some nights, he would sit in front of the TV, watching *The Late Show* and then hours of late-late shows, hoping somehow to postpone the dawn and another day of fear and scrubbing.

He sought psychiatric help, but was given a laundry list of misdiagnoses, including schizophrenia. Thirty days in a psychiatric hospital did little good, nor did another two weeks in a second hospital. "Nobody had a clue" as to what was wrong with him, Brian says. Their solution seemed to be "to give me lots of stuff to make me sleep."

He remembers almost nothing about the first five months of 1985. "Sara told me later that people we knew had died during that time, while I just lay in bed, absolutely zoned out. I had tremendous bouts of depression and I would cry frantically because I was just going crazy inside."

Then one night they happened to be watching *20/20* on television, when there was a feature on people with OCD. Sara recalled, "I was so relieved that this thing had a name." Brian said, "A bell went off." He now knew what he had. The feature had mentioned the UCLA outpatient program for OCD patients, and Brian called. When he got hold of me, he was so relieved that he broke down and cried.

Brian's is a classic, and severe, case of OCD, and his progress has been up-and-down, depending on how faithfully he takes his medication and how faithfully he practices the Four Steps of behavioral therapy and attends the OCD therapy groups.

If he works hard at it, he is able to keep his symptoms under control, but he has failed to learn the most important lesson: Only constant vigilance defeats OCD. Until he does, he will suffer the consequences, and Sara will have to suffer with him. When his OCD is really bad, Sara says, it is so extreme that "he uses paper towels and sandwich bags to open doors. And we can't go to church because there is a man there who owns a battery company." As long as Brian takes Paxil in the prescribed dosage, he is able to fight off depression and suicidal tendencies.

When she feels able to face the consequences—which almost

inevitably include angry outbursts—Sara tries to force him to confront reality, to acknowledge that this thing that is bothering him is not battery acid—it is OCD. Sometimes he will, sometimes he won't. Most of the time, he won't. She says, "OCD is this giant monster that sits over in the corner. He's eating us alive, but we're not supposed to notice."

The acid problem is, in itself, hard enough to live with. Sara says, "He has ruined more things trying to prevent acid contamination than if we'd sprayed daily with the stuff." Their driveway and lawn are inundated with baking soda and ammonia. He even cleans under the bushes. The sinks are pitted from the ammonia, and Sara says she expects the pipes to disintegrate and collapse some day.

"We spend three to four hundred dollars a month on baking soda and ammonia. It's so frustrating to watch the waste. It's ruined our clothes, shoes, and carpet." Brian watches where she walks and may decide later to retrieve her shoes from her closet and clean them. He turned a favorite pair of blue suede shoes a hideous green by dousing them in ammonia.

The money wasted is money they cannot afford to throw away. He was a partner in a car dealership that fell victim to overexpansion, recession, and the rerouting of a major freeway in the early 1990s. It was a financial disaster that left him broke. Because of his OCD, his job performance since has been shaky. His current sales job requires a great deal of driving—and he cannot keep appointments with clients if he finds that he will have to drive on streets where there might have been an acid spill.

Although money is tight, Brian still feels compelled to buy things he doesn't need. His closet is filled with suits and ties he's never worn. "He doesn't want to get them contaminated," Sara explains. Once, she went to a department store to buy him a birthday gift and, undecided, asked the saleswoman for an idea. When the saleswoman suggested a tie, Sara quickly chose something else. As the saleswoman was ringing up the purchase, she noticed the name on the credit card and said, "No, he sure doesn't need a tie." She recognized him as the man who couldn't stop buying ties.

Brian buys hammers and other tools in duplicate and once had to rent a garage to store all the stuff he was hoarding. Sara observes,

"We could have put his son through college with what he's invested on this disease."

He will buy and buy—and then a great guilt will seize him. Because he has OCD, he will reason, he must deny himself everything. "Everything," Sara says, "shampoos, haircuts . . . but then he will reward himself to the same extent that he has denied himself" and the buy-and-scrimp cycle will repeat.

But the greater toll on his family has been the emotional one. "If you're sick from the neck down, everyone will help you," Sara says. "If you are sick up above, there is this shame. A woman stays with her husband who's terminally ill and she's a saint. But I'm told I've got to be 'out of my mind' to stay with Brian. I ask people, 'Would I not be kind to him if he had polio or heart disease?'"

Many times, angry and frustrated, she has thought of leaving. "I've actually gotten in the car and driven until my gas tank was almost empty, not knowing where I was going. Finally, I'd pull over and wonder, 'Where am I?'

"I've told him I want a divorce. That's when he starts taking his pills by the gallon and calls the doctor and starts going to the group." But only until the marital crisis blows over.

There are many reasons why she has stayed: She is 56, and this is her third marriage; her first husband was a schizophrenic, her second an alcoholic. There is the matter of commitment. "He needs me terribly." And, she says, "Even the unstable, if it's constant, becomes secure."

When he is himself, she knows, he is a kind, loving, and charming man—the man she married, the man he was before he became so overwhelmed by his disease and not able to think of anything but his own needs.

Sara hates the role she is forced to play in her marriage. "I have become the mother, the watchdog, the critic. I hound. I nag. I try to control. I cry. I give up. Then there is nothing. Just apathy and sadness. What a waste—of him, of me, of time, money, everything."

Most of all, there is the dreadful loneliness. "I am alone most of the time, whether Brian is home or not. He doesn't think of me anymore. He is always thinking his own thoughts, always thinking of battery acid. I have never experienced loneliness like this. Even being divorced was not this lonely."

Most of the time, she is "contaminated," so physical intimacy between them is out of the question. "He won't even touch anything I have touched or use the same towel or the same cup." The problem is compounded by the fact that she works at an auto dealership. In Brian's mind, that means only one thing: battery acid.

Sometimes, she has reached out to hug him and has seen "stark terror" on his face. Or she might take his arm, and "he just recoils." Over time, she has learned to stifle her feelings, not to initiate any show of affection, so as not to be rebuffed. "I am no longer an equal, no longer feminine, no longer a love object."

"OCD isolates you like no other disease," Sara says. "It tries to keep your family and friends away. You can't plan get-togethers or holidays. It controls where you drive, walk, shop, see movies, every aspect of your life. Nothing is left untouched."

She smiles and says, "If I didn't have a sense of humor, I'd have done myself in—or him."

When he gets really bad—which is when he slacks off on his medication and behavior therapy—she worries that he will be suicidal. "I don't want to come home from work," she says, "and wonder if he's hung himself in the garage."

Sometimes Sara struggles to keep her sanity. She will sit and recite multiplication tables, just to focus on something besides his illness. For three years, she was in therapy. And, she has taken up hobbies with a vengeance—"I craft myself to death."

But her real strength comes from "a deep, abiding religious faith," combined with coping skills she learned from living with an alcoholic. "I will relive the good times mentally and use them over and over" to get through the bad times.

Still, she has to take medication to control her heart palpitations. And she overeats: "I haven't yet learned that food doesn't cure anything." Once, when Brian was out of town, she ordered pounds of pasta from a favorite Italian restaurant where they cannot go because it is "contaminated" and systematically ate her way through all of it.

A few years back, Brian and Sara decided to take their sons to Hawaii. "The vacation that I'd dreamed about," Brian says. "I thought we were going to have a great time." But the second day, they decided to take an offshore snorkeling excursion. As luck would have it, the owner of the boat asked everyone to remove his or her shoes before boarding. He then opened a storage compartment and put the shoes inside. Brian froze when he saw that there were batteries stored in that compartment.

From that moment, Sara says, "Everything we had on was contaminated and everything we bought was contaminated. It ruined the whole vacation."

"I was living in a virtual hell for the whole five or six days we were there," Brian recalls. "I didn't even wear my shoes off the boat. I just left them there. But I couldn't possibly clean everywhere where my kids wore their tennis shoes and I wasn't going to grab their shoes off their feet and get them new ones."

For a long time, Sara was very supportive of Brian. At his most desperate, he considered having brain surgery, but she talked him out of it. By the time he sought help at UCLA, she had consulted an attorney about a divorce. Brian states, "I begged her to do it. I said, 'Honey, I don't see me getting any better and I can't possibly put you through this for the rest of your life. Go out and find somebody else. Let's get this thing over with.'"

She didn't. For one thing, she didn't think he could make it on his own. And she worried constantly that he would take his own life. Brian remembers, "I had bought that book that tells 450 ways to kill yourself. I'd learned how to cut my wrists and all sorts of other things. I never tried but, boy, I sure contemplated it. I remember telling a doctor at UCLA, 'You know how bad I am today? I'm so bad that there's not a person in one of those beds on the cancer ward that I wouldn't change places with.'"

Sara talks about her weariness, her loneliness. Sometimes she is just too tired to fight his OCD, so she gives in to it, even though she knows that will not help him to get well.

She says, "I've tried not to buy into his illness, not to be codependent, not to be an enabler. But those times the house becomes a true war zone. There is no peace. So, if he thinks there is battery acid on a certain street, I agree not to drive on it so he can have peace of mind. I'm running around the edges, trying to keep everything peaceful." When she feels strong enough, she will force the issue and make him confront his disease. And he will go back to doing his behavior therapy and taking his medication. Then things markedly improve.

The worst part, Sara says, is that "he's in this alone and I'm in it alone." Rare are the occasions when he's honest about what's bothering him—it's not battery acid, it's OCD—but at those times she feels very comforted. Most of the time, "the beast is eating both of us, and we're both pretending that it's not touching anybody."

Sara longs to hear Brian say, "You're great for staying with me," but he never does. She doesn't think he understands what he's putting her through. After all, *he* is the one who gets up at night to scrub the streets, not her. Her friends tell her, "You've got to have your head examined." But she cannot bear to think "what he would be like and live like without me." So she stays.

Because he knows where he can get help, she is hopeful that sooner or later he will decide to conquer his disease because he must—for his sake and for theirs. Meanwhile, she says, "He's wasting his life, and I'm wasting mine watching him wasting his. I want him back with me. I want us to be in this together. I'm sure he's lonely, the same as I am."

It's not easy to know why Brian continues to go through such extended periods of noncompliance with his medication and behavior therapy when it is obvious to everyone, including him, that he shows consistent and marked improvement when he complies. From a classical psychotherapy perspective, it's clear that he has "emotional conflicts" about getting better, but it has not been easy getting to the root of what they are. The pattern of his cooperation with his treatment plan is somewhat hopeful in that the periods of remission are getting somewhat longer, but things remain much too inconsistent.

The moral of this story is that not everyone avails themselves to the same degree of the opportunity to get better. Some people seem to cling to their suffering more than do others. We are hopeful that Brian will eventually sort himself out and follow the combined medication-behavior therapy treatment regimen that has proved effective for him.

JOEL AND HIS PARENTS

Steven and Carol, both academics, at first indulged their 14-year-old son, Joel, in his newfound interest in subscribing to newspapers from different cities.

What they didn't know was that Joel had no intellectual interest in those newspapers. In fact, he wasn't even reading them. He was hoarding them. Stacks and stacks of newspapers were piling up in his room. "It was a real fire hazard," Joel says.

Carol remembers, "If you went into his room, it would hit you in the face, this tremendous, overpowering smell. And you'd suddenly realize that it was newsprint." Carol and Steven did the logical thing: They took the newspapers—by then thousands of pounds of newspapers—out into the yard and asked Joel to sort out the ones he wished to keep. He started to make choices but then, she says, "he just kind of cracked up. He couldn't do it." Even though he never read those papers, he was obsessed with the idea that he "had to preserve this information." For a long time, Joel was able to rationalize that his "collecting" made sense.

His parents thought it was a bit odd. They had no way of knowing that it was, in reality, the first stage of an OCD hoarding compulsion that was to get completely out of control. Soon, Carol says, "We started to find old food containers. He was saving things like McDonald's wrappers. I'd root around and find them all over the house. At first, Steven thought, 'Okay, he's making a collection,' and he'd allow him to keep one sample of each." But before long, Joel would be scouting the alley, sifting through other people's trash cans in search of food wrappers. And then he began hoarding junk mail. Carol had to take all the junk mail to school as soon as it came to the house and dispose of it there.

Obviously, Carol and Steven were beginning to see a disturbing pattern in their son's behavior, yet they were completely puzzled about what might be going on in his head. Thinking back, they recalled an episode several years earlier that had seemed harmless at the beginning: Joel had suddenly taken an interest in making videotapes. But his was no normal teenage experimentation. Soon he was taping compulsively and indiscriminately; the recorder was on all

day long. Of course, he never played any of the tapes. Taping in and
of itself had become a life-consuming activity.

Joel explained his hoarding by saying that he was into recycling,
but, Carol noticed, "Nothing actually got recycled." It just got
stashed away.

To their relief, the hoarding obsession eventually began to go
away. Joel did not throw away the mounds of junk in his room—he
was too sick to deal with it—but he stopped bringing in more junk.
Carol and Steven reasoned, "Well, maybe this was just an adolescent
problem." They consulted a psychiatrist who suggested that coming-
of-age pressures and anger can cause teenagers to do all manner of
strange things.

Life seemed to move along quite normally for several years, and
then, on Joel's 16th birthday, Carol and Steven took him to his
favorite restaurant for dinner. But Joel couldn't eat. They asked to
change tables, thinking that might help, but Joel was able to force
down only a few forkfuls. Joel explained that he had been thinking
for some time about converting to an organic vegetarian diet and
now, all of a sudden, he felt confused and put off by his food. Like
many young people, he had interests and concerns about the environment that were leading him in the direction of not wanting to see
animals killed for meat. Carol and Steven understood; certainly
didn't object; and, in fact, tried to incorporate his new dietary pref-
erences into their lifestyle as much as was practical. At this stage,
Joel would still drink milk and would eat meat occasionally if someone else had prepared it.

Soon, however, Joel began to exhibit signs of extreme worry over
things being "unclean." He began washing his hands repeatedly,
using huge quantities of water, and taking long showers. Carol and
Steven began to suspect that it was more than an ecological awareness that was behind Joel's ever-more-rigid eating habits. Later, they
would understand that he had started to equate "nonorganic" with
"unclean." He had begun to spend hours sorting through vegetables
at health-food stores. Once he brought the vegetables home, he
would have to wash them for hours. Even after the greens became
limp and soggy, he couldn't always bring himself to believe that they
were clean enough to eat. Steven remembers, "It was not only the

vegetarianism, which we could understand, but the minute examination of every possible contaminant, these long, agonizing sessions." Joel was going through a growth spurt and was quite thin for his height, and his parents began to worry that he was starting to become undernourished.

About this time, the compulsive washing was getting out of control. Whereas he had always been extremely punctual, now Joel could not get to school on time. Whenever he was leaving the house, Steven recalled, "he had to go through increasingly lengthy sessions of washing. They got longer and longer and more intense. He couldn't explain, except to say that he had to. I didn't know what to do. Shouting wouldn't have done any good, obviously. That would have just made him more anxious and maybe would have made it worse. Once or twice I thought, 'Well, look, maybe I can shock him out of this by turning off the main shutoff valve and cutting off the water.' Well, that created terrible consternation. And, in the end, it didn't really save anything because things got so bad that he couldn't go out if he couldn't wash, so it was just a vicious cycle. Eventually, I realized, of course, that this wasn't helping. Not only that, but I couldn't do that more than once or twice without breaking the plumbing. You know, if you keep turning the main valve off and back on, you've got trouble. So I gave up on that."

Now, Carol and Steven knew that whatever this power was that had taken control of their son, it was stronger than any of them.

Everyone's life was being turned upside down. Because Joel could not dry his hands on towels others might have used, he took to just shaking his hands and letting the water splash on the floor. He would let the water rise so high in the sink when he washed that it would slosh over. Both Carol and Steven slipped on the wet floors and fell. They had to buy big commercial mops to combat the deluge. Joel's hands were getting raw and red. Looking back, they describe life at home during that time as "an endurance contest." Joel couldn't pinpoint the "contamination." It wasn't a fear of germs, exactly, but just a feeling of "ick spreading everywhere. One thing would touch another thing that would touch another thing."

He could not sit down to a meal without first jumping up to wash and rewash his plate and utensils. Carol and Steven emptied the kitchen cupboards, relined them, and washed all the dishes in the dishwasher before replacing them. It proved to be wasted effort because Joel was still not convinced that things were clean.

Pretty soon, he began avoiding going to the bathroom, so he would not have to wash his hands afterward. At school, he remembers, "I didn't go to the bathroom at all because I didn't want people to see me wash my hands over and over. Of course, they must have known that something was wrong with me because I was arriving at school ten, twenty, or thirty minutes late with my hands white from soap."

By now, Joel was washing his clothes compulsively, as well. Carol says, "He would take seven or eight hours to wash them and then he had to wash the dryer before he could put them in." She could no longer be trusted to wash his clothes properly. As he took each item out of the dryer separately (with one hand), he would rush upstairs to his room with it, holding it at arm's length as though it were about to explode, touching nothing on the way. Water rationing was in effect in parched southern California, and the family was exceeding its quota by far and being penalized. Steven installed water-saving taps and showerheads, but it was futile. Joel—who before his illness had been very drought conscious—just let the water run longer. Carol and Steven would make little jokes about Howard Hughes, but to no avail. Joel was going through piles of towels and huge amounts of non-animal-based soap. Carol says, "We were beginning to live in fear that they were going to turn off our water." In desperation, Steven rigged up a lock for the clothes washer. Joel broke it off. Sometimes he would hang over the washing machine, compulsively turning the controls for hours. One time, out of patience, Steven hit him, hoping to bring him back to reality. But deep down, he knew that would not help. Steven tried to take away the towels that Joel had laid on the floor to absorb the overflow from the sink as he washed. Joel went into a panic and began knocking over chairs and tables.

Joel had been seeing a psychiatrist who told Carol and Steven that if the situation got totally out of control, they might have to call the police. They figured this was such a situation and dialed 911. Joel responded by striking Carol, trying to tear the phone off the wall, and running outdoors. He was gone when the police arrived.

Clearly, a crisis point had been reached. By now, Joel could touch nothing after washing and rewashing his hands. He took to using his knee to change channels on the television and would try to "knee" his way out of the house to go to school. Whereas once he had hoarded newspapers, now he couldn't read a newspaper because he couldn't stand to get newsprint on his hands.

Joel had abandoned all of his hobbies, including amateur radio and gardening, to concentrate on his compulsions. Ironically, while he expended all this energy on keeping himself and his food clean, his room was becoming a disaster area because of his inability to touch anything "dirty." Stacks and stacks of newspapers sat in the backyard, untouched, but if anyone suggested throwing them away, Joel would panic and start screaming. He rarely smiled anymore or communicated with his parents, except in a combative and adversarial way. He had begun to realize that he was losing control of his life, that he was letting his schoolwork slip—he had always been a top student—and he cried frequently, wringing his hands in frustration. He was a senior in high school, but had little interest in senior activities and left college applications unopened. An entire day could be spent doing laundry and bathing.

Joel's food fears were increasing. He could still drink milk, but only one brand. His compulsive washing left him no time for breakfast or lunch. He insisted on cooking his own vegetarian dinner, but this was a long and messy process because he could now use only one hand, even after repeatedly washing both. Salads were out, since he could not get the greens clean enough. His skin was becoming more and more irritated, but when Carol and Steven tried to cure the washing problem by refusing to buy more of his special soap, he started using his shampoo to wash. He spent much of his time standing around with his arms bent and his hands clenched, doing nothing and avoiding touching anything. Whereas he once enjoyed riding his bike to the health-food store, he now had to be driven there. One day, Carol and Steven came home to find Joel standing in the dark, hands clenched, unable to bring himself to touch the light switch. His shoes were a disgrace, but he rejected the idea of new shoes. New shoes would be stiff—and dirty—and he would have to touch them to put them on instead of just stepping on them and forcing his feet into them.

Carol and Steven tried to get Joel to talk about his anxieties, but he would either remain silent or change the subject. Only general, light conversation was possible.

Inevitably, all this turmoil began to be reflected in plummeting grades. Whereas once Joel had been extremely organized and his work very thorough, his reports and papers were now last-minute efforts banged out on the computer with little thought or fact-finding. (His keyboard and mouse could still be touched.) Rarely was he able to concentrate well enough to study for exams. Fortunately, he had applied to several University of California campuses before he was incapacitated by his OCD, and several acceptances had arrived. Carol and Steven urged him to read the literature, thinking it would boost his ego, but he showed little interest. Ultimately, after a perfunctory visit to several campuses, he decided—without much enthusiasm—on San Diego. With his lackluster senior-year grades, his parents feared that UCSD might withdraw its offer—or that, at the last minute, Joel would decide just to stay home and do nothing.

As a family, Carol, Steven, and Joel rarely sat down together for a meal. It was too nerve-racking. If either parent prepared food in Joel's presence, there was a long battle about whether it was clean. Carol and Steven began to describe his fixation as "molecularism"— if there could possibly be contamination, no matter how small or how imaginary, an object was unclean and unusable. Joel could not wear any clothes if they accidentally touched the floor or if Carol or Steven touched them. His washing compulsion escalated. The drains began to spring leaks, and Steven would have to place buckets beneath them and empty them regularly. The wall behind the sink was constantly drenched from Joel throwing water against it to clean it. Crumpled paper towels by the hundreds were scattered around the house. Carol and Steven were becoming hostages in their own home. "We found ourselves snacking our food when it wouldn't agitate him. He couldn't stand to have us near him in the house." Joel complained incessantly that "the house is dirty." In reality, it was he who was making it so, dropping things everywhere.

Joel's food obsessions were getting worse. Because everything was unclean—including his parents—he could eat nothing that they had cooked. And he could eat nothing off their plates or utensils. He had begun to subsist on commercially packaged organic vegetarian meals and organic juices drunk straight from the bottle. By now, he could not use the telephone or open a door. The movies were his only recreation. He would take the bus to the movie theater, carrying with him his own special snack food.

There were frequent family explosions. Joel was frustrated and angry. On the one hand, he had the normal teenager's love-hate relationship with his parents, but, on the other hand, he was also abnormally dependent on them in ludicrous ways—for example, to open a door. Physically, he was exhausted from long hours of compulsive activity and a diet that was totally out of balance. He no longer slept in his bed, but just fell asleep stretched across a chair, exhausted. Later, as his obsessive rituals became too painful, he took to sleeping in a sleeping bag to avoid having to shower and change his clothes come morning.

To make matters worse, he had developed an obsession that certain areas of the house were infested with imaginary bugs. Steven had to buy him a package of throwaway plastic gloves because even his computer was now sometimes contaminated. But Joel would complain that the gloves weren't long enough or that bug "particles" had somehow found their way inside the gloves.

His senior class at school was taking a trip to Europe, but Joel had no interest in going. He all but crawled on his knees through his last year of high school.

Just before Joel lost the ability to function at all—when he could still go outside—he happened upon Judith Rapoport's *The Boy Who Couldn't Stop Washing* at a campus bookstore and eagerly flipped through the pages. About the same time, Carol stumbled on the book and brought home several copies. She and Steven devoured it from cover to cover, but Joel could not; he couldn't pick up anything that they had touched. All three of them now knew what Joel had, and after a number of inquiries, Carol and Steven were able to get him to contact me at UCLA. "That," says Steven, "is the first time we got the full picture. That was the beginning of our understanding."

Joel began to comprehend that he had a medical problem caused by a chemical imbalance in the brain, but his physical reserve was so low that he could do little to combat it. By this time, he was house-bound. He couldn't go out without showering, but he hadn't the stamina to face the ordeal of an eight- or ten-hour shower. One Saturday morning Joel awakened Steven; he was sobbing and explained that he'd had a nocturnal emission and would now have to shower. Steven agreed and suggested some shortcuts that might curtail the length of the shower, but to no avail. On that occasion, Joel showered for seven hours.

Joel still washed his hands repeatedly, but couldn't bring himself to turn off the faucets when he finished and risk getting his hands dirty all over again. One day, Carol and Steven came home to find that the faucet had been running all day. Sometimes Joel would wake them up at night, pleading for one of them to turn off the faucet.

He could no longer drink tap water, only bottled. With greater urgency and frequency, he would ask his parents to make special trips to buy emergency food or drink or special anticontamination supplies. They rejected or deferred many of these appeals, repeatedly reminding Joel that they had a limited capacity to cater to his illogical needs.

His showering ritual had become so painful that he simply stopped showering. The very thought of starting a shower was, in Joel's mind, a challenge of the magnitude of "crossing the desert" on foot. "Once," Steven remembers, "he went twenty-one days before he built up the courage to take a shower. And that was only so we could take him to the hospital." All along, Joel had firmly rejected the idea of medication because medicine might be contaminated. Everyone, including Joel, had come to realize that hospitalization was his only hope. He wasn't functioning. He was, as he says, "frozen."

Taking that shower was a milestone. Steven says, "It takes a heck of a lot of courage to do these things when your OCD is so bad. You know, it's easy to say to somebody, 'Come on, why don't you take a shower and get out of here?' But it's horrible, it's just horrible. He told us how he would get into the shower and start washing, but then some part that he'd washed would get dripped on and he'd have to rewash. He would even get to the point where he'd almost pass out in the shower because of the hot steam. And of course, his body would be just raw afterward. When he went into the hospital, the outer layer of skin on his hands and arms was basically gone, all the way up beyond the elbow."

Joel was in the hospital for ten weeks, which wiped out the family's medical insurance for "mental disorders." Because he had finished high school, even though he wasn't yet 18, he was placed in the adult ward, which was very important to him because it meant he could be part of my group. In the hospital, everything was monitored, including the length of patients' showers. Steven says, "They had a big, beefy guy who hauled people out of showers naked. They had to do that." The therapy included exposure-and-response-prevention exercises wherein Joel would be told to touch "contaminated" objects, such as bathroom doorknobs.

For weeks, Joel made tiny improvements, would reach a plateau, and then would make another series of small improvements. During this time, he got up the courage to try medication, which helped to relieve his anxiety. Still, there were crises in the hospital; strangers would touch his clothing, and he would demand of his parents, "Take it away. I can't deal with it." Repeatedly, he would ask Carol and Steven to bring him brand-new clothing and to throw out the old. They knew they could never satisfy his demands because the new clothing would have to be brought in "uncontaminated" packages. They knew, too, that they would wind up spending all their time bringing clothing to the hospital, that they could not afford to replace everything that had been laundered by the staff and thus rendered unwearable. They actually considered presenting him with an ultimatum: Either he wore what was there or he could wear hospital gowns. But they knew this would be too upsetting and humiliating to someone with his anxieties. Ultimately, they hit on a plan to bring one set of "clean" clothing on each visit. They would seal it tightly and give it to a staff person to give directly to Joel. This seemed to work.

Just before the end of the ten weeks, Joel's condition took a significant turn for the better. Once home, he was determined not to regress. He began going faithfully to the OCD outpatient program at UCLA and to the weekly meetings of the OCD therapy group.

He still had multiple anxieties, but he was able to control his compulsive rituals. If he found himself starting to think contamination thoughts, he would force himself to Refocus on something else. The family's awful episode was behind them. After about six months of work on his behavior therapy as an outpatient, the washing compulsions were 99 percent gone. Joel was able to enroll at UCLA, even though he was still struggling with concentration problems.

The moment of truth, Carol says, was when Joel said one day, "I've decided that I can't be better than other people. I'm not going to be able to be cleaner than other people." And she knew he was going to be okay when he did the hardest thing of all: He touched the flusher on the toilet. Steven says, "Joel was extremely fortunate to be able to get to the right help, the right people, so quickly. If he hadn't gotten into a good treatment program early on—less than a year after he had clear-cut OCD—it could have gone on for years and years." Of course, having parents who sought appropriate treatment and persisted in their support as he worked on his behavior therapy also played a critical role.

Carol and Steven remain alert to any signs of backsliding and will confront Joel right away if they notice, say, that he is having trouble deciding whether he is washing something the "right" way. He is usually able to reassure them that everything is under control. He has become very effective at Relabeling and Active Revaluing. As a matter of choice, he still eats a vegetarian diet, but he can eat off plates and utensils like everyone else.

Because he was having concentration problems, Joel temporarily dropped out of college and took a volunteer job at UCLA Medical Center, which led to a part-time paid job. In private psychiatric counseling, he began working on overcoming such things as performance anxiety. Steven resisted the urge to ask his son, "Why don't you just do X-Y-Z? Why don't you try to concentrate?" He knew, "It isn't that easy for someone who's been through all this. For him, it's work, hard work. He's a young guy, and he's been through a lot. What difference does it make if he goes to college this quarter or next quarter?" In time, Joel was strong enough to leave home and enroll at a large out-of-state university, where he is studying computer sciences.

"This terrible episode is behind us," Steven says. "He'll find himself."

ANNA AND HER BOYFRIEND

Anna's earliest memory of having a major obsession was when she was in fifth grade and at Girl Scout camp. She had looked forward to having a wonderful time, as she had at past camps. But one day a girl who was bunking nearby happened to tell Anna about her sister, who had a severe kidney disease, and to describe the symptoms in vivid detail. Anna says, "For days, the thought of this sick sister whom I had never met stuck in my mind and refused to leave. It didn't make a lot of sense that I would feel so bad about a total stranger, but I did." Camp became a sad experience, and it wasn't until Anna returned home that she was able to put these painful thoughts away.

Years later, an equally inexplicable and illogical obsessional thought—this one focused on unfounded fears and doubts about her boyfriend's faithfulness—would drive him up the wall and almost lead to the breakup of their relationship before she learned that she was not a jealous shrew, she was a woman with severe OCD.

As a child, Anna was a worrier and, for most of her life, she had suffered from anxieties and insecurities. During her sophomore year in high school, she had her first real romance, with a good-looking boy a year ahead of her. They started going steady. "We decided we loved each other. We confided the most intimate details of our lives to each other." One day, he confessed to her that he liked to masturbate while looking at a picture of supermodel Cheryl Tiegs in a bikini. Anna began to obsess about this, over and over picturing him doing this, until she would become sick to her stomach. "Why am I thinking this?" she asked herself, but she couldn't find an answer. Later, she learned that it was more her boyfriend's suppressed homosexuality than her lack of sex appeal that made him fantasize about Tiegs while being less than amorous toward her. Still, it was hard for her to shake her obsession with Tiegs. It was the late 1970s, and Tiegs's picture was everywhere. Each time she saw it, Anna felt a wave of revulsion combined with a fear that her intense obsessions would flare up again.

Anna analyzed herself and decided that she was hypersensitive and jealous by nature and wondered how she'd ever be able to sustain relationships with men in the future if such trivial issues were so painful to her. In college, she became involved with a man who was a drug abuser. Although she tried to be open-minded about his drug habit at first, she soon began to ruminate on it. She had to know how he used drugs and with whom. Somehow, she got it in her mind that his drug problem was her fault. This thought led her to see a school psychiatrist who, on the basis of a fifteen-minute consultation, concluded that her real problem was that she was obsessed with her mother's breasts. Anna, quite rightly, didn't see what possible connection there was between such an obsession and her ruminations and increasingly frequent panic attacks.

Eventually, she was diagnosed with agoraphobia, an abnormal fear of leaving home. This is not an uncommon complication in people who get spontaneous panic attacks. "I was told that my panic attacks were probably due to having been raised in a perfectionist household and never having been taught to express anger effectively." Although we now believe that panic attacks, like OCD, are due mainly to biological factors, that explanation eased her fears that she'd gone crazy. Assertiveness training and exposure therapy to situations and places that brought on the attacks—such as crowds or dark spaces—eased her awful symptoms, the feelings of terror, the fear that she was having a heart attack.

Although she and her boyfriend had long since broken up, she still obsessed off and on about his drug habit. Then, the summer after college graduation, Anna was seized by a new, more overwhelming, obsession: death. "I began to wonder how anyone could make it through the day, knowing that sooner or later death would choke off life and make existence meaningless." She began to search for signs that she was losing her mind.

She went on to graduate school and met Guy. "Each time I had been involved romantically for any length of time, obsessions had resulted. By the time I met Guy, my less-than-healthy relationships with men in the past had made me especially sensitive to trouble, and I worried about the possible ways a man could destroy me, even if unwittingly. I knew I was prone to selecting men with serious problems of their own, and too many times I had felt the effects of this on my delicate mental balance. Ironically, it was probably this desire to protect myself from hurt that led to my most intense bout ever with OCD."

Guy was the innocent victim.

"For once," Anna says, "I had selected a trustworthy and supportive companion. Then I started in on him. First, I became obsessed with the idea that he had used drugs"—he hadn't—"and questioned him endlessly about this. Though he was faithful and loving, I began to obsess about his past romantic history"—even about whether he had ever read girlie magazines. Scores of conversations would begin with, "Have you been in love before?" "When exactly did you see this person last?" "Why don't you see her anymore?" "Do you think about her?" Anna wanted to know when he had looked at the magazines, why, where the magazines had come from, when he last looked at one, when he first looked at one, the total number of times he had looked at them, and which magazines.

And she demanded instant answers. "Not surprisingly," she says, "Guy hated these conversations, which would end with both of us angry. He was angry because he felt I was needlessly suspicious and distrustful. My anger stemmed from the feeling that his answers were vague and obstructionist." She spent hours checking and rechecking his answers, mentally reciting the facts he'd told her, searching for any discrepancies. "Often, hearing an answer once wasn't enough. If he gave an answer to a question I had already asked, and that answer didn't fit exactly with his previous account, this caused me tremendous mental anguish. I took these inconsistencies as proof that Guy had initially been untruthful."

Guy felt bewildered and mistreated. Anna felt vulnerable, fearful, and ashamed that she couldn't control herself. By the time they had been dating for about a year, she had begun to develop psychosomatic ailments and was contemplating suicide, in an abstract sort of way. She had read about a man suffering from mental problems who had shot himself in the head and miraculously "cured" himself by eliminating the rotten spot in his brain, a distorted and misleading account, as it turned out. "I fantasized about a similar cure for myself." She was now convinced that she was, at heart, a shrewish, jealous, demanding, difficult, unhappy person—and she hated that person.

As a teenager, Guy had lived in Europe, and together they made a summer trip that included visits to his old haunts and reunions with old friends. Anna was consumed with a need to know exactly what role they'd played in his life. How long had he known the women? Had he dated them in high school? "I would always start out by answering her," Guy says, "but by the fifth time she asked the question, it got to be completely stupid. I would ask her, 'Why are you asking me this?' And she'd just say, 'I need to know. I need to be sure.'" Sometimes, he would answer her in an offhanded, abstract fashion, thinking that would satisfy her: "Oh, I saw her for the last time three years ago in August." But later, in casual conversation, the woman would mention that it was actually four years ago or that it was July instead of August, and Anna would begin another barrage of questioning.

In her mind, one of two things had to be happening to her: Either Guy was lying to her or she was going crazy. Because she never wrote down all the details of his answers, she was never quite sure whether the discrepancies in his answers were real or imagined. So she would want him to prove that she had just imagined that he'd told her different stories.

Anna hit upon a solution. She told Guy she was going to start writing down everything he told her. At this point he put his foot down. "No, you're not. That's the worst thing you could do." He was right. He says, "I knew if she asked me, 'Did you ever go out and get drunk with this person?' I could say yes or no, and that was that. But if I said no and then she asked me, 'Well, when was the last time you saw this person?' I would probably not be able to say in the kind of detail she thought was necessary," and she would launch into another round of harassment.

During the first years of their relationship, they made several trips to Europe, where his family lived. Although he didn't know it at the time, Guy began to use behavior therapy to help Anna. He recognized that if she got too tired, this obsession of hers "would be ready to pounce," so he tried to plan their travel accordingly. He also planned their daily activities ahead, understanding that when she was busy, she was not asking all those silly questions.

On their second trip abroad, they stayed with his family in their small home. That turned out to be a mistake. Guy's mother thought her son had brought home a severely disturbed young woman and had little patience with her strange problems. She had much bigger worries—her husband had recently suffered a heart attack. She made her impatience obvious, which of course only increased Anna's stress and exacerbated her OCD obsessions. Guy's mother would tell her, "Well, deep down you must really want to be doing this. There must be some special urge in you." Anna, in desperation, would tell her, "No, no! You don't understand." The conflict was making both Anna and Guy miserable. "I just lost it," Anna says. "I wanted to kill myself because I was obsessing and obsessing and starting to do all these really crazy things. I just became obsessed with trying to reconstruct his life before me—although he'd actually had an extremely tame life before me."

She grilled him about every woman he had ever dated. "What did she look like?" "What did you eat when you went out with her?" "Where exactly did you go?" What did they have for an appetizer, main course, dessert? Did they sit down to eat at noon or four minutes past? What did they talk about? Anna was distraught. "I had no idea what was going on and I felt really horrible because I was basically torturing my boyfriend with all these crazy questions. He got very upset. He thought I was just doing it for fun or something. He is a very sensitive guy and he thought I didn't trust him, which in a way was true. But neither of us knew what this thing was. We had no clue. I had already been through therapy for my panic attacks, so I knew what panic attacks were, but this was something totally new. [About 10–15 percent of people with OCD get panic attacks as well.] I knew there was something seriously wrong and that I had to see a psychiatrist, but I was in Europe, so I had to sort of live through the rest of that summer."

Deep down, she knew that Guy was "a really steady, nice guy." She'd never seen any untoward behavior; in all the time she'd known him, she'd never even seen him drink too much. Deep down, she understood that because of her own insecurities, she was trying to sabotage a wonderful relationship. What she did not know was that she had OCD. That summer, when she was at her worst, Guy asked her to marry him. "Really crazy, huh?" he laughs now. Soon, however, both began having serious doubts about a future together. Anna remembers, "We had a number of confrontations where I was screaming at him, saying he'd lied to me because I'd asked him if something had happened on Wednesday or Thursday or whatever and he would have gotten it wrong. I'd think, 'Okay. I'm going to have to break up with this guy. He's lying.'" In reality, he was just trying to get her off his back. He wouldn't remember each answer he'd given her, but she would.

Back in Los Angeles, they sought help for her and were referred to me at the UCLA Neuropsychiatric Institute. By this time, they were living together and were both in stressful periods of their lives. She was in graduate school, and he was starting a job in academia— a job to which he could not devote full attention. Guy looks back on this time as "sort of a daze. We were trying to get through this mess, and I wasn't sure whether Anna was the problem or if I was totally incompetent as a teacher."

I diagnosed a classic case of OCD. This was nine years ago, and Anna was one of the first patients to whom I was able to explain, with some certainty, that the problem was the chemical imbalance in her brain I call "Brain Lock." Told that she had a brain disease, Anna was greatly relieved and anxious to begin treatment. The Four Steps of behavior therapy had not yet fully evolved, but for the first time I applied the fifteen-minute rule in a systematic fashion.

Whereas family members sometimes try to sabotage the treatment of a person with OCD because they are fearful that the person will change, will refuse to continue to be the family doormat, or whatever, Guy was eager to help Anna. He understood, "This was not the person I loved. This was not her doing these crazy things. It was *happening* to her, and she was in pain." Early in treatment, there were many times when it would have been easier for him just to answer her questions, but he understood that doing so would not help her get well. So he set some ground rules: He would answer one question, not a long string of them, and then make her wait fifteen minutes before he would answer another. They would fight, and she would cry, but Guy had the insight to see that the fifteen-minute rule was more than just a waiting period; it was an implicit recognition that her questions were ridiculous, that they weren't her—they were her OCD.

He says, "It was hard for her to choose who to trust. When I said, 'This is your OCD,' she would demand to know if maybe it was just a question that I didn't want to answer." He constantly reassured her, "It's just the OCD. Don't worry about it." Very calmly, he would tell her, "I can answer your questions if you really want me to," but he would always remind her that the problem was not her need to know the answers. Her problem was OCD. "The first three months were just traumatic, the antagonism between her and me." She would stalk out of the room, slamming the door, or just sit on the bed crying. Since they lived in a small apartment, each would give the other space, literally and figuratively. One would go into the kitchen and the other into the bedroom for fifteen minutes. Sometimes, Guy acknowledges, they were putting the fifteen-minute rule into play, but not in a constructive manner: "One of us would just go off and sulk for a while."

As Anna's treatment progressed, Guy was able to say to her, "Do you really want me to answer your question?" and she would say no. A big step forward. "On those occasions," Guy says, "she was so happy. We both knew that there was no real point in my answering the question. She'd already asked the question in the past, and I'd already answered it, but she'd forgotten the answer. Therefore, by osmosis, there could be nothing to be worried about."

Anna hated what OCD had done to her, and she was motivated to work hard to get well. For weeks at a time, she would be able to resist asking questions. He says, "Anna knew that she had to get on with her life and that if she could get rid of this thing, she could." In the short term, the trade-off was not an easy one to make: fifteen minutes of waiting in very real anguish with the promise of long-term relief versus the very real and immediate relief she could get by asking her questions. Guy says, "Deep inside, Anna knew that it was just her brain doing this to her, so the value of carrying out the compulsion really fell when she identified it as OCD. Every week that goes by, every week that this thing preys on your life, the value of not succumbing to the negative impulse increases. Anna would use words like, 'I have to remain vigilant.'" Guy knew that she was in terrible pain because she would start frantically checking and rechecking things around the house. She would become moody and withdrawn. "If I'd come home half an hour late, she'd be very upset. I hadn't done what I said I was going to do when I said I was going to do it."

As the months went by, she became increasingly confident that she could control the symptoms of OCD. Guy was her partner in behavior therapy. He would say, "Look, you're getting down because you're feeling a little bit more of the OCD today. But over the last week, it really hasn't been that bad." Or, "It's been pretty bad this week, I know that."

Anna had eighteen months of weekly outpatient behavior therapy—with small dosages of medication as her waterwings. During this time, she says, "Guy learned a lot about how to handle me. Before, he used to just get mad and say, 'You're torturing me. Stop doing this.' But once he realized what it was, he was very strong about saying to me, 'I am not going to participate in this obsession. I am not going to answer your questions. You can do whatever you want, you won't make me answer these questions. So take your fifteen minutes, come back in fifteen minutes, and we'll talk.' I credit him a lot for my recovery. So many family members are just not helpful at all, but he was really there for me, pointing out when it was OCD. Many times, of course, I didn't believe him. I'd say, 'Oh, no, it's not. This is real. I really need some help.' And I'd be desperate for him to answer one of my questions or to verify some fact— but he just wouldn't do it. I got very mad at him sometimes, but it helped. It really helped. Before treatment, this would have infuriated me as a suspicious obstruction. Now, however, I could see it was a positive step for my own good."

Guy is well aware of how much effort Anna—with his help—put into getting well. "In some ways," he says, "we were lucky because I was implicated just by the very nature of her OCD. It's not clear to me that if she'd had a serious hand-washing problem, I'd have been involved in quite the same way. It was easy for me to see that there was a problem and to participate in the therapy because I was so involved."

Now and then, Anna still has one of her crazy thoughts. They tend to be "What if?" questions that are unanswerable. Lying in bed one night, she began obsessing, "What if my husband is gay?" But she quickly turned to Guy and told him she was having this crazy thought and that she knew it was OCD. He said, "Yeah, you're right. It's OCD. It's ridiculous." And he went back to sleep.

Anna completed a demanding doctoral program, and both she and Guy have rewarding teaching careers. They have been happily married for four years and have a baby.

Anna now describes her life as "normal."

KEY POINTS TO REMEMBER

•OCD always involves the family.

•Be aware of how OCD symptoms affect your loved ones.

•Be aware of using OCD symptoms as a way of distancing yourself from the needs of your loved ones.

•Avoid at all costs using OCD symptoms as a way of demonstrating anger or annoyance at your loved ones.

•Help family members learn more about OCD and the Four Steps to help them avoid nonproductive criticism and facilitating your symptoms.

•Family members can make excellent cotherapists. Encourage them to help, not criticize.

•Mutual acceptance in the context of constructive interaction is very conducive to improved performance of the Four Steps.

7

The Four Steps and Other Disorders

Overeating, Substance Abuse, Pathological Gambling, and Compulsive Sexual Behavior

People frequently ask what the difference is between treating obsessive-compulsive disorder (OCD) and other disorders, such as eating disorders. How does this Four-Step method apply to other common conditions that may also be related to OCD? As with OCD, the serotonin circuits seem to be involved in the treatment of eating disorders and other types of impulse-control disorders like pathological gambling, drug and alcohol abuse, and compulsive sexual behavior.

The major difference between treating OCD with the Four Steps and treating these other disorders is that with OCD, people always find the urge to do the compulsive behaviors unpleasant. They complain not only that they wash and check too much but that they feel totally besieged by urges to wash and check, which they themselves view as entirely inappropriate and want to get rid of once and for all.

Unfortunately, from the perspective of treatment, the desire for change is not so straightforward with the eating and substance-abuse disorders, compulsive gambling, and sexual behaviors. Clearly, people who have eating, drug, gambling, and sexually related behavioral problems find the excessive nature and the poor impulse control surrounding those behaviors problematic. Then again, people obviously don't want to stop eating altogether, and many drug abusers would prefer to be able to use drugs in a controlled fashion. The same is true for gambling and, even more strongly, for the sexual behaviors. So the key problem in treatment is, how much can people with these disorders make the excessive, problematic behaviors "genuinely ego-dystonic," that is, how much can they come to find their behaviors genuinely foreign to their own notion of who they are and what they want, as people with OCD do with the urge to wash and check?

HIDDEN AGENDAS

Because of this difference, applying the Four Steps to the eating, drug, compulsive gambling, and sexual behaviors requires additional work. You can think of this work as the need for additional steps. People with the impulse-control problems have to do a lot more work than even an OCD person does to clarify the role that these behaviors play in their lives and how much they really want to stop doing them. People with OCD also have a lot of hidden reasons to cling to their own compulsive behaviors as an excuse for not fully dealing with some of the genuine difficulties that reality brings. These reasons are often related to their relationships with their families and their fear of taking on greater personal responsibility.

However, it is also true that people with OCD genuinely do not enjoy on almost any level washing things over and over again and checking things over and over again. They also quite clearly recognize these behaviors as foreign to them, so getting them to acknowledge, at least to some degree, that they may be using these behaviors to fend off dealing with other unpleasant or anxiety-provoking aspects of reality, especially those that involve interpersonal relationships, is often not that difficult. The other impulse-control problems are sometimes considerably more complex, primarily because many people with these problems genuinely enjoy certain aspects of the pathological behavior—whether it is eating, taking drugs, gambling, or sex. These behaviors have what's called in classical behavioral therapy theory "primary-reinforcing properties." In other words, people as well as animals can be induced to work and exert effort to attain food, sex, or drugs that cause pleasant feelings.

This fact is extremely well known by many people in addition to professional mental health workers. So, the key difficulty that we have to deal with before we can apply even the Relabel step to the general category of impulse-control problems is how much a person really wants to stop doing this behavior and how much he or she is willing to let go of the pleasure experienced by doing the behavior— especially when the problems are in their early stages, before the behaviors become totally pathological.

As you can see, there is more of a need for what is commonly called willpower in overcoming the urge to eat, to drink or take drugs, to gamble, or to engage in sexual activity than there is in getting a person to stop washing or checking. Therein lies the dilemma. When people say "That's not me—that's my OCD," they almost immediately realize that they don't want to check or don't want to wash. Much of the effort involved in perfecting your performance of the Four Steps revolves around further deepening your insight into the fact that this urge is not really you and is just caused by a false message from your brain. But this job is considerably more straight-forward than it is for those who have eating, drinking, drug, gambling, or sexual problems. The key factor that determines how applicable the Four Steps are to problems of impulse control is the degree to which the person with the problem is able to separate his or her own self-concept from the behavior that is causing the difficulties.

CALLING AN URGE AN URGE

Even for people with OCD, much effort is required, especially to become profoundly aware of the difference between them and the OCD. But OCD is genuinely ego-dystonic: People view the urge to wash and the urge to check as foreign to them. The degree to which a person with impulse-control problems can come to the realization that "It's not me—it's just my inappropriate urge to eat, drink, take drugs, gamble, or have sex" tells us the degree to which the Four Steps will be helpful to them as a means of doing cognitive-behavioral therapy. In this regard, you can also begin to get a deeper understanding of the meaning of the Reattribute step. Although the

Reattribute step helps you understand that the urge to wash and the urge to check are caused by false messages coming from the brain, many people come to understand that part of the urge is related to an emotional need to avoid intimate interpersonal relationships and unwanted personal responsibilities.

Once we begin to grasp how these emotional factors play a role in Reattributing inappropriate obsessive-compulsive urges to their true cause, we become more aware of the kind of mental processes that a person with impulse-control problems must learn to use. People with impulse-control problems must begin to get a good grasp of the difference between who they really are and who they really *want* to be and the urge to eat, get high, gamble, or have inappropriate sex. As they begin to see this relationship more clearly, which may in itself require traditional, emotionally related psychotherapy, they will then be able to effectively use the Four Steps and genuinely apply the OCD battle cry, "It's not me—it's just my inappropriate urge." As their insight deepens, they will increasingly perceive the difference between who they are and what that urge to act in an impulsive manner is. From my perspective, although brain biochemistry plays a significant role in these inappropriate urges, it in no way decreases the amount of personal responsibility a person must take for how he or she responds to these inappropriate urges. This is just as true for impulse-control problems as it is for OCD. The fact that your brain may be sending you a painful message that's difficult to deal with does not decrease your responsibility for coping with the problem in a healthy manner and performing functional, rather than destructive, behaviors. This is where the Refocus step is as genuinely applicable to people with impulse-control problems as it is to people with OCD.

LOOKING INSIDE OURSELVES

Ultimately, of course, the first two steps of the Four Steps are designed largely to enhance a person's ability to perform the Refocus step under his or her own reconnaissance. This is what the Impartial Spectator is all about: *trying to observe your own behavior as if you were observing the behavior of another.* Once your ability to do so increases, you are able to Refocus on new and more adaptive behaviors. Of course, it's very important to remember that these two processes are interactive and reinforce one another. The more you Refocus your behaviors, the stronger your Impartial Spectator becomes. And the stronger your Impartial Spectator becomes, the more readily you are able to Refocus your attention and change your behaviors to something more functional and healthy. This truth is also as applicable to people with impulse-control problems as it is to people with OCD. The challenge for people with impulse-control problems who wish to begin the process of the Four Steps is to look honestly into their own motives and their own goals for the future and to do the work required to separate their emotional lives from compulsive eating, drinking, gambling, or whatever.

When people do that, they begin to be able to utilize the Relabel and Reattribute steps more effectively, and they are on their way to creating an adaptive armamentarium of healthy behaviors to Refocus on, just as a person with OCD does.

To summarize: People with OCD have an advantage in starting the Four Steps because they already know that they are different from their urge to wash or urge to check. People with impulse-control problems need to arrive at that same realization. Once they do, they can apply the Four Steps in a similar manner to the way people with OCD do.

A final word concerning urges to pull hair out, which is the cardinal symptom of the OCD-related condition, trichotillomania. There is one very practical piece of advice I can give: When doing the Refocus step and trying to switch gears away from hair pulling, it is particularly important to develop alternate behaviors that involve the use of the hands. Many people learn to knit, crochet, do needlepoint, make pottery, play a musical instrument, or perform any of a variety of activities that involve using the hands. You can even do things as simple as squeezing a rubber ball or, when things get really difficult, clasping your hands together. Dr. Don Jefferys of Melbourne, Australia, reports that wearing the type of rubber finger guards used by people who count money or sort paper can be very helpful. It makes the hair much more difficult to pull, leading to a decrease in the urge. Some people are even helped by sitting on their hands for fifteen minutes. Again, as always with the Refocus step, you try to use greater delays and notice even subtle changes in the urge after fifteen minutes or so pass.

Another very important point for people who pull their hair out is to try to become aware as quickly as you can when your hands have moved into your hair because people with trichotillomania can start pulling their hair without realizing it, just like chain smokers can light a cigarette without even realizing that they've done it. (By the way, everything I've just said about drug abuse and the Four Steps applies to quitting smoking.) Sometimes, as a joke, I have told patients with trichotillomania to get into the habit of saying things like, "It's ten o'clock. Do I know where my hands are?" It actually helps and is, in fact, another way in which the Impartial Spectator brings mindful awareness. Automatic behaviors can sneak up on you and very easily take control; mindful awareness is your best ally in fending off unwanted destructive behaviors.

KEY POINTS TO REMEMBER

•The Four Steps can be applied to almost any behavior you genuinely want to change.

•The key to Relabeling and Reattributing is clearly seeing the difference between you and the behavior you want to change.

•Learn to consult your Impartial Spectator as much as possible in moments of weakness—this is how you can determine your true goals and interests.

8

The Four Steps and Traditional Approaches to Behavior Therapy

(Prepared in collaboration with Paula W. Stoessel, Ph.D., and Karron Maidment, R.N., UCLA Department of Psychiatry)

The treatment of obsessive-compulsive disorder (OCD) was revolutionized in the 1970s and 1980s by the development of behavior therapy techniques called exposure and response prevention. Here, I will briefly describe further developments of these now classical techniques at UCLA in the 1990s in the context of our work with the Four Steps of cognitive-biobehavioral self-treatment.

PART I: THE CLASSICAL APPLICATION OF EXPOSURE AND RESPONSE PREVENTION FOR OCD

Let's begin by presenting an overview of classical behavioral therapy techniques. Whether treatment is done in the UCLA hospital or at the UCLA OCD treatment center on an outpatient basis, all people with OCD progress through the following stages: (1) assessment, including education; (2) collaborative design of treatment by the behavior therapist and the person; (3) exposure and response prevention; and (4) post-treatment follow-up.

1. ASSESSMENT

After the diagnosis of OCD is established by a thorough evaluation, including a structured interview, the person is clearly taught the proper meaning of the words *obsession* and *compulsion*, as explained in the Introduction.

Once the person is clear about the true nature of obsessions and compulsions, a complete profile of all the person's obsessions and compulsions is established. Included in this list of obsessions are internal and external cues that cause obsessions to occur and those associated with physical or bodily complaints or ailments. Compulsions include things that are inappropriately avoided and all types of rituals, as well as more typical compulsive behaviors, such as washing and checking.

At this point, the therapist explains the treatment and presents the rationale for treatment in behavioral terms, as follows:

Exposure and response prevention is designed to break up two habitual associations: (1) the association between obsessions and anxiety and (2) the association between anxiety and the performance of compulsive behaviors in an attempt to get relief from anxiety.

In addition to presenting this classical behavioral approach to OCD treatment, the behavior therapist explains the neurobiology of OCD, as described in Chapter Two, which helps the person conceptualize this disorder as a medical problem. The medical model frees the person from self-blame, destigmatizes OCD, and helps the person overcome the shame of having this disorder. At UCLA, we emphasize that the biological aspects of this disorder may be influenced by genetics, but that genetics and biology in no way interfere with the response to behavior therapy. In fact, behavior therapy, as well as psychotropic medication (see Chapter Nine), has been found to be efficacious in the treatment of the underlying biology of OCD.

2. COLLABORATIVE DESIGN OF TREATMENT

The treatment design is a collaborative effort between the behavior therapist and the person with OCD. Each obsession and each compulsion are assigned a value that indicates subjective units of distress, or SUDS, on a scale of 0 to 100, in which the item at 100 is the most anxiety-provoking to confront. Obsessions and compulsions are then arranged in a behavioral hierarchy, with the least fear-provoking items at the bottom and the most at the top. (This is what Professor Gallagher, at the beginning of Chapter One, failed to do.)

Generally, 10 to 15 items are represented on a person's hierarchy, and the treatment begins at a SUDS of about 50.

A hypothetical hierarchy of a patient with contamination fears might be:

SUDS

100 urine

95 toilet seats

85 handle on toilet

80 toilet paper roll

75 bathroom doorknob

70 faucet handles in bathroom

50 sticky substances like jelly

An OCD patient with primarily checking concerns might construct the following hierarchy:

SUDS

100 stove burners

95 light switches

90 kitchen appliance plugs

85 heater

80 bathroom heater

70 locks

60 doors

50 television

These hypothetical hierarchies are simplified for the purpose of clarity. It should be noted that many people with OCD have very complex obsessions and compulsions. However, the goals of behavior therapy are the same, regardless of the complexity.

3. EXPOSURE AND RESPONSE PREVENTION

Once the hierarchy has been constructed, the person is ready to begin treatment. As with the design of the treatment plan, the person is encouraged to collaborate with the therapist to develop assignments.

Exposures are conducted during the therapy session and again at home. The first assignment begins at a SUDS of approximately 50, and then progressive assignments move up the hierarchy until all items on the hierarchy have been addressed. The person is anxious during exposures, but his or her anxiety decreases over the next ninety minutes or so. (Reminder: These are the classical behavior therapy techniques that are done with the therapist's assistance. When the Four Steps are used in self-treatment, the tasks are broken down into smaller bits, and the fifteen-minute rule is used, as described in Chapter Three.) Each time the exposure is repeated, the anxiety level lessens. If there is no anxiety, the exposure is not difficult enough. If the anxiety is too overwhelming, the assignment must be adjusted so it is appropriate.

At UCLA, we ask people with OCD to do exposures at least twice a day and to refrain from responding with a compulsion until the anxiety level goes down. This exposure is repeated until the initial anxiety, or SUDS, of the exposure becomes manageable; then the next item in the hierarchy is confronted. An example of an initial exposure for the man with contamination fears would be to put jelly on his hand and to have him refrain from washing until his anxiety decreased. He might begin this exposure with a SUDS level of 90, indicating that the jelly made him extremely anxious, and then end it ninety minutes later with a SUDS of 30. The therapist would be present or easily reachable the entire time. The second time he did this exposure, the beginning SUDS would probably be around 75 or 80 and would decrease to less than 30. The SUDS will continue to decrease with each exposure. The woman who checks would be asked to leave home to come to the therapy session without checking the television and not to return to check until the session was completed. As with the man with contamination fears, the woman's initial anxiety, or SUDS, would be high at the start, but would decrease over time within a given exposure. The intensity of symptoms tends to decrease with each subsequent exposure and response prevention. However, since the initial anxiety and resulting SUDS scores can be quite high as the hierarchy gets more difficult, more assistance from the therapist may be needed.

Through exposure to the obsession without responding with a compulsion, the person breaks the association between the obsession and anxiety, since the anxiety goes down each time the exposure to the obsession is repeated. In addition, the compulsion no longer serves the function of reducing anxiety. So, the loop between the obsession and compulsion that was once so demanding, fear-producing, and self-perpetuating is broken. In other words, the person must confront the obsessive fears generated by an obsession and not act on the compulsion in order to break the cycle of obsessions and compulsions. This change in thoughts (obsessions) and feelings (anxiety) is accomplished by changes in behavior (compulsions).

4. POST-TREATMENT FOLLOW-UP

The person with OCD who has completed every item on his or her hierarchy is encouraged to follow up as an outpatient, or at least to have telephone contact for the next six months. If a new symptom emerges, the person is taught to continue to do exposure and response prevention twice a day, as he or she did during treatment.

PART II: APPLYING THE FOUR STEPS

The Four Steps can be combined with these classical treatment techniques very effectively. By regularly using the Relabel step, people with OCD become increasingly aware of their more subtle symptoms and the things they avoid doing because of their fear of OCD symptoms. Relabeling helps them create a complete symptom profile when preparing a SUDS behavior therapy hierarchy. The regular use of the Relabel and Reattribute steps helps them manage their responses to anxiety, which, in turn, enables them to do the exercises in exposure and response prevention. This process can lead them to work their way up the SUDS hierarchy more assertively.

In the Refocus step during therapist-assisted exposure and response prevention, the person with OCD focuses his or her attention on the support of and interaction with the therapist while waiting for the anxiety from the exposure to an OCD-inducing stimulus to subside. When you work on your own, as described in Chapter Three, you can Refocus on other constructive behaviors and use the fifteen-minute rule as a rule-of-thumb time-delay period for response prevention. Of course, you should always try to lengthen each time-delay period or put together strings of fifteen-minute periods. Always remember to continue to Relabel and Reattribute during these periods. The idea is not to wait passively, but to Actively Revalue the urges as nothing but OCD symptoms that you are not going to allow to control your life anymore. As you get better control of your behavioral responses, you are also improving your own brain function. Breaking the loop that uses anxiety and fear to tightly bind obsessive thoughts to compulsive behaviors leads you to a progressive Revaluing of the obsessions and urges and results in further decreases in anxiety.

The use of a behavioral hierarchy based on the SUDS scale as a way of creating structured exercises in exposure and response prevention is an excellent approach to doing behavior therapy and applying the Four Steps.

KEY POINTS TO REMEMBER

•Create a behavioral hierarchy.

•Start working on the less anxiety-provoking symptoms and achieve successes before proceeding up the hierarchy. Don't overwhelm yourself. Regular, steady progress is what you're aiming for.

•Use the fifteen-minute rule and try to put sequences of time-delay periods together.

•Use the Four Steps on a consistent basis.

9

OCD and Medication

My research for over twenty years has largely been on the biological and medication side of psychiatry, and I remain an advocate of the proper use of psychopharmaceuticals. But what exactly is the proper use of medications in treating OCD? Well, I can tell you right now that I'm not a big fan of the "take this pill and wait to get better" school of psychiatry. It's too passive, requires too little directed effort by the person, and puts too much of the responsibility for the success of treatment on the doctor finding the "right formula."

Throughout this book, I have repeatedly referred to the "water-wings" approach to using medications, a term that I coined in the course of my work with people whose ability to do the Four Steps seemed enhanced by adding medication. It simply refers to the fact that in the early stages of treatment many people with OCD (typically about one-half to two-thirds) found that by making the symptoms less intense, medications made it easier to do the Refocus step. (However, it should be stressed that all the people in the behavior-therapy-brain-imaging studies we did at UCLA were totally medication-free.) Thus, the medication functions like waterwings do in helping a child to learn to swim: It reduces the fear and makes it easier to "float along" while you're learning the strokes. The analogy seems particularly apt because just as children who are learning to swim can function with less and less air in the waterwings and eventually do without them, people with OCD who do the Four Steps can get by with lower and lower doses of medication as the weeks go by and they keep working on their behavior therapy. Eventually, many of them end up on low doses or no medication at all. As our research has shown, doing the Four Steps alone changes brain chemistry in almost exactly the same way as medication does.

The medications studied so far that have been consistently helpful in treating OCD all interact with a chemical in the brain called serotonin. Serotonin is one of many brain neurotransmitters—chemicals that help to transmit signals from one nerve cell to another. After a neurotransmitter is released by a nerve cell, one main way in which it becomes deactivated is by being picked up by a "pump" and taken back up into the nerve cell. The complex molecules that pick up neurotransmitters to deactivate them are thus called "reuptake pumps." One of the most widely used groups of medications prescribed by doctors today is called selective serotonin reuptake inhibitors or SSRIs, which selectively block or inhibit the reuptake pump that deactivates serotonin.

Three SSRIs that have been approved by the Food and Drug Administration (FDA) for treating OCD are fluoxetine (Prozac), paroxetine (Paxil), and flovoxamine (Luvox). The only other medication approved by the FDA at this time for the treatment of OCD is clomipramine (Anafranil), which is also a reuptake inhibitor, but is an older drug from the early days of psychopharmacology, is not selective, and acts significantly on neurotransmitters other than serotonin. One other SSRI with reasonable research support for treating OCD that has not yet been approved by the FDA for that purpose is sertraline (Zoloft). Probably the most important thing to remember to get the maximum OCD treatment effect from these medications is that they take a few months to show their full effect. The general principle is that you must take any one of these medications for three months to determine if it is effective for treating your OCD. Of course, in any particular case, you should follow your doctor's instructions. (An interesting side point is that all these SSRIs are also effective in treating depression, generally in about half the time it takes them to treat OCD.)

Even though it takes three months to see the full effects of these medications on OCD symptoms (which generally means about a 50 percent decrease in the severity of symptoms), they *can* make it easier for you to do the Four Steps considerably faster than that. Unfortunately, no research has been conducted to show whether behavior therapy can make medications work faster, but I believe, after treating many hundreds of OCD patients with both behavior therapy and medication, that it definitely does. It certainly makes sense that it might, given that behavior therapy itself changes how the brain works in the same way that medications do. There's no doubt that a lot of research still needs to be done in the mental health field.

One medication that the FDA approved for treating anxiety works mainly by acting on serotonin but not by acting on the reuptake pump. It's called buspirone (BuSpar), and though it's not particularly effective in decreasing the intensity of OCD symptoms on its own, it is quite helpful for people who get too anxious when they try to do behavior therapy. It seems particularly helpful for the cognitive part of the treatment, when people get so frightened by the OCD that they forget to Relabel and Reattribute or get so anxious that they can't Refocus and realize, "It's not me—it's OCD." BuSpar is a mild medication, is generally fairly easy to tolerate, and usually takes about two to four weeks to begin to work effectively. It also combines quite smoothly with the SSRIs and can even block some of the side effects of that group of medications, if your doctor wants to use them together.

So if you're being overwhelmed by OCD or think that you could use some waterwings to help you learn to do the Four Steps, by all means talk to your doctor about the possibility of using medication. But please remember this: You must do the work. Whatever you sow, that you will also reap.

KEY POINTS TO REMEMBER

•Medications are like waterwings or training wheels—they can help keep things under control as you learn the Four Steps.

•Allow several months for things to reach an equilibrium.

•Lower doses of medication *slowly*.

•As the dose comes down, the OCD symptoms may well get stronger. Use the Four Steps to manage your responses in a controlled fashion.

•As your brain changes by doing the Four Steps, the need for medication almost always decreases.

10

University of Hamburg Obsession-Compulsion Inventory Screening Form

Do you wash your hands after you feel you have come too close to an animal or dirty object?   1.   True   False

Do you reposition tablecloths or rugs because you think they are not exactly right?   2.   True   False

Are there days when you have to think about certain words or images so much that you are unable to do anything else?   3.   True   False

Is it often impossible for you to stop repeating (if only to yourself) a sentence already spoken?   4.   True   False

During the day do you think several times about work you have already finished?   5.   True   False

Do you find that you cannot stop counting during certain activities?   6.   True   False

Do you sometimes try to distract yourself from a thought about your partner doing something he or she would not want you to know about?   7.   True   False

Are there any activities you cannot finish before having counted to a certain number?   8.   True   False

Do you sometimes consciously distract yourself from the thought of hurting or killing yourself?   9.   True   False

During the course of the day, do you often remember a certain word, picture, or sentence?   10.   True   False

Do you check the cleanliness of public seats, such as those in buses or taxis, before you sit down?   11.   True   False

Do you sometimes repeat aloud what has already been spoken, although you try to prevent yourself from doing it?
12.   True   False

Having left your home, do you constantly have to think about whether everything is in order there?   13.   True   False

Before starting to dress, do you think about exactly how to do it?
14.   True   False

Did you ever find yourself counting things for no reason?
15.   True   False

Was there ever a day when you could not think about anything else except hurting or killing yourself?   16.   True   False

Do you wash your hands after reading the newspaper?
17.   True   False

Did you ever notice that you touch things several times before or after you have used them?   18.   True   False

Have you ever touched switches on electric devices several times and counted despite trying not to?   19.   True   False

Do you check books or magazines for dog-ears and straighten them immediately?   20.   True   False

Do you fold newspapers back to the original way after reading them?   21.   True   False

Does the thought often occur to you that you might get sick or go blind or crazy?   22.   True   False

Are there days when you can think only about hurting or killing someone?   23.   True   False

After going to bed, do you get up again to check all electrical devices?   24.   True   False

Does counting the number of times you touch switches of electrical devices interfere with your everyday activities?
                                                25.   True   False

Do you rearrange objects on your desk, in your cupboard, or other places repeatedly, even though nothing's been touched since you last arranged them?   26.   True   False

Do you check the return address immediately before you mail a letter?   27.   True   False

SCORING

A. Calculate the total number of answers circled true for questions 3, 4, 5, 6, 7, 8, 9, 10, 13, 14, 15, 16, 22, and 23. These are obsessions.
 If the *total* number of true answers circled for these questions is
 1 or 2: You probably do not have clinically significant obsessions.
 3, 4, 5, or 6: You probably have obsessions that are clinically significant.
 7–14: You definitely have obsessions that are clinically significant.

B. Calculate the total number of answers circled true for questions 1, 2, 11, 12, 17, 18, 19, 20, 21, 24, 25, 26, and 27. These are compulsions.
 If the *total* number of true answers circled for these questions is
 1, 2, or 3: You probably do not have clinically significant compulsions.
 4, 5, 6, or 7: You probably have clinically significant compulsions.
 8–13: You definitely have compulsions that are clinically significant.

Source: Dr. Iver Hand and Dr. Rudiger Klepsch, University of Hamburg, Germany.

If you want further information on OCD, please contact the Obsessive-Compulsive Foundation National Headquarters, P.O. Box 70, Milford, CT 06460, a nonprofit organization, at (203) 878-5669; fax (203) 874-2826.

11

An OCD Patient's Diary of Four-Step Self-Treatment

Note: One of our patients kept these notes on how to apply the Four Steps to his own symptoms early in treatment. They are presented only as an example. Other people may organize their symptoms quite differently.

BREAK THE ENDLESS LOOP. MONSTER ANALOGY.
RECOGNIZE OCD THOUGHTS.

1. RELABEL immediately as:

A.   Obsessive Thought
Obsessive Idea
Obsessive Phrase
Obsessive Word (number of letters, symmetry, associations).
Obsessive Image

Types: Violent. Sexual. Excrement. Blasphemy. Loved one. Future-deprivation of pleasure. Self-punishment. (Scrupulosity.) Bad person. (Blaming myself. Intention. Do I mean that?)

Excuses: False wish, hope. Subtle-twist anger. Subtle-twist half-reality. Contamination. Need to be perfect. Need to confess. What if? Bad person. Need for reassurance.

B. Anxiety—temporary. Guilt. Sad. Nervous.

C. Compulsions-Mental. Right Feeling—Need For. Negate. Replace with Positive. Ruminate. Counting. Compulsions-Visible. Confess. Seeking reassurance. Tapping.

2. REATTRIBUTE. Medical condition. Biochemical imbalance. Gating theory: stuck in gear (caudate nucleus/putamen/striatum). False message: Car alarm. Static. Ego-alien. Genetic illness.

IT'S NOT ME—IT'S MY OCD. OUT OF MY CONTROL DISORDER. BLAME IT ON THE BRAIN.

A. ANTICIPATE. Prepare. Shall not fear. Blame it on the brain.

B. ACCEPT. Serenity prayer. Stature. Not because of me, but *despite* me.

3. REFOCUS. Turn away (other cheek). Do another behavior. Just say *know*. Put on hold—delay compulsions. Ignore.

4. REVALUE. Devalue-false messages. Who cares if it doesn't go away? It's not real anyway. Apathy—indifference. Humor. Sarcasm. Don't be polemical—it's just a chemical.

PART III

Self-Treatment Manual for the Four-Step Method

If you have obsessive thoughts and compulsive behaviors, you will be relieved to learn of significant advances in the treatment of this condition. Over the past twenty years, behavior therapy has been shown to be extremely effective in treating obsessive-compulsive disorder (OCD).

The concept of self-treatment as part of a behavior-therapy approach is a major advance. In this manual, I will teach you how to become your own behavioral therapist. By learning some basic facts about OCD, and recognizing that it is a medical condition that responds to treatment, you will be able to overcome the urges to do compulsive behaviors and will master new ways to cope with bothersome, obsessive thoughts.

At UCLA, we call this approach "cognitive-biobehavioral self-treatment." The word *cognitive* is from the Latin word "to know"; knowledge plays an important role in this approach to teaching basic behavior therapy techniques. Research has shown that exposure and response prevention are very effective behavior therapy techniques for treating OCD. In traditional exposure and response prevention, people with OCD learn—under the continuing guidance of a professional therapist—to expose themselves to stimuli that intensify their obsessive thoughts and compulsive urges and then learn how to resist responding to those thoughts and urges in a compulsive manner. For example, people who obsess irrationally about contamination from dirt may be instructed to hold something dirty in their hands and then not wash for at least three hours. We've made some modifications in this method to allow you to do it on your own.

The technique is called response prevention because you learn to prevent your habitual compulsive responses and to replace them with new, more constructive behaviors. We call our method "biobehavioral" because we use new knowledge about the biological basis of OCD to help you control your anxious responses and to increase your ability to resist the bothersome symptoms of OCD. Our treatment differs from classic exposure and response prevention in one important way: We have developed a four-step method that enhances your ability to do exposure and response prevention on your own without a therapist being present.

The basic principle is that by understanding what these thoughts and urges really are, you can learn to manage the fear and anxiety that OCD causes. Managing your fear, in turn, will allow you to control your behavioral responses much more effectively. You will use biological knowledge and cognitive awareness to help you perform exposure and response prevention on your own. This strategy has four basic steps:

> **Step 1: Relabel**
>
> **Step 2: Reattribute**
>
> **Step 3: Refocus**
>
> **Step 4: Revalue**

The goal is to perform these steps daily. (The first three steps are especially important at the beginning of treatment.) Self-treatment is an essential part of this technique for learning to manage your responses to OCD on a day-to-day basis. Let's begin by learning the Four Steps.

STEP 1: RELABEL

The critical first step is to learn to recognize obsessive thoughts and compulsive urges. You don't want to do this in a merely superficial way; rather, you must work to gain a deep understanding that the feeling that is so bothersome at the moment is an obsessive feeling or a compulsive urge. To do so, it is important to increase your *mindful awareness* that these intrusive thoughts and urges are symptoms of a medical disorder.

Whereas simple, everyday awareness is almost automatic and usually quite superficial, mindful awareness is deeper and more precise and is achieved only through focused effort. It requires the conscious recognition and mental registration of the obsessive or compulsive symptom. You should literally make mental notes, such as, "This thought is an *obsession;* this urge is a *compulsive* urge." You must make the effort to manage the intense biologically mediated thoughts and urges that intrude so insistently into consciousness. This means expending the necessary effort to maintain your awareness of what we call the Impartial Spectator, the observing power within us that gives each person the capacity to recognize what's real and what's just a symptom and to fend off the pathological urge until it begins to fade and recede.

The goal of Step 1 is to learn to Relabel intrusive thoughts and urges in your own mind as obsessions and compulsions—and to do so assertively. Start calling them that; use the labels *obsession* and *compulsion.* For example, train yourself to say, "I don't think or feel that my hands are dirty. I'm having an obsession that my hands are dirty." Or, "I don't feel that I have the need to wash my hands. I'm having a compulsive urge to perform the compulsion of washing my hands." (The technique is the same for other obsessions and compulsions, including compulsive checking of doors or appliances and needless counting.) You must learn to recognize the intrusive, obsessive thoughts and urges as OCD.

In the Relabeling step, the basic idea is: *Call an obsessive thought or compulsive urge what it really is.* Assertively Relabel it so you can begin to understand that the feeling is just a false alarm, with little or no basis in reality. As the result of much scientific research we now know that these urges are caused by biological imbalances in the brain. By calling them what they really are—obsessions and compulsions—you begin to understand that they do not really mean what they say. They are simply false messages coming from the brain.

It is important to remember that just Relabeling these thoughts and urges won't make them go away. In fact, the worst thing you can do is to *try* to make them vanish. It won't work because the thoughts and urges have a biological cause that is beyond your control. What you *can* control is your behavioral response to those urges. By Relabeling, you begin to understand that no matter how real they feel, what they are saying is not real. The goal: to learn to resist them.

Recent scientific research on OCD has found that by learning to resist obsessions and compulsions through behavior therapy, you can actually change the biochemistry that is causing the OCD symptoms. But keep in mind that the process of changing the underlying biological problem, and by doing so changing the urge itself, may take weeks or even months. It requires patience and persistent effort. Trying to make these thoughts and urges go away in seconds or minutes will cause only frustration, demoralization, and stress. It will, in fact, tend to make the urges worse. Probably the most important thing to learn in this behavioral treatment is that your responses to the thoughts and urges are within your control, no matter how strong and bothersome they may be. The goal is to control your *responses* to the thoughts and urges, not to control the thoughts and urges themselves.

The next two steps are designed to help you learn new ways to control your behavioral responses to OCD symptoms.

STEP 2: REATTRIBUTE

The key to our self-directed behavioral therapy approach to treating OCD can be summed up in one sentence: "It's not me—it's my OCD." That is our battle cry. It is a reminder that OCD thoughts and urges are not meaningful, that they are false messages from the brain. Self-directed behavior therapy lets you gain a deeper understanding of this truth.

You are working toward a deep understanding of why the urge to check that lock or why the thought that "my hands are dirty" can be so powerful and overwhelming. If you know the thought makes no sense, why do you respond to it? Understanding why the thought is so strong and why it won't go away is the key to increasing your willpower and enabling you to fight off the urge to wash or check.

The goal is to learn to Reattribute the intensity of the thought or urge to its real cause, to recognize that the feeling and the discomfort are due to a biochemical imbalance in the brain. It is OCD—a medical condition. Acknowledging it as such is the first step toward developing a deeper understanding that these symptoms are not what they seem to be. You learn not to take them at face value.

Deep inside the brain lies a structure called the *caudate nucleus*. Scientists worldwide have studied this structure and believe that, in people with OCD, the caudate nucleus may be malfunctioning. Think of the caudate nucleus as a processing center or filtering station for the very complicated messages generated by the front part of the brain, which is probably the part used in thinking, planning, and understanding. Together with its sister structure, the *putamen*, which lies next to it, the caudate nucleus functions like an automatic transmission in a car. The caudate nucleus and the putamen, which together are called the *striatum*, take in messages from very complicated parts of the brain—those that control body movement, physical feelings, and the thinking and planning that involve those movements and feelings. They function in unison like an automatic transmission, assuring the smooth transition from one behavior to another. Typically, when anyone decides to make a movement, intruding movements and misdirected feelings are filtered out automatically so that the desired movement can be performed rapidly and efficiently. There is a quick, smooth shifting of gears.

During a normal day, we make many rapid shifts of behavior, smoothly and easily and usually without thinking about them. It is the functioning of the caudate nucleus and the putamen that makes this possible. In OCD, the problem seems to be that the smooth, efficient filtering and the shifting of thoughts and behavior are disrupted by a glitch in the caudate nucleus.

As a result of this malfunction, the front of the brain becomes overactive and uses excessive energy. It's like having your car stuck in a ditch. You spin and spin and spin your wheels, but without traction you can't get out of that ditch. With OCD, too much energy is being used in a frontal part of the brain called the *orbital cortex*. It's as if the orbital cortex, which has an error-detection circuit, becomes stuck in gear. This is probably why OCD causes people to get a "something is wrong" feeling that won't go away. You have to do the work to get it out of gear—to shift the gears. You have a manual, rather than an automatic, transmission. In fact, the person with OCD has a sticky manual transmission; he or she must shift the gears. This takes great effort because the brain tends to get "stuck in gear." But, whereas an automobile transmission is made of metal and can't fix itself, people with OCD can teach themselves how to shift gears through self-directed behavior therapy. In doing so, they can actually fix this broken gearshift in the brain. We now know that you can change your own brain biochemistry.

The key to the Reattribute step is to realize that the awful intrusiveness and ferocious intensity of OCD thoughts are due to a medical condition. Underlying problems in brain biochemistry are causing these thoughts and urges to be so intrusive. That is why they won't go away. By doing this Four-Step Method of self-directed behavior therapy, you can change the brain's biochemistry. This takes weeks or even months of hard work. In the meantime, understanding the role the brain plays in OCD thoughts and urges will help you to avoid one of the most demoralizing and destructive things people with OCD almost invariably do: the frustrating attempt to "get rid of" the thoughts and urges. There is nothing you can do to make them go away immediately. But remember: You don't have to act on them. Don't take them at face value. Don't listen to them. You know what they are. They are false messages from the brain that are due to a medical condition called OCD. Use this knowledge to avoid acting on them. The most effective thing you can do—something that will help you change your brain for the better in the long run—is to learn to put these thoughts and feelings aside and go on to the next behavior. This is what we mean by shifting gears: Do another behavior. Trying to make them go away will only pile stress on stress—and stress just makes OCD thoughts and urges worse.

Using the Reattribute step will also help you to avoid performing rituals in a vain attempt to "get the right feeling" (for example, a sense of "evenness" or a sense of completion). Knowing that the urge to get that "right feeling" is caused by a biochemical imbalance in the brain, you can learn to ignore the urge and move on. Remember, "It's not me—it's my OCD." By refusing to listen to the urge or to act on it, you will actually change your brain and make the feeling lessen. If you take the urge at face value and act on it, you may get momentary relief, but within a very short time the urge will just get more intense. This is perhaps the most important lesson that people with OCD must learn. It will help you avoid being the "sucker" and taking the false bait of OCD every time.

The Relabel and Reattribute steps are usually performed together to bring about a deeper understanding of what is really happening when an OCD thought or urge causes you such intense pain. You Relabel it, call it what it is—an obsession or a compulsion. Use mindful awareness to get beyond a superficial understanding of OCD and to gain the more profound understanding that the thoughts and urges are nothing more than fallout from a medical condition.

STEP 3: REFOCUS

The Refocus step is where the real work is done. In the beginning, you may think of it as the "no pain, no gain" step. Mental exercise is like a physical workout. In Refocusing, you have work to do: You must shift the gears yourself. *With effort and focused mindfulness, you are going to do what the caudate nucleus normally does easily and automatically,* which is to let you know when to switch to another behavior. Think of a surgeon scrubbing his hands before surgery: The surgeon doesn't need to wait for a timer to go off to know when it's time to stop scrubbing. After a while, the behavior is simply automatic. After a while he gets a "feel" for when he's scrubbed enough. But people with OCD can't get the feeling that something is done once it's done. The automatic pilot is broken. Fortunately, doing the Four Steps can usually fix it.

In Refocusing, the idea is to work around the OCD thoughts and urges by shifting attention to something else, if only for a few minutes. Early on, you may choose some specific behavior to replace compulsive washing or checking. Any constructive, pleasant behavior will do. Hobbies are particularly good. For example, you may decide to take a walk, exercise, listen to music, read, play a computer game, knit, or shoot a basketball.

When the thought comes, you first Relabel it as an obsessive thought or a compulsive urge and then Reattribute it to the fact that you have OCD—a medical problem. Then Refocus your attention to this other behavior that you have chosen. Start the process of Refocusing by refusing to take the obsessive-compulsive symptoms at face value. Say to yourself, "I'm experiencing a symptom of OCD. I need to do another behavior."

You must train yourself in a new method of responding to the thoughts and urges, redirecting your attention to something other than the OCD symptoms. The goal of treatment is to stop responding to the OCD symptoms while acknowledging that, for the short term, these uncomfortable feelings will continue to bother you. You begin to "work around" them by doing another behavior. You learn that even though the OCD feeling is there, it doesn't have to control what you do. You make the decision about what you're going to do, rather than respond to OCD thoughts and urges as a robot would. By Refocusing, you reclaim your decision-making power. Those biochemical glitches in your brain are no longer running the show.

The Fifteen-Minute Rule

Refocusing isn't easy. It would be dishonest to say that dismissing the thoughts and urges and moving on does not take significant effort and even tolerance of some pain. But only by learning to resist OCD symptoms can you change the brain and, in time, decrease the pain. To help you manage this task, we have developed the fifteen-minute rule. The idea is to delay your response to an obsessive thought or to your urge to perform a compulsive behavior by letting some time elapse—preferably at least fifteen minutes—before you even consider acting on the urge or thought. In the beginning or whenever the urges are very intense, you may need to set a shorter waiting time, say five minutes, as your goal. But the principle is always the same: Never perform the compulsion without some time delay. Remember, *this is not a passive waiting period.* It is a time to perform actively the Relabeling, Reattributing, and Refocusing steps. You should have mindful awareness that you are Relabeling those uncomfortable feelings as OCD and Reattributing them to a biochemical imbalance in the brain. These feelings are caused by OCD; they are not what they seem to be. They are faulty messages coming from the brain.

Then you must *do another behavior*—any pleasant, constructive behavior will do. After the set period has lapsed, reassess the urge. Ask yourself if there's been any change in intensity and make note of any change. Even the smallest decrease may give you the courage to wait longer. You will be learning that the longer you wait, the more the urge will change. The goal will always be fifteen minutes or more. As you keep practicing, the same amount of effort will result in a greater decrease in intensity. So, in general, the more you practice the fifteen-minute rule, the easier it gets. Before long, you may make it twenty minutes or thirty minutes or more.

It's What You Do That Counts

It is vitally important to Refocus attention away from the urge or thought and onto any other reasonable task or activity. Don't wait for the thought or feeling to go away. Don't expect it to go away right away. And, by all means, *don't do what your OCD is telling you to do.* Rather, engage in any constructive activity of your choosing. You'll see that instigating a time delay between the onset of the urge and even considering acting on it will make the urge fade and change. What is more important, even if the urge changes hardly at all, as sometimes happens, you learn that you can have some control over your response to this faulty message from the brain.

This application of mindful awareness and the Impartial Spectator will be empowering to you, especially after years of feeling at the mercy of a bizarre and seemingly inexplicable force. The long-range goal of the Refocus step is, of course, never again to perform a compulsive behavior in response to an OCD thought or urge. But the intermediate goal is to impose a time delay before performing any compulsion. You're learning not to allow OCD feelings to determine what you do.

Sometimes the urge will be too strong, and you will perform the compulsion. This is not an invitation to beat yourself up. Keep in mind: As you do the Four Steps and your behavior changes, your thoughts and feelings will also change. If you give in and perform a compulsion after a time delay and an attempt to Refocus, make a special effort to continue to Relabel the behavior and to acknowledge that this time the OCD overwhelmed you. Remind yourself, "I'm not washing my hands because they are dirty, but because of my OCD. The OCD won this round, but next time I'll wait longer." In this way, even performing a compulsive behavior can contain an element of behavior therapy. This is very important to realize: Relabeling a compulsive behavior *as* a compulsive behavior is a form of behavior therapy and is *much* better than doing a compulsion without making a clear mental note about what it is.

A tip for those who are fighting checking behaviors—checking locks, stoves, and other appliances: If your problem is, say, checking the door lock, try to lock the door with extra attention and mindful awareness the first time. This way, you'll have a good mental picture to refer to when the compulsive urge arises. Anticipating that the urge to check is going to arise in you, you should lock the door the first time in a slow and deliberate manner, making mental notes, such as "The door is now locked. I can see that the door is locked." You want a clear mental image of that locked door, so when the urge to check the door seizes you, you will be able to Relabel it immediately and say, "That's an obsessive idea. It is OCD." You will Reattribute the intensity and intrusiveness of the urge to check again to your OCD. You will remember, "It's not me—it's just my brain."

You will Refocus and begin to "work around" the OCD urges by doing another behavior, with a ready mental picture of having locked that door because you did it so carefully and attentively the first time. You can use that knowledge to help you Refocus actively on doing another behavior, even as you Relabel and Reattribute the urge to check that has arisen, as you anticipated it would.

Keeping a Journal

It is important to keep a behavior-therapy journal as a record of your successful Refocusing efforts. It need not be anything fancy. The idea is simply to have a written record to remind you of your successes in self-directed behavior therapy. The journal is important because you can refer back to it to see which behaviors most helped you to Refocus. But—and this is equally important—it helps you to build confidence as you see your list of achievements grow. In the heat of battle against a compulsive urge, it isn't always easy to remember which behavior to Refocus on. Keeping a journal will help you to shift gears when the going gets tough, when the obsessive thought or compulsive urge heats up, and will train your mind to remember what has worked in the past. As your list of successes gets longer, it will be inspirational.

Record only your successes. There is no need to record your failures. You have to learn to give yourself a pat on the back. This is something people with OCD need to learn to do more of. Make sure to give yourself encouragement by consciously acknowledging your successful use of Refocusing behaviors as a job well done. Reinforce that success by recording it in your behavior-therapy journal and giving yourself a little reward, even if it's only to tell yourself how terrific you are for working so hard to help yourself. Many people find that even something as simple as jotting down one Refocusing behavior a day, and calling it the "Play of the day," contributes significantly to their self-esteem.

STEP 4: REVALUE

The goal of the first three steps is to use your knowledge of OCD as a medical condition caused by a biochemical imbalance in the brain to help you clarify that this feeling is not what it appears to be and to refuse to take the thoughts and urges at face value, to avoid performing compulsive rituals, and to Refocus on constructive behaviors. You can think of the Relabel and Reattribute steps as a team effort, working together with the Refocusing step. The combined effect of these three steps is much greater than the sum of their individual parts. The process of Relabeling and Reattributing intensifies the learning that takes place during the hard work of Refocusing. As a result, you begin to Revalue those thoughts and urges that, before behavior therapy, would invariably lead you to perform compulsive behaviors. After adequate training in the first three steps, you are able in time to place a much lower value on the OCD thoughts and urges.

We have used the concept of the "Impartial Spectator," developed by 18th-century philosopher Adam Smith, to help you understand more clearly what you are actually achieving while performing the Four Steps of cognitive biobehavioral therapy. Smith described the Impartial Spectator as being like a person inside us who we carry around at all times, a person aware of all our feelings, states, and circumstances. Once we make the effort to strengthen the Impartial Spectator's perspective, we can call up our own Impartial Spectator at any time and literally watch ourselves in action. In other words, we can witness our own actions and feelings as someone not involved would, as a disinterested observer. As Smith described it, "We suppose ourselves the spectators of our own behavior." He understood that keeping the perspective of the Impartial Spectator clearly in mind, which is essentially the same as using mindful awareness, is hard work, especially under painful circumstances, and requires the "utmost and most fatiguing exertions." The hard work of which he wrote seems closely related to the intense efforts you must make in performing the Four Steps.

People with OCD must work hard to manage the biologically induced urges that intrude into conscious awareness. You must strive to maintain awareness of the Impartial Spectator, the observing power within that gives you the capacity to fend off pathological urges until they begin to fade. You must use your knowledge that OCD symptoms are just meaningless signals, false messages from the brain, so you can Refocus and shift gears. You must gather your mental resources, always keeping in mind, "It's not me—it's my OCD. It's not me—it's just my brain." Although in the short run, you can't change your feelings, you *can* change your behavior. By changing your behavior, you find that your feelings also change in time. The tug-of-war comes down to this: Who's in charge here, you or OCD? Even when the OCD overwhelms you, and you give in and perform the compulsion, you must realize that it's just OCD and vow to fight harder the next time.

With compulsive behaviors, simply observing the fifteen-minute rule with consistency and Refocusing on another behavior will usually cause the Revalue step to kick in, which means realizing that the feeling is not worth paying attention to and not taking it at face value, remembering that it's OCD and that it is caused by a medical problem. The result is that you place a much lower value on—devalue—the OCD feeling. For obsessive thoughts, you must try to enhance this process by Revaluing in an even more active way. Two substeps—the two A's—aid you in Step 2: Reattribute: Anticipate and Accept. When you use these two A's, you are doing Active

Revaluing. Anticipate means "be prepared," know the feeling is coming, so be ready for it; don't be taken by surprise. Accept means don't waste energy beating yourself up because you have these bad feelings. You know what's causing them and that you have to work around them. Whatever the content of your obsession—whether it is violent or sexual or is manifested in one of dozens of other ways— you know that it can occur hundreds of times a day. You want to stop reacting each time as though it were a new thought, something unexpected. Refuse to let it shock you; refuse to let it get you down on yourself. By anticipating your particular obsessive thought, you can recognize it the instant it occurs and Relabel it immediately. You will simultaneously, and actively, Revalue it. When the obsession occurs, you will be prepared. You will know, "That's just my stupid obsession. It has no meaning. That's just my brain. There's no need to pay attention to it." Remember: You can't make the thought go away, but neither do you need to pay attention to it. You can learn to go on to the next behavior. There is no need to dwell on the thought. Move ahead. This is where the second A—Accept—comes in. Think of the screaming car alarm that disturbs and distracts you. Don't dwell on it. Don't say, "I can't do another thing until that blankety-blank car alarm shuts off." Simply try to ignore it and get on with things.

You learned in Step 2 that the bothersome obsessive thought is caused by OCD and is related to a biochemical imbalance in the brain. In the Acceptance substep of Reattributing, you realize that truth in a very deep, perhaps even spiritual, way. Do not get down on yourself; it makes no sense to criticize your inner motives just because of an imbalance in the brain. By accepting that the obsessive thought is there despite you, not because of you, you can decrease the terrible stress that repetitive obsessive thoughts usually cause. Always keep in mind, "It's not me—it's the OCD. It's not me—it's just my brain." Don't beat yourself up trying to make the thought go away because in the short run, it will not. Most important, don't ruminate and don't fantasize about the consequences of acting out a terrible obsessive thought. You won't act it out because you don't really want to. Let go of all the negative, demeaning judgments about "the kinds of people who get thoughts like this." For obsessions, the fifteen-minute rule can be shortened to a one-minute rule, even a fifteen-second rule. There is no need to dwell on that thought, even though it lingers in your mind. You can still go on—indeed, you must go on—to the next thought and the next behavior. In this way, Refocusing is like a martial art. An obsessive thought or compulsive urge is very strong, but also quite stupid. If you stand right in front of it and take the full brunt of its power, trying to drive it from your mind, it will defeat you every time. You have to step aside, work around it, and go on to the next behavior. You are learning to keep your wits about you in the face of a powerful opponent. The lesson here goes far beyond overcoming OCD: By taking charge of your actions, you take charge of your mind—and of your life.

CONCLUSION

We who have OCD must learn to train our minds not to take intruding feelings at face value. We have to learn that these feelings mislead us. In a gradual but tempered way, we're going to change our responses to the feelings and resist them. We have a new view of the truth. In this way, we gain new insights into the truth. We learn that even persistent, intrusive feelings are transient and impermanent and will recede if not acted on. And, of course, we always remember that these feelings tend to intensify and overwhelm us when we give in to them. We must learn to recognize the urge for what it is—and to resist it. In the course of performing this Four-Step Method of behavioral self-treatment, we are laying the foundation for building true personal mastery and the art of self-command. Through constructive resistance to OCD feelings and urges, we increase our self-esteem and experience a sense of freedom. Our ability to make conscious, self-directed choices is enhanced.

By understanding this process by which we empower ourselves to fight OCD and by clearly appreciating the control one gains by training the mind to overcome compulsive or automatic responses to intrusive thoughts or feelings, we gain a deepening insight into how to take back our lives. Changing our brain chemistry is a happy consequence of this life-affirming action. True freedom lies along this path of a clarified perception of genuine self-interest.

QUICK SUMMARY OF THE FOUR STEPS OF COGNITIVE-BIOBEHAVIORAL SELF-TREATMENT FOR OCD

Step 1: RELABEL
Recognize that the intrusive obsessive thoughts and urges are the RESULT OF OCD.

Step 2: REATTRIBUTE
Realize that the intensity and intrusiveness of the thought or urge is CAUSED BY OCD; it is probably related to a biochemical imbalance in the brain.

Step 3: REFOCUS
Work around the OCD thoughts by focusing your attention on something else, at least for a few minutes: DO ANOTHER BEHAVIOR.

Step 4: REVALUE
Do not take the OCD thought at face value. It is not significant in itself.